AN ETHOS OF COMPASSION AND

THE INTEGRITY OF CREATION

AN ETHOS OF COMPASSION AND

THE INTEGRITY OF CREATION

Brian J. Walsh, Hendrik Hart and Robert E. VanderVennen

Editors

University Press of America, Inc.
Lanham • New York • London

Copyright © 1995 by
University Press of America,® Inc.
4720 Boston Way
Lanham, Maryland 20706

3 Henrietta Street
London, WC2E 8LU England

Co-published by arrangement with the Institute for Christian Studies,
Ontario, Canada

Library of Congress Cataloging-in-Publication Data

An ethos of compassion and the integrity of Creation / Brian J. Walsh,
Hendrik Hart, and Robert E. VanderVennen, editors.
p.   cm.
Plenary addresses given at a conference held in June 1992 in Toronto,
Ont., to mark the 25th anniversary of the opening of the Institute for
Christian Studies.
Includes bibliographical references.
1. Order--Religious aspects--Christianity--Congresses. 2. Creation--
Religious aspects--Christianity--Congresses. 3. Reformed Church--
Doctrines. 4. Sociology, Christian (Reformed Church)--Congresses.
5. Theology, Doctrinal--History--20th century. I. Walsh, Brian J. II.
Hart, Hendrik. III. VanderVennen, Robert E. IV. Institute for
Christian Studies.
BT78.E   1995   230'.42 --dc20   95-33406 CIP

ISBN 0-7618-0102-2 (cloth: alk: ppr.)
ISBN 0-7618-0103-0 (pbk: alk: ppr.)

The Institute for Christian Studies
designates this book as the

1995 ROBERT LEE CARVILL MEMORIAL BOOK

in grateful tribute to the service
and inspiration he has given.

Contents

Contributors

Contributors

Atie Th. Brüggemann-Kruijff is Researcher in the Philosophy Department of the Vrije Universiteit, Amsterdam

Jonathan and Adrienne Chaplin live in Oxford, England, where Jonathan is on the faculty in political theory at Plater College, Oxford University

John Cooper is Professor of Philosophical Theology at Calvin Theological Seminary, Grand Rapids, Michigan

Calvin B. DeWitt is Professor of Environmental Studies at the University of Wisconsin, Madison, Wisconsin, and Director of the AuSable Institute, Mancelona, Michigan

Harry Fernhout is President of the Institute for Christian Studies

Langdon Gilkey is Professor Emeritus at the Divinity School of the University of Chicago, Chicago, Illinois

Sander Griffioen is Professor of Social Philosophy at the Vrije Universiteit, Amsterdam

Carroll Guen Hart holds the Ph.D. degree from the combined program of the Institute for Christian Studies and the Vrije Universiteit

John E. Hare is Professor of Philosophy at Calvin College, Grand Rapids, Michigan

Hendrik Hart is Senior Member in Systematic Philosophy at the Institute for Christian Studies

Sylvia C. Keesmaat is Senior Member in Biblical Studies and Hermeneutics at the Institute for Christian Studies

J. Richard Middleton is Assistant Professor of Hebrew Scriptures at Colgate-Rochester Divinity School, Rochester, New York

James Olthuis is Senior Member in Philosophical Theology at the Institute for Christian Studies

Elaine Storkey is Director of the Institute for Contemporary Christianity in London, England

Johan van der Hoeven is Professor of Philosophy at the Vrije Universiteit, Amsterdam

Allen D. Verhey is Blekkink Professor of Religion at Hope College, Holland, Michigan

Brian J. Walsh is Senior Member in Worldview Studies at the Institute for Christian Studies

Albert M. Wolters is Professor of Religion and Theology at Redeemer College, Ancaster, Ontario

Nicholas Wolterstorff is Noah Porter Professor of Philosophical Theology at Yale University, New Haven, Connecticut

Introduction

This book presents the plenary addresses given at a conference held in Toronto in June, 1992, to mark the twenty-fifth anniversary of the opening of the Institute for Christian Studies. Over 175 scholars and laypersons responded to the invitation to celebrate this milestone and to spend four days reflecting on the theme "An Ethos of Compassion and the Integrity of Creation." Co-sponsoring the conference with the Institute were the Vrije Universiteit in Amsterdam and Calvin College in Grand Rapids, Michigan.

The phrase the "Integrity of Creation" in the conference theme refers to a conception central to the thought tradition of the Reformed branch of Christianity which gave birth to the Institute for Christian Studies. This tradition understands the created world as a place lovingly and reliably ordered by God as an environment in which life can flourish. This strong emphasis on integral, life-giving order in creation provides the basis and impetus to this tradition's emphasis on the scholar's vocation; the academic pursuit of knowledge is, in fact, an investigation of the rich and reliable storehouse of creation. The theme of "creation order," then, is woven into the Institute's historical understanding of its academic task.

A key goal of the conference was to consider anew the strengths and weaknesses of this orientation to creation order. Does the understanding of order which has characterized the Institute's intellectual tradition have the strength and vitality to make a creative contribution to contemporary culture, a prominent feature of which is its sense of disorientation and loss of order? In the words of the conference brochure:

> A consistent characteristic of a post-modern culture is the questioning of traditional certainties. Many of us experience a shaking of the normative ground on which we stand, a crisis in our normative environment. Such a crisis is precipitated by cultural developments as diverse as the emergence of new medical technologies, shifts in patterns of sexual relations, the rise of cultural pluralism, the New Age movement, the question of a new world order, and how we respond to the environmental crisis. In the academy old assusmsptions have been shaken by recent developments in epistemology and ontology.

This crisis of normativity is not simply "out there," in the secular world. Vexing questions concerning traditional understandings of creation order also dominate the agenda in Christian circles, including the branch of the Reformed community of faith which maintains the ICS. The question of the respective normative roles of male and female are the subject of intense debate, particularly in the institutional church. Issues regarding medical ethics are similarly troubling.

Contemporary encounters with issues of order and normativity, not only on a broad cultural scale but also in narrower community settings, have generated an increased awareness that particular interpretations of order can be misused as instruments of oppression. The justification by North American Christians of slavery on the basis of understandings of the order of things is a classic case in point. More recently, the interpretation of order held by many South African Christians helped shore up the ideology of *apartheid*. Many see a parallel dynamic at work in contemporary discussions of gender relations. This raises the question of whether and how an understanding of the world which invests heavily in an emphasis on normativity and order can remain sufficiently attentive to the human capacity to oppress other people and to the reality of suffering. More particularly, has the community and intellectual tradition which spawned ICS adequately accounted for these realities?

> How does an emphasis on normative "order" for creation provide us with a healing orientation in very disorienting times? What are the limits of such a perspective? And how does such a perspective respect the integrity of creation and also evoke and ethos of compassion? (Conference brochure).

These were among the questions the anniversary conference sought to address.

Since the conference was hosted by an institution which seeks biblical direction in higher learning, each day began with a Scripture meditation led by Richard Middleton. These meditations, grouped as "Parables of Compassion and Judgment," are included in this volume.

In his opening keynote address Brian Walsh used the metaphor of "Setting the Table" to organize his effort to orient participants to the conference theme.

The conference agenda then turned to the philosophical understanding of creation order in the Institute's Reformed intellectual tradition. Albert Wolters provided his "diagnosis" of this central motif by means of "Creation Order: A Historical Look at Our Heritage." Hendrik Hart provided a "prognosis" by means of his "Critique and Refinement" of creation order. Their contributions, and the comments of their respondents, follow.

Allen Verhey and his respondents took up the challenge of addressing issues of Scripture interpretation relevant to the conference theme under the rubric "Biblical hermeneutics and an Ethos of Compassion."

The conference was designed to deal not only with the somewhat theoretical philosophical and theological dimensions of the theme, but also with specific issues of order and normativity troubling Christians today. The topics selected for attention in plenary sessions were issues of the environment, gender relations, and sexual ethics. The presenters on these topics were, respectively, Calvin De Witt, Elaine Storkey and James Olthuis.

To avoid a purely "in-house" discussion, some respected scholars from other Christian backgrounds were invited to give their perspectives on the theme. Langdon Gilkey's essay generated exactly the kind of "open-house" discussion the conference planners had in mind.

A series of eight workshops was an essential part of the conference program. They dealt with topics such as medical ethics, order and evolution in science, international political order, order and artistic freedom, and the challenges facing Christian higher education. While the workshop leaders provided many creative elaborations on the main theme, space limitations made it impossible for us to include their presentations in this book.

A sensitive summary of the conference, provided by ICS alumnae Adrienne and Jonathan Chaplin, concludes this volume.

The contributors to this book all clearly affirm that the order in our life-experience is God-given and real. This orderedness is a gift; it provides the context for life to flourish. At the same time is a call; as responsible image bearers of God, humans are called actively to shape a way of life. However, as the Chaplins note in their summary, the contributors differ considerably in their assessment of the degree to which this orderedness is both given and accessible. Consequently, they also differ considerably in their assessment of the necessary and permissable breadth of free human response to that order.

Given these differences, some of the conference presentations generated significant controversy both among the conferees and within the ICS. Intense debate emerged particularly around views expressed on contemporary vexing issues of normativity. James Olthuis's paper on "When is Sex Against Nature," exploring the possible normativity of certain same-sex relationships in a fallen world, was the flashpoint for very sharp differences. Partly as a result of substantial critical feedback, the published version of Olthuis's essay represents a significant revision and refinement of his conference talk.

That the conference generated sharp debate and strong feelings was, one could say, an enactment of the theme. The "order" of academic interaction is characterized by the give and take of ideas, and by taking issue with views expressed. To possess integrity this process must be infused with a willingness to listen and bear with one another through differences—intellectual compassion, if you will. This spirit of bearing with one another allows people who differ profoundly on specific issues to stay together in their shared commitment to live as academic followers of Christ in troubled times. This spirit, manifested in the essays in this volume, is a precious gift. May those who read these pages also share in this spirit.

Harry Fernhout
President, Institute for Christian Studies

Parables of Compassion and Judgment:

Opening Meditations For a Creation-Order Tradition

J. Richard Middleton

This twenty-fifth anniversary conference intends to celebrate and examine the reformational heritage and tradition of the Institute for Christian Studies. Many of us here have found this tradition to be a rich intellectual and spiritual feast, a hearty banquet that has sustained us in our journey of faith over the years, and that has us coming back for more. Others of us, new to the table perhaps, find the taste of this meal unusual, with some unfamiliar ingredients and intriguing flavours. But, old or new, we are all invited to sit at table together these next three days, to taste and sample the offerings of the reformational tradition.

One of the things we will explore together is whether this feast is just an old, tried and true, "meat and potatoes" meal, or whether it holds the potential for the sort of nuanced flavouring and spicing that would result in an appealing array of mouthwatering dishes. The question is: Is this reformational banquet ultimately just a bland, monochrome lunch that sticks to your insides? And that's good for you, so eat up! Or, can this meal be served up as a multicultural smorgasbord, characterized by a truly international cuisine, including dishes the like of Japanese sushi, fettucini alfredo, Atlantic lobster tails, hot and sour soup, tandoori chicken and Jamaican curry goat?

How Hungry Are We? The Parable of the Banquet

Now, every feast, every meal, is a cultural affair, coloured by local customs and traditions. In the gospel of Luke, chapter 14, we find Jesus invited to a Sabbath meal at the house of a prominent Pharisee. There he tells a parable. Although I will focus on three different parables of Jesus in these meditations, Luke 14 provides us with a good point of entry, with its setting at a Sabbath meal. This would be what in current Jewish tradition is termed a *seder* supper *(seder* referring to "order," thus a meal ordered according to the tradition). Luke 14 is thus eminently suitable for us as the starting point for our reflections on creation order in the context of our own tradition.

> One Sabbath, when Jesus went to eat in the house of a prominent Pharisee, he was being carefully watched.... Jesus said to his host, "When you give a luncheon or dinner, do not invite your friends, your brothers or relatives, or your rich neighbours; if you do, they may invite you back and so you will be repaid. But when you give a banquet, invite the poor, the crippled, the lame, the blind, and you will be blessed. Although they cannot repay you, you will be repaid at the resurrection of the righteous."
>
> When one of those at the table with him heard this, he said to Jesus, "Blessed is the man who will eat at the feast in the kingdom of God."
>
> Jesus replied: "A certain man was preparing a great banquet and invited many guests. At the time of the banquet he sent his servant to tell those who had been invited, 'Come for everything is now ready.'
>
> "But they all alike began to make excuses. The first said, 'I have just bought a field, and I must go and see it. Please excuse me.'
>
> "Another said, 'I have just bought five yoke of oxen, and I'm on my way to try them out. Please excuse me.'
>
> "Still another said, 'I just got married, so I can't come.'
>
> "The servant came back and reported this to his master. Then the owner of the house became angry and ordered his servant, 'Go out quickly into the streets and alleys of the town and bring in the poor, the crippled, the blind and the lame.'
>
> " 'Sir,' the servant said, 'what you ordered has been done, but there is still room.'
>
> "Then the master told his servant, 'Go out to the roads and country lanes and make them come in, so that my house will be full.' I tell you not one of those men who were invited will get a taste of my banquet." (Luke 14:1, 12-24)

The gospels tell us that when Jesus lived and ministered in Galilee and Judea he gave and attended many parties. Indeed, he partied so much that he was accused of being a drunkard and a glutton (Luke 7:34). And the kind of people he hung out with! Tax collectors, that despised profession of Jews who collected taxes from fellow Jews on behalf of the Roman empire, often with force, and for a cut of the profits. And moral and social outcasts, like prostitutes, lepers, poor people, and in general "sinners." Whole categories of people who just weren't up to scratch, if you were an upright moral and religious person in first century Judaism.

It is no wonder, therefore, that in Luke 15:1-2, we read: "Now the tax collectors and 'sinners' were all gathering around him [Jesus] to hear him. But the Pharisees and the teachers of the law [the upright religious people] muttered, 'This man welcomes sinners and eats with them.' "

The Pharisees and the teachers of the law knew that Jesus' constant partying with the "riff-raff" wasn't just of bit of charitable slumming on his part. Being good Jews, they knew that the Scriptures (and much Jewish literature since then) portrayed the Kingdom of God as a party, a sumptuous feast, a banquet which the Messiah was preparing for all who were truly hungry for righteousness, for healing, for forgiveness. It would be a great party where all who were hungry would be satisfied, where all who were lonely would be welcomed with open arms into a fellowship of grace and given a place to belong. It would be an incredible celebration where tears would be wiped away and where joy would overtake sorrow.

The Kingdom of God—God's healing rule over creation—was coming, and it would be a party to ring out the old year of suffering and pain, of injustice and fear, and to ring in the new year, the year of the Lord's favour, the new age of grace and renewal and salvation.

And these Pharisees and teachers of the law knew that Jesus' hanging around with the riff-raff and untouchables of Jewish society was a sign, a portent, a visible parable of what *he* thought that final banquet was going to be like. And so they were offended.

They may well have known Isaiah 25:6-9, which not only portrays the Kingdom of God as a party, but says that Jews and Gentiles (i.e., pagans) will be there on equal footing. Nevertheless their attitude was more like that of the Qumran community in the first century. Also known as the Essenes, this was a group of purist Jews who regarded the nation of Israel (including the Pharisees and teachers of the law) as hopelessly corrupt. So they founded a separatist sect, an alternative community, out in the desert by the Dead Sea. In one of their writings called "The Messianic Rule" they describe the great feast of the Kingdom of God. According to that text, no Gentiles will be there. Moreover, from among the Jews, only the righteous, wise and perfect leaders (all *men*) will be there, and they will be organized in ranks, depending on just how righteous they were. The text specifically says that no one is allowed to this banquet—to this table fellowship with the Messiah—who is "smitten in his flesh, or paralyzed in his feet or hands, or lame, or blind, or deaf, or dumb, or smitten in his flesh with a visible blemish" (1 QSa 2:11-22). No imperfect, "defective" people allowed! That's what the sign says outside the doors of this feast.

So it's interesting that when Jesus is at a dinner given by a Pharisee, he pointedly tells the host (Luke 14:12-13): When you give a banquet, *don't* invite your family or your friends, or your rich neighbours. Because they might return the favour. Instead, invite the poor, the crippled, the lame, the blind—precisely the people excluded by "The Messianic Rule." Invite them, says Jesus, because they can't repay you.

Jesus knew (as the Pharisees also knew) that how you live *now* is integrally connected with your future destiny. Specifically, our attitude *today*, in the here and now, to "undesirable" people—and to fellowship with them in something as simple as sharing a meal—is ultimately indicative of our attitude to joining in the eschatological feast of the Kingdom of God. No wonder the upright religious people were upset with Jesus. It's as if he were saying that God had no standards!

But we're running ahead of the story. When Jesus tells his host that he is to invite the undesirables, those in genuine need, who can't repay him, some pious old gentleman is touched and says, "Blessed is the man who will eat at the feast in the kingdom of God!" To which the appropriate response would be something like, "Amen!... Let it be so!... How right you are!" But Jesus is always overstepping the bounds of propriety at these meals—doing things like healing people on the Sabbath, telling the host who to invite. And here, instead of simply saying "Amen!" he tells a troubling story, a parable.

A wealthy man gave a great dinner. And he invited many guests. He would have to be wealthy to afford a large party. And his guests would likely be of his own social station. The way these banquets worked in the old days was that, based on how many accepted, the host prepared a meal of the appropriate size, slaughtering a chicken, a duck, a goat, a sheep or a calf. When the day of the banquet came and the food was cooked and the meal prepared (it would be evening by this time), he sent his servant to those who had previously accepted the invitation to tell them, "Food's on! It's time to come now." The butler, in other words, rang up the guests on the phone to tell them that "high table" was prepared.

But, surprisingly, they all began to make excuses. One said, "Sorry, old chap, but I've just bought some property. I've just this minute struck a real estate deal with my agent (he's on call-waiting right now). I've just faxed payment and I've simply *got* to go and see this property that I've paid for. I've got to go check it out. Please excuse me!"

The second said, "Look, I've just bought five used tractors (yoke of oxen, I mean). The salesman is on the other line. And I've got to go inspect them to see if they're working mechanically, and what model and make they are. Having already paid for them, I've need to see if I got my money's worth. Please excuse me!"

These excuses are paper-thin. They're even insulting. No intelligent person would believe them. But at least they make a form of politeness: "Please excuse me!"

Not so with the third guest. He breaks the pattern of even the semblance of politeness. He simply says, "Hey look, I got married. So ... I can't come. Bye!" I got married? Well, a lot of us did. He doesn't even say I *just* got married. That's in the NIV, but not in the Greek. Besides, a wedding and a dinner party wouldn't be scheduled on the same day in a first century village. This guest doesn't even make an attempt at apology.

These three well-to-do invited guests, who had previously sent in their RSVPs and had reserved seats at the banquet, back out at the last minute. Why? What's behind these crazy excuses?

It's not explicitly stated. But, given the offence the Pharisees and teachers of the law took at Jesus' eating with tax collectors and sinners (15:1-2), as well as the general tenor of Luke's gospel as a whole, we can guess at the reason. It's quite likely that the invited guests had second thoughts about this party when they realized that the host was the sort of man to invite riff-raff. And, being so concerned with their image and status, they quickly found something else to do—anything, so long as they didn't have to associate with people like that. What it came down to was that they didn't *need* that badly to be there. They simply weren't *that* hungry!

Yes, in principle, they of course wanted to be at the party. Of course, we recognize our need for God. And, in principle, we've put in a formal acceptance to God's invitation to salvation. For some of us that acceptance was a long time ago, pledged at our baptism, confirmed at our public confession of faith. For me, it was through conversion, some thirty years ago. For others of us it hasn't been so long. We've accepted the invitation only recently. But whatever the circumstances, we've sent in our RSVP to this feast and we figure we've got a reserved place in the Kingdom of God.

The trouble comes when the summons to eat arrives. The food is ready *now*. Remember, there was no refrigeration in those days. If the invited guests don't come when called, the meal won't last. And so, when the excuses start pouring in, the host is understandably angry.

So he says: If those with reserved seats aren't hungry, don't sense their own need for this feast, then go find others who are starving. Go out quickly into the city streets and bring in the poor, the crippled, the blind and the lame. *They* know their need. Go bring in the outcasts of Israel. There is plenty food for them. If the keepers of the tradition as so numb to their own hunger, there are many others who yearn for what the tradition has to offer. Invite them to the table.

And the servant returns and says to the host, "I've done as you've said, but there is still room." So the master says: Go *outside* the city, into the country lanes and roads, and make them come in. Go to the ones foreseen in Isaiah 49:6, where God said,

> It is too small a thing for you to be my servant
> > to restore the tribes of Jacob
> > and bring back those of Israel I have kept.
> I will also make you a light for the Gentiles,
> > that you may bring my salvation to the ends of the earth.

Go, in other words, *outside* Israel, to the nasty *goyim*, to the pagans, the really unclean. And make them come in. "Compel" them to come in.

In the Middle East it was expected that you have to refuse a dinner invitation the first couple of times, because your host might be inviting you out of simple politeness. So you've got to let him convince you that it's for real. Especially if you're from a lower social or economic stratum, there's no way he could mean it. This is too good to be true. The offer is unbelievable! Who me? Invited to God's banquet? So, take them by the arm, says the host, and walk them in.

Notice that this last set of instructions isn't fulfilled within the parable as Jesus tells it. The instructions are given, but there is no report on what happens next. Jesus indeed came, as he himself put it, to the lost sheep of the house of Israel (to the needy within the city, to those among his people who were hungry for salvation). But he commissioned his disciples (who were recruited precisely from that group) to take the good news to all nations, to spread the word of the feast Messiah was preparing even further afield.

And as Christ's disciples today, members of a church composed of Jews and Gentiles (testimony to the obedience of the first Christians), it is *our* calling to continue this mission. The offer is still open. God still invites to this sumptuous feast the needy, the outcasts, the unclean—dare I say it, the anti-normative. This banquet is not for those whose lives are well-ordered, but precisely for those who are broken, those in pain, the abused, the powerless, the voiceless. I came, said Jesus, not to call the righteous, but sinners. It is not the healthy, but the sick who need healing. It is not the satiated, but the starving who need food.

Who do we identify with in this parable? Do we see ourselves in the long-time invitees, looking with disdain on the broken of this world, guarding—indeed hoarding—our tradition, to keep it "pure"? Would we, in the name of creation order, bar the door to this feast and block the path to healing for those who really need it? If so—if we refuse to sit at table with the unclean—perhaps we are simply deluding ourselves about which table we are in fact sitting at. We may be deluding ourselves about which feast we are attending. For the Messianic feast will be filled with riff-raff.

Or do we identify with the needy, whether those invited to the banquet in the second and third rounds or the servant who does the inviting? In the last analysis, there is no fundamental distinction between them. Evangelism, the old saying goes, is one beggar telling others where to find bread. Indeed, it is only those who know their deep need who will actively seek out others to share the feast. The self-satisfied do not evangelize. They are self-enclosed. And if we take Jesus seriously, those people exclude themselves from the feast. Having returned an RSVP is not enough. You have to be hungry enough to come now. Your hunger has to override your dislike of the riff-raff. The Messianic feast isn't a fast food restaurant; and there is no take-out menu. Only the needy will be at this banquet, so get used to eating with needy people.

The question for us, then, as long-term custodians of a creation-order tradition, is whether we are open to sitting at table with those whom this tradition has marginalized as unclean, even as anti-normative. Indeed, the question is whether we will actively *invite* the marginal, who are in pain, to the table. Or, on the contrary, do we have second thoughts about joining the feast? Second thoughts about whether we are at the right banquet at all, when we look at the changes being wrought in the reformational tradition. It seems that the teachers of the law (the custodians of order) in Jesus' day judged that *his* banquet wasn't one they were going to attend. So the question for us moves towards this: Are *we* in danger of mistakenly identifying *our* articulation of creation order, our well-prepared meal, with the genuine banquet of God's Kingdom?

Jesus concludes the parable with an abrasive personal statement addressed to those listening. This is his only explicit "application" and it is indicated by the shift to "you" plural in Greek, whereas the master in the parable had been addressing the servant in the singular. As contemporary hearers of the parable, this concluding statement is addressed to us too: I tell you, said Jesus, not one of those who were originally invited shall eat at *my* banquet.

Now I'm uncomfortable ending my meditations on this parable with this remark by Jesus. I'd prefer to stay with the open-ended set of questions I just listed. I have genuinely raised these possibilities as questions, not as finalized judgements. This is not just because I don't want to destroy the provocative nature of the parable by bringing it to premature closure. I raise these questions also because I believe the future is genuinely open for us.

On the Old and the New: Torah and Gospel

But there is another consideration. I'm aware of the diversity of Scripture and the differing theological and practical emphases of different texts. I'm aware that the Lukan concern for the marginalized, evident in the parable of the banquet, is "balanced," if you will, or complemented by a somewhat different emphasis on tradition in Matthew's gospel. It is in Matthew, after all, that Jesus says:

> Do not think that I have come to abolish the Law or the Prophets; I have not come to abolish them but to fulfil them. I tell you the truth, until heaven and earth disappear, not the smallest letter, not the least stroke of a pen, will by any means disappear from the Law until everything is accomplished. Anyone who breaks one of the least of these commandments and teaches others to do the same will be called least in the kingdom of heaven, but whoever practices and teaches these commands will be called great in the kingdom of heaven. For I tell you that unless your righteousness surpasses that of the Pharisees and the teachers of the law, you will certainly not enter the kingdom of heaven. (Matthew 5:17-20)

So my second parable is Matthean. It's also somewhat more didactic than the parable of the banquet. It is also a different sort of parable, different on formal grounds. The parable of the banquet is what might be called an "allegorical" parable, and it contains a number of implied or unstated correspondences. It raises the question of who is represented by the banquet master, the servant, the banquet, the various categories of invited guests. Other allegorical parables are the parables of the sower and of the tenants in the vineyard. Each has a number of correspondences.

My second parable is much simpler, with a narrower one-to-one correspondence. It consists in a more or less extended similitude or comparison. *This* is like *that*. Longer, more extended similitudes have been called "exemplary stories" and include parables like the lost coin, the mustard seed, the pearl of great price, the leaven, and the fishnet. Indeed, our present parable comes after Jesus has just told the parables listed above. Then he asks the disciples, "Have you understand all these things?" And they answer, unhesitatingly, "Yes" (Matthew 13:51). This prompts Jesus to tell one more parable.

> He said to them, "Therefore every teacher of the law who has been instructed about the kingdom of heaven is like the owner of a house who brings out of his storeroom new treasures as well as old."

Every custodian or articulator of normative order who, discerning the times, has feasted at the banquet of God's inbreaking Kingdom, having been instructed in that Kingdom, that person is like a householder who reaches deep into her treasure chest and takes out the old stuff, rich in ancient tradition *and* the sparkling new.

It's not enough just to polish off the old china and set the table, to use the same old recipes. Torah by itself is not adequate, Jesus says to aspiring teachers of Torah. For Torah is updated by and fulfilled in *Euangellion* (Gospel). But gospel does not repudiate Torah. Indeed, as Jesus says in Matthew 5, creation will pass away, but not Torah. Not creation order. Nevertheless, those teachers who have been genuinely instructed in God's coming Kingdom, who really understand the parables of the Kingdom, also get to take out the new china and try new recipes. But new or old, God's purpose—God's creational intent—is the same. God wants us to eat well. To be satisfied. To enjoy the feast. God wants shalom. The question is: What contributes to shalom?

On this point I find Tom Wright's notion of the biblical story as an unfinished drama, with the church standing between the coming of Jesus and the eschaton, quite heuristic. Standing where we are, *in media res*, we are called to contribute responsibly to the unfolding and resolution of the story. It is not enough simply to repeat what occurred in earlier stages of the drama, to recite the script *verbatim*. It's not enough to take the old stuff out of the storeroom, to set the banquet with the old china, to serve up the old recipes. That's just not adequate.

For example, it's obvious to us now that the Bible doesn't have the last word on slavery. Slavery is never abolished *within* the pages of Scripture. It was modified in a humanitarian direction, limitations were placed on the institution, perhaps. And the seeds of the destruction of slavery are planted in Scripture, certainly in Paul's instructions to Philemon about Onesimus. But it wasn't until a later act of the drama, indeed, a much later act—in the nineteenth century—that the church clearly heard God say, "Slavery is an abomination."

The teacher of the law, or the custodian of creation order, who has *not* been instructed in the present and coming Kingdom of God simply serves up the old stuff.

But that can be enslaving. Instead, we must hear what the Spirit is saying to the churches. And today if you hear his voice, do not harden your heart, as in the wilderness. Yes, it is difficult to journey in the wilderness. And God's word for wilderness times is not the same as for settled landed situations. Yearning for the good old days of creation order can be like yearning for eternal static Egyptian *Ma'at*, which at least guaranteed a meal for the Israelites (the flesh pots of Egypt), even though it was a meal eaten in slavery. And Paul says in Galatians that trying to go *back* to Torah and just repeat it, today, leads to slavery (Gal. 4:1-11; 5:1-6).

And yet we're stuck with Matthew. If it is not enough to repeat the old verities, neither is it enough to ignore them, to take out just the new stuff. It's inadequate, if I read this parable rightly, in its Matthean context, to simply innovate, to improvise without consideration of what has gone before, without being deeply embedded in the biblical story, without immersing ourselves in the script we have before us, discerning its plot and being permeated by its spirit and overarching thrust.

But once we are so immersed, once we discern the direction of the plot, it becomes our task to plot our lives in terms of the biblical story. We are called to discern where that story is leading us *today*, to see what improvisation is appropriate, even required of us *now*, based on God's overarching desire for the healing of the world.

Torah is not to be jettisoned for gospel. Neither, I dare to suggest, should it become functionally secondary, superseded by a new emphasis on gospel. That also misconstrues the relationship between them. Rather, Torah is to be re-interpreted and re-articulated *as* gospel. If the notion of "creation order" has become, in our articulations, oppressively static, legalistic and heteronomous, then let the reformation continue! *Ecclesia reformata semper reformanda*!

As teachers of the law trained in the Kingdom, it is our responsibility to discern, in humility—and in community—the trajectories of Scripture concerning the issues put before us on the table at this conference. Of course, I have my opinions (studied opinions) about these issues, and so do we all. But we dare not simply rehearse our studied, deeply held opinions, while writing off those we disagree with. Because, like it or not, there's going to be only *one* Messianic banquet. It's not a take-out menu, where you can still get a bite if you don't like the company. This is a sit-down affair, with table fellowship. To sit at table with Jesus means to engage in community building and mutual struggle to understand God's leading with all who call upon his name.

When Jesus asked the disciples, "Do you understand all these things?" they unhesitatingly said, "Yes!" But as Mark's gospel in particular makes clear, they hadn't *begun* to understand. If you trace the word "understand" in Matthew 13 you'll see that it occurs some six times. Two of those times are in the parable of the sower, where those who hear *and understand* are compared to good soil, which bears fruit and yields a hundred-fold, sixty-fold, thirty-fold.

The question before us is, how fruitful is our tradition in articulating what God is saying to the churches and to the world? Another way to put it is, Do *we* really understand the gospel of the Kingdom?

I realize I've put a whole series of questions on the table so far. And I know that questions alone can't nourish us. We need answers too. But let's not answer too hastily. Let's not be presumptuous. Instead, may our earnest questions addressed in prayer to God give us such a hunger for shalom that we would be driven communally to cook up a meal for our times, a deeply satisfying feast of a compassionate creation order, for all who would attend. A feast at which Christ might be present, that would be a parabolic anticipation of the day when we will eat bread with him in the eschatological Kingdom.

Risking All on God's Grace: The Most Difficult Parable

My third and final parable, the "unjust steward," is universally acknowledged as being *the* single most perplexing parable in the gospel corpus. As parables go it is difficult to classify. It is has been called an "open" parable. That is perhaps not a very satisfying name, but it does signal that there are parables which are *not* very satisfying, which are so riddling and problematic in their interpretation (both in Jesus' day and our own) that they challenge us to undergo a paradigm shift. But a shift to what is not entirely clear. There is an under-determined residue in such parables. An open parable is a conundrum that raises more questions than it answers. And that is part of what this twenty-fifth anniversary conference is about, reflecting on conundrums of normativity. In that case, the parable of the unjust steward is particularly apt for us in the reformational tradition as a catalyst for our reflection.

But a warning: this is a dangerous, unstable, destabilizing parable. It is dangerous, first of all, for me. Apart from the fact that such a difficult parable is easily susceptible of misinterpretation, I am risking the judgement that this text can (and does) speak to our task at hand in this conference. More fundamentally, however, I believe we are *all* at risk as hearers of this parable if we fail to discern its message. We would be like the hard ground upon which the seed fell in the parable of the sower, the ground which represents those who hear but do not understand the message because the Evil One snatches it away.

But this is a dangerous, destabilizing parable also because it asks us as modern western people (and as Calvinists) to suspend our very notions of morality, our sense of what's right and wrong, if we are first of all to even *hear* the parable. In many non-western cultures, including the Middle East, this problem does not exist to the same degree. Many cultures celebrate the rascal, the trickster who beats the system, even by underhanded methods. We, however, don't see things that way. We have a cultural bias (indeed, a theological bias) against this story. What are we to do with a "hero" who is so patently anti-normative?

Jesus told his disciples: "There was a rich man whose manager was accused of wasting his possessions. So he called him in and asked him, 'What is this I hear about you? Give an account of your management, because you cannot be manager any longer.'

"The manager said to himself, 'What shall I do now? My master is taking away my job. I'm not strong enough to dig, and I'm ashamed to beg—I know what I'll do so that, when I lose my job here, people will welcome me into their houses.'

"So he called in each one of his master's debtors. He asked the first, 'How much do you owe my master?'

" 'Eight hundred gallons of olive oil,' he replied.

"The manager told him, 'Take your bill, sit down quickly, and make it four hundred.'

"Then he asked the second, 'And how much do you owe?'

" 'A thousand bushels of wheat,' he replied.

"He told him, 'Take your bill and make it eight hundred.'

"The master commended the dishonest manager because he had acted shrewdly." (Luke 16:1-8a)

In this story we have a steward or a manager who has been found out. He has squandered his master's possessions, with which he has been entrusted (much like the prodigal son in Luke 15:13). Is this some particularly evil person? Or does he stand for all of us, as *we* have been found out by the gospel of the Kingdom? As we have been found out by God, our Master, for squandering our stewardship of this world, with which we have been entrusted?

Upon being found out this manager is fired on the spot. Turn in the account books, the master says, you can no longer be manager.

With his world fallen to pieces, with no ground upon which to stand, the steward begins a salvage operation. He doesn't defend himself. He makes no excuses. He doesn't protest. He doesn't plead, he doesn't try to keep his job. His silence indicates he knows where he stands. But he turns his mind to the future, to the issue of his *survival*. He is self-interested, and he begins to scheme.

He first considers farm labour—but he's not strong enough. Then he considers begging—but he would be ashamed. I know, he says! I know what I'll do so that they will accept me into their dwellings. I know what I'll do so I'll still have a place in the human community. And (if we attend to v. 9) so I'll have a place in the heavenly community, with God and the angelic host.

Quickly he calls his master's debtors. Quickly—before word gets out that he is fired. He acts deceptively, *as if* he were still a representative or agent of the master. And he reduces the debts. He forgives one debt by half and another by twenty percent. He represents (falsely?) the master as generous and gracious. The debtors are surprised and pleased. Wow! This is some master. He can count on our votes at the next town council. This is some steward. What a wily guy. How did you do it?

How did you get him to agree to this? Come by for a drink anytime. If there's anything I can do for you, just ask.

Wouldn't it be interesting if the parable ended there. Suppose that was all we had and we were required to complete the story. What would happen next if we were writing the conclusion?

Would we even come close to what Jesus said? The master commended the unjust steward; he praised the dishonest manager. Not for his dishonesty or un-righteousness (verses 10-13, though outside the present parable, make it clear that Jesus isn't valorizing deception). But the manager is praised for his shrewd, wise action.

But in what sense was his action wise? Well, the steward was wise not to make excuses for his injustice; when he was found out, he didn't try to justify himself. Unlike the Pharisees (see v. 15), he was honest about his own guilt. Also unlike the Pharisees, referred to here as the "people of the light" (v. 8), the steward makes friends of those he has to deal with (v. 9). In this the "people of this world," says Jesus, surpass the supposedly righteous, "the people of the light," who separate themselves from sinners, who set up a barrier between themselves and others.

But the parable implies something more. It is never clearly stated, and that's part of the difficulty in interpreting its point. It is risky to try to discern just why the unjust steward was judged wise. But I want to take the risk of suggesting that, most fundamentally of all, the steward is wise because he discerned something crucial about his master, something which provides the motivation for his admittedly dishonest actions. When he was fired, the steward discovered that his master was not concerned only with justice. Certainly, he would not acquit the guilty, that much was clear (cf. Exodus 34:7b). And yet, being fired was all that happened to the steward. There was no scolding or reprimand. More surprisingly, he was not put in jail; he was not even made to pay up for his squandering. He simply did not receive the punishment he genuinely deserved. Thus the steward discerned that the master was a generous, gracious man. The master, though just, was also compassionate.

And the Kingdom of God which comes in Jesus—and is proclaimed in his parables—exposes our injustice, yet offers us grace. In the light of Jesus, the tax collectors and prostitutes were exposed in their sin. Yet not ultimately for judge-ment, but for mercy and forgiveness. God is a God of grace. This was clearly *not* something the Pharisees had discerned in their wholesale condemnation of "sin-ners." But the Kingdom of God which comes in the person of Jesus is a Kingdom of grace, which invites tax collectors and prostitutes, *and Pharisees* to the Messianic feast, on condition only that they not justify themselves. On condition that they discern that salvation—if it is possible at all for sinners (which is what we all are)—lies in risking everything in a reckless scheme that takes seriously God's gracious compassion offered to the unjust.

The Pharisees (in v. 14) sneer at Jesus. Who does this guy think he is? Presumptuous bastard! And Jesus says to them: You're the ones who are trying to justify yourselves (v. 15), unlike the steward, who *knew* he was unjust. But he saw, behind his master's justice—he discerned, beyond condemnation—a glimmer of compassion. And he took bold, scheming, seemingly foolhardy steps, in light of that discernment.

What the steward did was to represent the master to his debtors as a generous and gracious person. And the question of this parable is, was that an accurate representation? The steward risked all on the claim that it was. If he was wrong, then he would certainly be jailed this time. But if he was right, then perhaps, like the debtors, he could expect mercy, grace.

The issue before us at this conference is *not* our discernment of the normativity of sexual orientation or of feminism, etc. Important though they are, those are side-issues. Rather, the central issue at hand is a discernment of *God*. The question before us is how we represent our Master. De we represent God as a generous Lord, compassionate and gracious, slow to anger and abounding in love and faithfulness, willing to forgive our sin (Exodus 34:6-7a)? Or not?

As those entrusted with the stewardship of creation, called to image God, and—we believe—renewed in that stewardly, imaging task by Christ's redemption, the issue before us is: *What sort of God* do we image? Is this a God who guards his table, allowing no beggars to gather round seeking a hot meal? Is this God a harsh parent who tells us to eat up, strap in hand? Or is this the God who spreads a sumptuous feast for us, graciously offering a rich smorgasbord of mouthwatering dishes to all who are hungry?

Our discernment of God, this parable tells us, is disclosed in the sort of people we are. It is manifested in the way we represent God in the world.

And, like the steward, the way we represent God also discloses what our destiny is. Condemnation or praise. Judgement or grace. As Jesus taught in the Lord's prayer, God's forgiveness is available only to those who also grant forgiveness to others. God's compassion rests on those who themselves show compassion.

I am not here to decide on anyone's destiny. I'm not here to pronounce judgement on anyone. Yet as the parable of the banquet indicates, we can condemn ourselves. We can, indeed, exclude ourselves from the banquet. We can bring judgement on ourselves.

Or, we can, in a wild and desperate gamble, stake everything on the discernment that the God we serve is gracious.

An Ethos of Compassion and the Integrity of Creation:

Setting the Table

Brian J. Walsh

On Setting Tables when Jesus Is Coming to Dinner

In this opening chapter it is my task to "set the table" for this book on an ethos of compassion and the integrity of creation. Now the setting of tables is, at first glance, a pretty straightforward thing—make sure that there are the appropriate number of plates, spoons, forks, knives, glasses, napkins, etc., which will make the eating of the meal as civil and as comfortable as possible. But that very matter of civility and comfortability is not as simple as it might at first appear. In our cultural and intellectual context we might well ask "whose comfortability and which civility?"

I will give you an example. While it is the case that the ritual of a high table in a large dining hall is rooted in a hierarchical societal system of privilege and honour, it is also the case that those who dined at medieval high tables dined in the same hall as other members of the manor—the servants also ate in the same room.[1] Perhaps the food was different, but at least there was a sense that there was still a common fellowship—within tightly arranged bounds, no doubt—in a common eating hall. The later retreat of the lord of the manor from the high table in the dining hall to a private dining room with only his chosen companions may seem to be a breakdown of a hierarchical society, but it is in fact making that hierarchy all the more pronounced. The poor are now out of sight and out of mind and therefore the rich need to have no qualms about the luxuriousness of their meal since no one else is watching, nor do they need to notice if the poor are not receiving proper sustenance.

Of course, high tables still exist. I have had the mixed pleasure of eating at high table a number of times at Worcester College in Oxford. But during my dining at high table I have not quite had a sense that there is much common table fellowship going on. Perhaps that is because I am a middle class guy from the suburbs of Toronto and I find it difficult to feel too comfortable in a jacket, tie and academic gown. Or maybe the reason is that I so often find the conversation at high table to be rather contrived, affected and out of touch with at least my experience of reality. On one evening I was talking to this musicologist and I referred to Dylan and he thought that I was talking about Dylan Thomas, whoever he was!—"the man ain't got no culture."

Or maybe my dis-ease at high table has to do with the fact that the only other people seated in the dining hall are Oxford students, all of whom are of the same class as the high table diners, only of a lower status because of age and academic rank. In an Oxford dining hall the servants serve, they don't sit down anywhere in the hall and eat as well. So my problem with high table is one of feeling cultural dislocation personally and fundamental injustice societally. For example, I just don't know what would happen if the homeless folks who show up at the Gatehouse in Oxford for a sandwich and a cup of tea were to decide that they were going to dine in hall one night. You see *their* level of comfortability and *their* notions of civility are very different from the average Oxford don. How would you set a table if you knew that they were coming? Keep the good china and crystal in the sideboard and bring out the plastic picnic utensils?

Nonetheless, it is still my responsibility to set the table for this volume, as ambiguous as that may be. But the ambiguity is even deeper than I have presently suggested. As I have said, setting a table is a cultural act of producing a context of civility and comfortability. Such an act assumes all kinds of cultural mores. Will we have chopsticks or forks? Can we take the risk of putting knives on the table or is the possibility of violence too great? Who will sit where and why? What will be served? Will there be meat? If so, will it be beef, chicken, pork, lamb, or Uncle Charlie? And if it is Uncle Charlie, did he leave any instructions about who gets what part of his body? You think I am joking, but in endo-cannibalistic societies in which people eat their relatives, there tend to be very strict table manners and protocol when it comes to eating Uncle Charlie.[2]

Back to my questions about table-setting—how many places will be set? Who is invited? Why them and not others? What hints and rituals will there be to maintain a good level of civility at the meal? Now all of these things, and many others, go into setting a table. And while I may feel culturally ambivalent about the whole thing because I don't really know how to answer all of these questions (except for the one about Uncle Charlie—I never liked the guy and wouldn't take a bite out of him if he was the last meal on earth), there is another problem that haunts me. This problem is rooted in my Christian faith and in what I have come to know about Jesus. I have this sinking feeling that as soon as I set the table Jesus is going to come in and kick it over. After all, if he had no respect for the tables in the temple, where perfectly legitimate temple business was taking place, then how can I be so sure that my faltering table setting will fare any better?

One of the most consistent themes in gospel stories in which Jesus comes to dinner is that all kinds of codes of civility get thrown out the window with the result that certain guests, and often the host, experience a very unnerving discomfort. If it is true that eating is a primal ordering event in which we act out and legitimate a certain ordering of the world,[3] then we need to attend closely to the table fellowship of Jesus in its re-ordering power. The way in which Jesus radicalizes the rules of etiquette and holiness at dinner parties is experienced, in its context, as tampering with the very primal order and historical destiny of the world. I offer you one example.

Table-setting has to do with rules. And when Jesus speaks of the rule-enforcers of his day, the Pharisees, he mocks them for their frustration that neither he nor John the Baptist will play by the rules (Matthew 11:16-19, Luke 7:31-35). They are like a group of children complaining that Jesus and John would not join in their childish games. John refused to dance when they said dance, and Jesus refused to weep when they said weep. To John, who neither ate nor drank, they said, "He has a demon." And concerning Jesus, who seemed to have had a pretty good appetite, they said, "Here is a glutton and a drunkard, a friend of tax collectors and sinners." Jesus concludes this discussion by enigmatically saying, "But wisdom is proved right by all her children." Or, to push the culinary metaphor a little further, "the proof of the pudding is in the eating."[4]

The story that Luke records for us immediately after this teaching picks up on the themes of weeping and eating (Luke 7:36-50). It seems that a Pharisee named Simon had invited Jesus to dinner and Jesus had accepted. Now one thing that we know about Pharisees is that table fellowship was central to their piety. Indeed, it has been suggested that "no fewer than 229 of the 341 rabbinic pericopae attributed to the houses of Shammai and Hillel pertain to table fellowship."[5] And for second temple Pharisees, table fellowship wasn't just a matter of the patterns of intimacy, and inclusion and exclusion, that were common to ancient Near Eastern peoples. Rather, "[F]or the Pharisees the meal had become a microcosm of Israel's intended historic structure as well as a model of Israel's destiny."[6] If Israel were to be a holy nation of priests, then Israelites must follow the rituals of cleanliness that are observed by officiating priests in the temple. And that also meant that anything, or anyone, that would serve to pollute or defile that meal must be avoided at all costs. Defilement of table fellowship is indicative of the defilement of Israel. And since Israel is the locus of the cleansing of a defiled creation, the very creation is ultimately at stake.

Unfortunately (at least for Simon the Pharisee), Jesus couldn't get around anonymously any more, so word got out that he was eating at Simon's house and a particular woman of ill-repute somehow slipped into the house. And as Jesus was reclining at table, she came up behind him, weeping. Remember that the Pharisees had complained that Jesus wouldn't play the weeping game, well here is a woman weeping in a Pharisee's home, and at a Pharisee's table. And with her tears she washes Jesus' feet. And as beautiful (and sensual) as that is, there is more. She also dries his feet with her hair, kisses his feet and then anoints them with perfume. The beauty of the scene sends chills up my spine. But not Simon's! Not daring to confront Jesus personally, Simon simply thinks to himself, "How can this man be a prophet of Israel, how can he be a holy man, if he can't even discern that the woman who is touching him is a sinner?" What Simon can't comprehend is why Jesus is allowing someone who is literally an untouchable to touch him. Why does Jesus, a prophet of Israel, put not only himself and his ministry, but the very destiny of Israel, indeed the very integrity and order of creation, at risk by allowing this woman to fondle his feet?

I will not here retell the whole story or explicate fully Jesus' response to Simon. But to catch the power of Jesus' response we have to view this situation from Simon's perspective. He had invited Jesus to table fellowship. He had invited him to anticipate and ritually enact the very destiny of Israel by eating a holy meal together with holy hands. As a pious Pharisee he had set the table with a meticulous eye to the holiness code. No unclean food was present. No unclean people were present. All hands had been properly washed. And then the whole event is put in jeopardy (and by symbolic extension, the very destiny of Israel is put in jeopardy) by this woman. So Simon is understandably mortified. However, he does not get too much sympathy from Jesus. In fact Jesus proceeds to compare what Simon understands to be orderly to what the woman deems to be in order.

> Simon, you see this woman here?
> Well, when I came into your house you gave me no water for my feet, but she has wet my feet with her tears and wiped them with her hair.
> You did not give me a kiss, but this woman has not stopped kissing my feet since she came in.
> You did not pour oil on my head, but she has anointed my feet with perfume.
> So here's the word, Simon: her sins are forgiven, for she has loved so deeply.

And then Jesus turned to the woman and said,

> Your sins are forgiven.... Your faith has saved you; go in peace.

I can just imagine the look of incredulity on Simon's face. "This woman has loved much? This woman has not stopped kissing you? Well, she sure has had enough practice at that, hasn't she? She's kissed almost every unclean man in this town. And she has loved deeply? Well, I guess! Given her lifestyle, that isn't so surprising!"

But even these things would not have been what would have thrown Simon for such a loop. It is the comparison that he wouldn't be able to handle. "You dare compare me to this loose woman who has flaunted her sexuality all over town?"

Even more than that, however, Simon would be perplexed at the content of the comparison. Yes, the woman did wash Jesus' feet, and she did kiss him, and she did anoint him with perfume. But so what? None of these things were required by the holiness code, and what Simon had done in providing water for Jesus' hands and a good kosher meal was enough, until that damn woman came in and ruined everything. But that, I think, is at least part of the point. True, this woman was unclean. True, she did not match up to the holiness code. True, she defiled the meal. But precisely in her defilement she sanctified the meal. Precisely in going beyond the holiness code, beyond the law and loving Jesus deeply with her tears, her lips and her perfume, does she demonstrate a faith that cleans the unclean, makes holy the defiled, shows a hospitality that is truly welcoming, and thereby demonstrates what the kingdom of God is all about. And that is why she departs with the messianic blessing of forgiveness and shalom.

Now this story, like most of the gospel stories, is shrouded in crisis. The very holiness code of the Pharisees, with its nationalistic expectations, was born in a context of the post-exilic crisis of being in the promised land yet still labouring under the rule of foreign empires. Maintaining ritual holiness was a way of remaining faithful to Torah when living under the rule of empires that were self-consciously assimilationist. Yet it is also clear that the ministry of Jesus as a whole, and particularly his patterns of table fellowship, only served to deepen the crisis. By eating with tax collectors and sinners he not only demonstrates an openness of the kingdom to such people, he also inaugurates a reconstitution of Israel that necessitates an abandoning of nationalistic pretensions and an embrace of a renewed understanding of the task of Israel in God's redemptive purposes.[7] And for the Pharisees, this entailed nothing less than a reorientation in their whole understanding of creation order.

It seems to me that we live in a culture and at a time that experiences a similar kind of crisis. To this I now turn.

The Malaise of Modernity

The crisis of second temple Judaism could legitimately be described as crisis of theodicy.[8] The very nomic foundations of Israel, and therefore the whole creation, were confronted with an anomic phenomena, namely foreign occupation of Israelite soil and thwarting of Israel's destiny, which did not seem as if it was going to go away. To use the language of Peter Berger, the "sacred canopy" of temple, Torah and land seemed to have collapsed.[9]

We live in a similar cultural situation. Our time is aptly described as a "time of troubles."[10] In one of my favourite images from the work of Langdon Gilkey, "An autumnal chill is in the air; its similarity to the chill in other periods of cultural decline is undeniable."[11] Ten years after Professor Gilkey first penned those words, however, it seems that the chill is no longer autumnal. It now feels as if we are in the depths of a cultural winter. The culture within which we live, and within which we formulate the questions that are before us in this book, is in radical decline.[12] That is to say, our normative environment, together with its codes of conduct, understanding of values, and legitimating story or worldview is presently in crisis. Such a worldview crisis gives rise to what Clifford Geertz calls the "gravest sort of anxiety."[13] In such a context the very normative ground on which one stands is uncertain. The old answers and the old stories are no longer convincing, and ultimate questions that once had some form of ultimate, faith-committed answers are reopened. Such reopening is usually horrific. Gilkey sums up our situation well:

> Everything seems to slip: our landscape, our institutions, our values, our way of life—and so the security and meaning, the sense of being at home in a world we can understand and deal with that they brought.[14]

To employ Berger again, this is a world in which our social constructions are increasingly hard to maintain, our plausibility structures cease to be plausible, and we are lost in a confused and terrifying anomie in which the nomic structures which quite literally provide us with a "world" in which to live dissipate, leaving us worldless and therefore "homeless."[15] We are, therefore, submerged "in a world of disorder, senselessness and madness."[16] This is an anomic and broken world of broken people "bending broken rules." That was a quote from Dylan—*Bob* Dylan:

Broken lines, broken strings
broken prayers, broken springs
broken idols, broken heads
people sleepin' in broken beds
ain't no use jivin'
ain't no use jokin'
everything is broken

Broken bottles, broken legs
broken switches, broken gates
broken dishes, broken pots
streets are filled with broken hearts
broken words never meant to be spoken
everything is broken

Seems like every time you stop and turn around
something else just hit the ground

Broken colours, broken saws
broken buckles, broken laws
broken bodies, broken bones
broken voices on broken phones

take a deep breath, feel like you're choking
everything is broken.[17]

We live in a world where it does indeed seem "like every time you stop and turn around / something else just hit the ground"—a world of broken idols, broken prayers, broken bodies, broken laws and terribly broken hearts. And well might our hearts be broken since our gods have failed us, by proving to be impotent to hear our prayers.[18] The question of late modernity is also a question of theodicy.

Or perhaps what we are talking about here is the *postmodern* condition. At once liberated from the past distortions, the past lies, yet also "cast adrift—exposed, unprotected and above all frightened."[19]

This experience of being at sea, adrift with little bearings, can be found in the music and lyrics of some of our best and most sensitive artists. Consider the Indigo Girls' song, "Closer to Fine":

I'm trying to tell you something about my life
Maybe give me insight between black and white
The best thing that you've ever done for me
Is to help me take my life less seriously, it's only life after all
Well darkness has a hunger that's insatiable
And lightness has a call that's hard to hear
I wrap my fear around me like a blanket
I sailed my ship of safety until I sank it, I'm crawling on your shores

Chorus:
I went to the doctor, I went to the mountains
I looked to the children, I drank from the fountains
There's more than one answer to these questions pointing me in a
crooked line
The less I seek my source for some definitive
The closer I am to fine

I went to see the doctor of philosophy
With a poster of Rasputin and a beard down to his knee
He never did marry or see a B-grade movie
He graded my performance, he said he could see through me
I spent four years prostrate to the higher mind, got my paper
And I was free

Chorus

I stopped by the bar at 3 a.m.
To seek solace in a bottle or possibly a friend

I woke up with a headache like my head against a board
Twice as cloudy as I'd been the night before
I went in seeking clarity

Chorus

We go to the Bible, we go through the workout
We read up on revival and we stand up for the lookout
There's more than one answer to these questions pointing me in a
crooked line
The less I seek my source for some definitive
The closer I am to fine.[20]

I do not refer to this song just because of its wonderful depiction of a four year undergraduate degree, or even for its depiction of philosophers (or by extension any scholar) who will presumptuously pronounce on all sorts of matters (especially the performance of their students) when they themselves have never really experienced some of the fundamental matters of life (B-grade movies and marriage—both of which bring up questions of normativity in often tragic ways!). Rather, I refer to this song because it begins to capture aesthetically and existentially the issues that we will confront in this book.

The purpose of the song is stated in the opening lines: "I'm trying to tell you something about my life / Maybe give me insight between black and white." This is a postmodern anthem about normativity. She depicts a context in which "darkness has a hunger that's insatiable" and "lightness has a call that's hard to hear." And that is a context in which fear is the most appropriate emotional response—indeed, a fear that is so tangible that it can be wrapped around you like a blanket. A context in which the "ship of safety" has been sunk.[21] This is a situation of radical questioning and the author tells the story of seeking answers in various sources [the doctor, the mountains (a reference to meditation or communion with nature?), the children and the fountain (a reference to the myth of the blessed naiveté of eternal youth?), philosophy, friendship, alcohol, the Bible, revivals, etc.]—seeking clarity and finding none. And finally she concludes that "There's more than one answer to these questions pointing me in a crooked line." But this answer is enough because, in the end, she decides that "The *less* I seek my source for some definitive / the closer I am to fine."

In a postmodern culture in which the assumed *doxa* of modernity has been deconstructed, or "de-doxified" (as Roland Barthe would put it),[22] it is hard to maintain what Charles Taylor calls a "horizon of significance"[23] with its possible points of orientation. To borrow a metaphor from immigration law, if "naturalization" is necessary in order to be a citizen in this world, then postmodern "denaturalization" has made all of us sojourners, without a home in this deeply disorienting civilization with all of its discontents. Consider the words of Bruce Cockburn:

> I need a helmet to protect my head
> I need earphones to hear what gets said
> I need a miracle to keep this little thread from snapping
>
> I know a lot about alienated man
> But we've all heard as much about that as we can stand
> It's just what happens when you let the time span catch you napping
>
> Two forward and one back
> Blind fingers groping for the right track
> What's to do when a stab and a pat on the back look like the same thing?
>
> Civilization and its discontents
> When all's been said and all the money's spent
> Trying to beat the system of the world's events
> Gets you nowhere.[24]

The music of this song aesthetically accentuates cultural disintegration. This is a world in which we need earphones to break through the cacophony of our cultural malaise. A world in which we are never really sure any more what's what. A world of blind fingers groping for the right track. A world in which all the money has been spent, but apparently to no avail—it gets you nowhere!

Of course, there is nothing new about all of this, is there? After all, what I have been talking about is something that "everybody knows":

> Everybody knows that the dice are loaded
> everybody rolls with their fingers crossed
> everybody knows the war is over
> everybody knows the good guys lost
> everybody knows the fight was fixed
> the poor stay poor, the rich get rich
> that's how it goes, everybody knows
>
> Everybody knows that the boat is leaking
> everybody knows the captain lied
> everybody got this broken feeling
> like their father or their dog just died
> everybody talking to their pockets
> everybody wants a box of chocolates
> and the long-stemmed rose, everybody knows.[25]

Not only are we cast adrift and frightened. The boat is leaking and we can't trust the captain. In fact when it comes right down to it, everybody knows that everything is fixed and the dice are loaded against us. No wonder everybody's got this broken feeling. How else can we feel?

"An Ethos of Compassion and the Integrity of Creation:" Seeking Biblical Direction

To summarize the above section: we live in an ethos of either confusion or denial in the midst of what we experience as a dis-integrating creation. To use the categories that Walter Brueggemann developed in his theological commentary on the Psalms, we live in a time of radical disorientation in which the old orientation no longer gives direction and a new orientation has not yet been found.[26] The purpose of this book (and the conference that was the occasion of these papers) is to begin to work together to seek such a reorientation and to consider whether prayerful reflection on "an ethos of *compassion* and the *integrity* of creation" might well be a way to go towards such reorientation. The chapters that follow test out that proposal.

But there is one thing that needs to be made clear at the outset. We come to our theme precisely from an experience of disorientation. Undoubtedly this is a disorientation experienced within the context of an orientation. Indeed, it is only in such a context that anyone can experience disorientation. And we seek for a reorientation that does not lead us to abandon our prior, grounding orientation, but that leads us to a reorientation which empowers us to address our cultural (and personal) malaise with sensitivity, hope and the transformative power of the gospel. In other words, the constant process of orientation, disorientation and reorientation is a life hermeneutic that is profoundly biblical. In the midst of a disquieting worldview crisis, simply singing the old songs of orientation over and over again amounts to little more than saying "peace, peace" when there is no peace. This is indeed dressing our postmodern wounds as if they were not serious.[27] Perhaps the songs we need for today are laments. We need to be singing the slow mournful tunes of the blues. Because it is only in singing laments that we begin to anticipate the *new* songs of reorientation. This book seeks such a new song. But if we are not prepared to lament, we will never be able to sing such a new song with integrity. I'll say more about this in a moment. My point here is simply that an experience of disorientation, or at the very least an ability to empathetically hear and resonate with the disorientation of others is a prerequisite for a fruitful and honest struggling towards reorientation together.

It is my job to set the table. And I hope that these pages have begun to do so. But so far all that we have before us are the plates, cutlery and perhaps some hunger for the meal itself. So far so good. It is not my job to serve up the meal—that is yet to come. But I feel that perhaps we still need an appetizer. So I will conclude this introductory chapter by placing some things on the table for us to begin chewing on.

I want to suggest, in a very beginning way, some biblical direction for our deliberations.

We are seeking to foster, in the academy, in the church, in our homes and in our world an *ethos* of compassion. By ethos, I propose that we accept the broad contours of Clifford Geertz's definition of the term: an ethos is the tone, character and quality of a people's life together, the moral and aesthetic style and mood of that life.[28] An ethos is, then, an attitudinal stance, a *Lebenshaltung*. While seldom fully articulated, it guides and directs those who live within its compass. And the issues we are addressing here are fundamentally about the crisis in the ethos of western culture as it is manifest in literally every dimension of our cultural lives.

If my depiction of our malaise in terms of an anxious anomie in which we feel dislocated, worldless and homeless is at all on target, then perhaps the first thing we need to reflect upon is the biblical view of creation order. Indeed, precisely because the creation is called, directed and ordered is it possible to be at-home in this world. The biblical theology of creation order tells us that we live in a moral universe in which there is normative direction for human life, and that parting from such direction results in nothing less than death. There are "orders, limits and boundaries within which humanness is possible, and beyond these there can only be trouble."[29] This is a creation theology in which "there is an ordered quality to life that will not be mocked."[30] This kind of creation theology, which is undoubtedly central to the grounding orientation of the reformational tradition in which the Institute for Christian Studies was born, is good news. In a time of ecological crisis we are just beginning to re-hear the biblical message of the wise interconnectedness of all things in this creation.[31] In a dis-integrating world we need a vision of integrality and coherence. And in the Scriptures such integrality and coherence is named *shalom*.[32]

Moreover, in the face of chaos, shalom is experienced precisely as order. When Israel is confronted with the chaos of life under the imperial rule of Egypt or Babylon, what is desperately needed is a revelation of the sovereign God who orders all creation and who therefore deposes and topples over all pretentious and idolatrous claims to sovereignty. At first glance, however, it would not seem that chaos was really the threat in either Egypt or Babylon. These were, after all, highly ordered and controlled societies. But order and chaos are terms that we use to judge the character of certain situations. And the Scriptures tend to view these situations "from below." So what the Egyptian Pharaoh or Babylonian emperor calls order, Yahweh calls chaos because oppressed Israelites experience this order as chaos. This is why these empires are so often identified with Rahab and Leviathan, the sea-monsters of chaos.[33] In this literature, chaos is not formless anarchy, but the repressively ordered, though graceless, power in which chaos presents itself as order.[34] This appears to be an ordering of creation, but it is in fact a masquerade, a false representation.

One of the central characteristics of false imperial order is that it is a construct of a royal ideology and must be cruelly imposed upon its subjects. Biblical creation order breaks through this kind of ideology by insisting that creation order is not a construction of kings and emperors, nor does it serve to legitimate such imperial arrangements. Rather the order of creation comes to us as a gift from the hand of a gracious God who brings about the liberation of people labouring under the weight of such imperial orders. Such a doctrine flies in the face of not only ancient Near Eastern emperors but also of late modernity. Creation order is not, ultimately, a product of our social construction of reality. Nor is a shalom-filled ordering of life an accomplishment of human technique. Creation order is a gift of a good, wise and loving Creator.

With every gift, however, a task is entailed. While an order is quite literally "given" to life, we are also called to "give order" to life. Such an ordering of life is constitutive to human culture-forming. And to a very large degree the issues before us in this book are at the intersection of order as given and order as task. If we only notice the given, indeed the gift-character of creation order, then we will likely succumb to the temptation of an authoritarian realism which will lack compassion. If, however, we only attend to the reality-constructing activity of ordering our own world, then we may have a lot of compassion but it will lack any creational integrity and direction. Indeed, without recognizing that order is a gift, it seems to me that it is not likely that we will form an ethos of compassion, but that we will end up absolutizing our particular historical order. Given the perverse self-justifying brokenness of fallen humanity, I can't imagine any other option.

But there is the rub. We are talking about creation order in a fallen world. And that is the ultimate source of our disorientation. Order language is inextricably language of legitimation. That which is orderly is legitimate. That which is disorderly is illegitimate. Expressed pain is seldom orderly. We need only think of racial riots in places like Los Angeles, Toronto and other North American cities to see that this is true. Indeed, we only need to think of our last domestic fight to see that this is true. The question is, what do we do with pain? In a programmatic essay on the shape of Old Testament theology, Brueggemann says, "What we make of pain [and pain-bearers] is perhaps the most telling factor for the question of life and the nature of our faith."[35] I think that he is right. And one of the defining characteristics of the imperial creation orders of the ancient Near East is that they ruled pain out of order. Pharaoh didn't "hear" the cry of the Israelites groaning under the oppression of his brick quotas because he had no ears to hear such crying within the constructs of his own world. Babylonian emperors were not noticed to respond to the pain of their vanquished and enslaved peoples because slavery was the real goal of humans in service of the gods and their imperial image-bearers. Such pain is disregarded or censored because if it was acknowledged it would then bring into question the legitimacy of the empire and the creation order that that empire is erected upon. This remains the case in our time. Brueggemann puts it this way:

> Where pain is not embraced, critical uneasiness about every crushing orthodoxy is banished. It is certain that, where there is the legitimation of

structure without the voice of pain embraced, there will be oppression without compassion.[36]

It seems to me that such legitimation of structure without embracing the voice of pain is a deadly temptation of western culture in general and reformational Christianity in particular.

When we talk about creation order and the embrace of pain we invariably find ourselves talking about the character of creation order. If creation order is an order of order, or an order of rationality, or an order of divine arbitrariness, then pain, and anything else that is disorderly, is ruled out of order and illegitimate. Well then, what kind of a creation order *could* embrace pain? Only a creation order before which pain could have a legitimate complaint? The biblical understanding of an earth which is full of the steadfast love of a God who loves justice and righteousness, conceives of such a creation order.[37] This is a covenantal creation order in which God is available for complaint.

A covenantal creation order is dialogic in character, not the monologue of the order-giver to the subjects of order. Since the relationship is one of covenant partnership the troubles of one partner impinge upon the other. Unlike his Babylonian and Egyptian rivals, Yahweh is involved in the pain of his people. In the psalms of lament, God is implicated in our disorientation. In a time of troubles, the biblical God has no luxury to remain trouble-free.[38] Only in a relationship of covenantal partnership could people be so bold as to rise above docile submissiveness and to raise a voice of protest before the throne of God. Lament gives voice to the pain of a world that does not seem to be very well ordered at all. Lament refuses to acquiesce to the chaos that goes under the name of order. Indeed, lament arises out of the profound sense of a lack of order, lack of justice and lack of integrity. And it legitimately asks God to intervene historically to bring about a renewal of shalom. It can also ask for such intervention, often with tears, wailing and a loud voice, because this God is always in the fray, always in the midst of our historical troubles. This God is always "with us" and if the place where we are is a place of pain, then this God will be with us in the only way that can help, that is, compassionately.

Compassion is a matter of suffering-with the other. In the face of pain the only other options are cold indifference or numbness. Both lead to death. The biblical God is a compassionate God who internalizes the hurt of the creation, who shares the grief of Israel and who weeps over Jerusalem. Earlier I asked: What do we do with pain? How is the threat of anomie, disorder, chaos and demonic evil met? In Jesus we have the answer. When God is most perfectly "with us," God does not impose more order on a disorderly world. Rather, God comes in the com-passionate one—indeed the one who went to a passion week. God deals with pain by bearing it. God deals with chaos by being subject to its fury.

To be the people of God is to take up a cross-bearing discipleship. It is this which sets the contours for an ethos of compassion. Without such compassion, the integrity of creation will be but an ideological dream.

And this brings us back, finally, to the woman who interrupted Simon's dinner party with Jesus. What gained her entry into that dinner, into Jesus' heart, and ultimately into the kingdom of God was her tears. She enters into Jesus' life, and ours, through her voiced pain. That voiced pain supersedes Simon's rules of table etiquette and in so doing transforms the way in which the destiny of Israel and the very order of the world are to be understood. Jesus' response was one of compassion.

In this book we celebrate the twenty-fifth anniversary of the Institute for Christian Studies. We celebrate the gift that the Lord has given to us in this school, and this tradition of Christian scholarship. One of the things that has always characterized the ICS community is the desire to sing a new song unto the Lord. We want to sing a new song in our reflections in this book. But that song must be composed with the voices of pain. So we need to hear voiced pain as we reflect on forming an ethos of compassion which will respect and restore the integrity of creation. We need to hear the pain of women who continue to suffer under the weight of patriarchy with its fluctuations between mild patronizing and wild violence. We need to hear the pain of gay people for whom the notion that heterosexuality is creationally normative is deeply confusing, and the insistence of straight Christians that gays must remain celibate is too painful to bear. We need to attend to the pain of the sick who succumb to the diseases of a toxic society only to be left wondering whether the toxicity of the medical establishment might only be complicating their problems. And ultimately, we need to hear the groaning of the whole creation as it cries out to its Creator, raising a voice of lament which is itself a voice of hope. Simply and baldly stated, if we don't hear that pain, even as we give voice to our own pain, then compassion will be impossible. And without compassion we will neither recognize God's redemptive creation order nor be agents of the restoration of creational integrity.

Notes

1. See Margaret Visser, *The Rituals of Dinner: The Origins, Evolution, Eccentricities, and Meaning of Table Manners* (Toronto: Harper Collins, 1991), 122.
2. Ibid., 4-17.
3. See Mary Douglas, *Purity and Danger: An Analysis of Concepts of Pollution and Taboo* (London: ARK, 1989, first published 1966).
4. R. T. France's interpretation of the verse in *Matthew,* Tyndale New Testament Commentaries (Leicester: InterVarsity Press and Grand Rapids: Eerdmans, 1985), 197.
5. Marcus Borg, *Conflict, Holiness and Politics in the Teachings of Jesus,* Studies in the Bible and Early Christianity, vol. 5 (Lewiston, N.Y. and Queenston, Ont.: Edwin Mellen Press, 1984), 80. Borg's estimation of the Pharisees is heavily dependent on the work of Jacob Neusner. There is, however, a battle raging within scholarship on second temple Judaism between Neusner and E. P. Sanders. Sanders comes to a more "liberal" interpretation of the shape and character of the Pharisee movement.

In this essay all I can do is note that debate and move on. I suspect that even Sanders would acknowledge that table fellowship was a significant (though not the most significant) aspect of the piety and worldview of second temple Phariseeism.

6. Ibid. Borg goes on to say, "Disputes about table fellowship were not matters of genteel etiquette, but about the shape of the community whose life truly manifests loyalty to Yahweh," 81.

7. I am indebted to N. Thomas Wright of Worcester College, Oxford, for not only introducing me to the dining practices of high table, but also for this understanding of Jesus' reconstitution of Israel. See his *The New Testament and the People of God* (London: SPCK and Minneapolis: Augsburg/Fortress, 1992); and his *New Tasks for a Renewed Church* (London: Hodder and Stoughton, 1992), esp. chs. 2 and 4. Similar themes are developed by Marcus Borg in *Jesus: A New Vision* (San Francisco: Harper and Row, 1987).

8. See Peter Berger's discussion of theodicy in *The Sacred Canopy: Elements of a Sociological Theory of Religion* (Garden City: Doubleday/Anchor Books edition, 1969, first published 1967), ch. 3.

9. Ibid., chs. 1 and 2.

10. See Arnold Toynbee, *A Study of History* (London: Oxford University Press, 1934), I, 53; and (1939), IV, 1-5. Langdon Gilkey employs this notion from Toynbee in his article "Theology for a Time of Troubles: How My Mind Has Changed," *Christian Century* 98 (April 29, 1981): 474-80. For further discussion of Gilkey's understanding of this "time of troubles," see my book, *Langdon Gilkey: Theologian for a Culture in Decline* (Lanham, MD: University Press of America), ch. 3.

11. *Society and the Sacred: Toward a Theology of Culture in Decline* (New York: Seabury, 1981), xi.

12. I have discussed the decline of modernity at further length in *Subversive Christianity: Imaging God in a Dangerous Time* (Bristol: Regius Press, 1992), chs. 2 and 3; and in *Who Turned Out the Lights? The Light of the Gospel in a Post-Enlightenment Culture.* An Inaugural Lecture (Toronto: Institute for Christian Studies, 1990).

13. *The Interpretation of Cultures* (New York: Basic Books, 1973), 99.

14. *Reaping the Whirlwind: A Christian Interpretation of History,* A Crossroad Book (New York: Seabury Press, 1976), 16.

15. See Peter Berger's appraisal of modernity's homelessness in *The Homeless Mind: Modernization and Consciousness* (New York: Random House, 1974). Similarly, Michael Walzer speaks of home as a "dense moral culture" in *Interpretation and Social Criticism* (Cambridge: Harvard University Press, 1987), 15-16. Perhaps the anomie that accompanies the worldview crisis of modernity is a matter of normative homelessness.

16. *Sacred Canopy*, 22.

17. "Everything is Broken" from the album *Oh Mercy.* © 1989 CBS Records Inc.

18. See Bob Goudzwaard, *Idols of our Time,* translated by Mark Vander Vennen (Downers Grove, IL: InterVarsity Press, 1984). See also the biblical taunt of the impotence of idols in passages like Psalm 115 and Isaiah 40:18f.

19. Jeremy Rifkin (with Ted Howard), *The Emerging Order: God in the Age of Scarcity* (New York: Putnam's Sons, 1979), 212.

20. From the album *Indigo Girls*. © 1988 Godhap Music (BMI).

21. The image of being shipwrecked is rich with metaphoric potential. I think of Bruce Cockburn's evocative song, "Ship-wrecked at the Stable Door," on the 1988 album, *Big Circumstance.*

22. Linda Hutcheon, *The Politics of Postmodernism* (London and New York: Routledge, 1989), 2-4.

23. *The Malaise of Modernity* (Toronto: Anansi, 1991), ch. 4.

24. Bruce Cockburn, "Civilization and its Discontents," from the album *Trouble with Normal.* © 1983 Golden Mountain Music Corp. Richard Middleton and I have explored the Christian relevance of Bruce Cockburn's artistry further in two other articles: "Dancing in the Dragon's Jaws: Imaging God at the End of the Twentieth Century," *The Crucible* 2, 3 (Spring 1992), and "Theology at the 'Rim of A Broken Wheel': Bruce Cockburn and Christian Faith in a Postmodern World," *Grail: An Ecumenical Journal* 9,2 (June 1993).

25. Leonard Cohen, "Everybody Knows" from the album *I'm Your Man.* © 1988 CBS Records Inc.

26. Walter Brueggemann, *The Message of the Psalms: A Theological Commentary,* Augsburg Old Testament Studies (Minneapolis: Augsburg, 1984).

27. See Jeremiah 8:11.

28. *The Interpretation of Cultures,* 89.

29. Walter Brueggemann, "A Shape for Old Testament Theology, I: Structure Legitimation," *Catholic Biblical Quarterly* 47,1 (Jan. 1985): 40. This article and its sequel, "A Shape for Old Testament Theology, II: Embrace of Pain," *Catholic Biblical Quarterly* 47, 3 (July 1985), are foundational to the following discussion.

30. Ibid., 41.

31. For example, see Loren Wilkinson et al., *Earthkeeping,* revised edition (Grand Rapids: Eerdmans, 1991); James A. Nash, *Loving Nature: Ecological Integrity and Christian Responsibility* (Nashville: Abingdon, 1991).

32. See Walter Brueggemann, *Living Toward a Vision: Biblical Reflections on Shalom,* second edition (New York: United Church Press, 1982); and Nicholas Wolterstorff, *Until Justice and Peace Embrace* (Grand Rapids: Eerdmans, 1984).

33. Cf. Psalms 68:28-31; 89:9-13; Isaiah 30:7; 51:9-11; Jeremiah 51:34-36, 42-44; Ezekiel 29:2-6, 32:2-4. For helpful and biblical reflection on creation and chaos see Bernhard Anderson, *Creation versus Chaos: The Reinterpretation of Mythical Symbolism in the Bible* (Philadelphia: Fortress, 1967, 1987); and Pedro Trigo, *Creation and History,* Robert R. Barr, trans., Theology and Liberation Series (Maryknoll, NY: Orbis, 1991).

34. See Brueggemann, *Living Toward a Vision,* 92.

35. "Shape of Old Testament Theology," I, 44.

36. "Shape of Old Testament Theology," II, 399.

37. See Psalm 33:5.

38. See "Shape of Old Testament Theology," II, 402.

Creation Order: A Historical Look at Our Heritage

Albert M. Wolters

Introduction

It is fitting that the Institute for Christian Studies in Toronto should celebrate its twenty-fifth anniversary with a conference on the idea of creation, since the Institute for Christian Studies has its roots in Dutch neo-Calvinism, in which the idea of creation played a particularly significant role. I think for example of Herman Bavinck, probably the greatest theologian of Dutch neo-Calvinism, whose thought was dominated by the theme "grace restores nature," by which he meant that salvation was essentially a restoration of creation in all its fullness.[1]

It is therefore also particularly fitting and symbolic that Bavinck visited Toronto exactly one hundred years ago, in 1892, and gave a lecture just a few blocks from the present location of ICS, on the topic "The influence of the Protestant Reformation on the moral and religious condition of communities and nations." The lecture was given to the Fifth General Council of the Alliance of Reformed Churches Holding the Presbyterian System, and was included in the proceedings of this international gathering.[2] According to his successor and biographer, Valentinus Hepp, Bavinck's 1892 speech in Toronto might just as well have been entitled "The Excellence of Calvinism," since it stressed the virtues of Calvinism as a world-transformative movement.[3] It is safe to assume that Bavinck had no inkling at that time that another international gathering in Toronto would be devoted to exploring the implications of this kind of Calvinism a century later, hosted by an institution that owed its origins to precisely the Dutch neo-Calvinism of which Bavinck was the foremost intellectual spokesman.

As a former historian of philosophy, and current biblical scholar, I will make my points about neo-Calvinism against a broad historical background. Neo-Calvinism as a historical reality is now a thing of the past; for us its heirs it may be useful to try to establish its distinctive features, at least with respect to the understanding of creation, in order to help us in determining what is living and what is dead in the neo-Calvinist heritage. For that a broad historical perspective can be useful. I begin with a sketch of the history of the notion of cosmic order.

Cosmic Order: History of an Idea

With the one significant exception of the modern West, it seems that all cultures have a notion of cosmic order, an overarching and stable framework of meaning in which everything finds a meaningful place. Consonant with this is the fact that virtually all religions teach a doctrine of cosmic order. In fact, if the Dutch missiologist J. H. Bavinck is to be believed, the notion of cosmic order is a structural component of religion in general.[4] Let me illustrate this overall point with a number of examples from the ancient civilizations which lie at the root of our own.

The major cultures of the ancient Near East are similar in holding to some overarching concept of cosmic order. In Egypt, for example, we have the idea of *Ma'at*, usually translated "justice" or "truth," which has been defined as "the constitutive order of creation established by the primeval creator deity to direct the harmonious regularity of the cosmos for all eternity."[5] In the ancient Mesopotamian civilizations we have the analogous concept of *me*. Consider the following quote from the eminent Sumerian scholar S. N. Kramer:

> The Sumerian theologians adduced what was for them a satisfying metaphysical inference to explain what kept the cosmic entities and cultural phenomena, once created, operating continuously and harmoniously without conflict and confusion; this was the concept designated by the Sumerian word *me*, the exact meaning of which is still uncertain. In general, it would seem to denote a set of rules and regulations assigned to each cosmic entity and cultural phenomenon for the purpose of keeping it operating forever in accordance with the plans laid down by the deity creating it.[6]

This Sumerian idea of *me* was taken over by the Assyrians and Babylonians, who expressed it by means of the Akkadian words *parsu, mesaru* and *kittu*.[7]

It is clear that Kramer's description of Sumerian *me* has some remarkable parallels with the modern theological concept of *Schöpfungsordnung*, or Herman Dooyeweerd's philosophical category of "individuality structure." Note that *me* refers not only to "cosmic entities," but also to "cultural phenomena." This fits in with the more general observation that the idea of an established order in the ideologies of the ancient Near East included the structures of human society and culture. In fact, as Richard J. Clifford has pointed out, it seems that the notion of creation in the ancient Near East referred *primarily* to the institutions of human society.[8]

Generally speaking, the gods are subject to, or identified with, the cosmic order, or else responsible for only a small part of it. Wisdom is the apprehension of this order.[9]

In many ways, the Bible fits into this overall picture of ancient Near Eastern conceptions of cosmic order. Its notion of creation is distinctive primarily in that the created order was established by a transcendent and sovereign Creator (although even here there are analogies in surrounding cultures). For Israel, there is nothing divine that is subject to, or identified with, the cosmic order. But it is like other ancient Near Eastern cultures in seeing the cosmic order (creation) as referring specifically to human society, and in being associated with wisdom. Furthermore, cosmic wisdom is cognitively available to humankind; this is probably the significance of the picture found in Proverbs 1 and 8 of Lady Wisdom calling out in public places to everyone.[10]

A characteristic feature of Israelite wisdom literature is the antithesis between wisdom (*hokma*), which is rooted in the fear of the Lord and conforms to the created order, and folly (*nebala*), which is an irreligious violation of the created order and thus acquires the strong sense of "outrage," especially of violations of the order for human sexuality.[11] Corresponding to this religious antithesis between wisdom and folly is the opposition between "the righteous" and "the wicked."

The close connection between wisdom and creation in the Old Testament has been a prominent theme in recent biblical studies, and is usually associated with the name of Gerhard von Rad.[12] It should be pointed out, however, that this connection had already been clearly understood by earlier scholars, for example James Fleming, who wrote that for the Israelite wise man "wisdom ... was wrought into the constitution of the universe," so that human wisdom can be defined as "ethical conformity to God's creation."[13]

We find a similar connection between wisdom and the cosmic order among the early Greeks. It has been pointed out by Burkhard Gladigow, in his important study *Sophia und Kosmos* that in early Greek thought there was a complementarity between cosmic order and wisdom. Correlate with *sophia* was the notion of *kosmos*, meaning "the world held in a divine order" (*die in einer göttlichen Ordnung gehaltenen Welt*). Wisdom was a question of "fitting oneself into" (*sich einzuordnen*) this cosmos.[14] In Greek thought this concept of cosmic order was closely tied to such other basic notions as *Ananke, Moira*, and *Heimarmene*, the necessary fate ordained by the gods, which in Heraclitus and Stoicism becomes identified with *Logos*, the rational order of the universe which can be grasped by reason. In this way the notions of *kosmos* and *sophia* become intellectualized in Greek philosophy, so that both order and wisdom come to be defined in strictly *rational* terms. It now becomes the special province of the *philosopher*, by means of his or her rationality, to discern the order of the world, now defined in terms of the metaphysical universals behind and in the reality of our experience. There is now little sense of the religious or ethical dimensions of this apprehension of the cosmic order. The tradition of autonomous rationality, with its corresponding "natural law," is born in Greek philosophy.

In the modern West, with the breakup of the medieval synthesis of the Bible and Greek philosophy, we see the rise of "humanism," here defined as the increasingly secular and anthropocentric mindset of modernity, with its emphasis on autonomous human freedom. In the basic outlook of humanism, two fundamental themes of the biblical tradition were increasingly marginalized: creation as God-ordained order, and antithesis as the religious opposition with respect to that order.[15] This process of marginalization culminated in Kant's "Copernican revolution" and its heirs in German idealism and in what Alvin Plantinga calls the "creative antirealism" of much contemporary thought. Whatever order there is in the world is posited by man,[16] not God, and the antithesis of biblical religion is domesticated or privatized, if not denied altogether.

Creation Order in Neo-Calvinism

Against this broad and sketchy background, let me make my remarks about creation order in neo-Calvinism, the soil in which the Institute for Christian Studies has its most immediate roots. In speaking of "neo-Calvinism," I mean the revival of orthodox Calvinism in the Netherlands in the nineteenth century, chiefly associated with the names Guillaume Groen van Prinsterer, Abraham Kuyper and Herman Bavinck, and the later movement for a Calvinistic philosophy in the Netherlands, chiefly associated with the names D. H. T. Vollenhoven and Herman Dooyeweerd. All these thinkers shared a basic "world and life view," and a concomitant approach to culture, which set them apart from other traditions of Christendom. In what follows I will lump them all together under the rubric "neo-Calvinism," and only occasionally note their differences. This simplification has the advantage of making it easier to highlight what is distinctive about their view of creation.

In a general way, it seems to me that the neo-Calvinist conception of creation can be defined in terms of three points of reference: the Greek, the humanistic, and the biblical notions of cosmic order. Neo-Calvinism opposed the humanist tradition (especially as embodied in neo-Kantianism) by seeking to recapture the biblical view of reality. It did this by strongly reasserting the twin biblical themes which humanism had marginalized, namely creation and antithesis, with the latter defined in terms of the former. Initially, the neo-Calvinists looked upon the Greek philosophical heritage as an ally in their struggle against contemporary humanism (for example in adopting the tradition of *Logos* speculation), but increasingly they sought to distance themselves from this tradition as well (especially in the work of Vollenhoven and Dooyeweerd).

As I see it, the idea of creation in neo-Calvinism can be conveniently outlined under seven headings: law, scope, dynamism, knowledge, constancy, history, and differentiation. In what follows, I will briefly illustrate each of these seven points by quotations from leading representatives of neo-Calvinism. I am well aware that I am oversimplifying matters to an astonishing degree. I hope that my critics will refine and correct the picture I have drawn, and that at least its main outlines will survive the scrutiny of those better versed in neo-Calvinist thought than I myself.

Law

For the neo-Calvinists, creation was defined by law. The order of creation was a *law*-order. This is hardly surprising, since a positive notion of law has always been a hallmark of Calvinism in general. If the sovereignty of God is a central, if not *the* central, theme of Calvinism, then God's law must needs be prominent also, since law and sovereignty go together. To say that God is sovereign is to say that what he says goes, that his word is law. This applies not only to soteriology, but also to cosmology. God lays down the law to all his creatures. Consequently, we find prominent in the vocabulary of the neo-Calvinists such terms as *levenswet*, the creational ordinance applicable to the life or functioning of a particular kind of creature, *wetsidee*, "law-idea" or "cosmonomic idea," and *ordinantiën*, the old-fashioned Dutch plural of the word designating a creation ordinance. When Kuyper became Prime Minister of the Netherlands in 1901, and assigned to his colleague Geesink the task of writing a series of articles outlining the basic contours of a Calvinistic world and life view, the latter did so under the characteristic title (also assigned by Kuyper) *Van's Heeren Ordinantiën*, "On the Ordinances of the Lord."[17]

The connection between creation and law is stated unequivocally by Kuyper himself:

> Everything that has been created was, in its creation, furnished by God with an unchangeable law of its existence. And because God has fully ordained such laws and ordinances for all life, therefore the Calvinist demands that all life be consecrated to His service, in strict obedience.[18]

Or we might repeat the oft-quoted words which Kuyper spoke at the twenty-fifth anniversary of *De Standaard* in 1897:

> One desire has been the ruling passion of my life. One high motive has acted like a spur upon my mind and soul. And sooner than that I should seek escape from the sacred necessity that is laid upon me, let the breath of life fail me. It is this: That in spite of all worldly opposition, God's holy ordinances shall be established again in the home, in the school and in the State for the good of the people; to carve as it were into the conscience of the nation the ordinances of the Lord, to which Bible and Creation bear witness, until the nation pays homage again to God.[19]

Three corollaries of the idea of creational law should also be briefly mentioned: the law-subject correlation, the distinction between principles and positivization, and the distinction between structure and direction.

If God lays down the law to each of his creatures, then we must accept both the distinction and correlation of law and subject; that is, the creational ordinance and the creature for which it holds. For every creature there is an ordinance, and for every ordinance there is something subject to it. This distinction was to become one of the categorial cornerstones of the philosophies of Vollenhoven and Dooyeweerd.

Secondly, it is significant that neo-Calvinism allowed for a diversity of implementation of creational ordinances, at least in the human sphere, according to different historical and cultural contexts. In other words, a distinction was made between the normative principles given in creation and their human positivization for different situations. Again, this is a categorial distinction which finds later systematic elaboration in philosophy (especially in the thought of Dooyeweerd), but we find it already in earlier neo-Calvinism. Consider the following statement in Bavinck's *Philosophy of Revelation*:

> Now the peculiarity of all revelation is, that while it posits principles and lays foundations, it charges men with the application of these principles and the building upon these foundations. Creation was the first revelation.... Thought and speech, life and history, science and art, have all had their commencement in principles which are laid down by God's creative power.[20]

Thirdly, we must mention the distinction between structure and direction, between the nature of a creaturely phenomenon as it is constituted and governed by its creational ordinance, and the duality which separates the ordained nature of a phenomenon from its factual nature in a fallen world, so that a direction toward creational lawfulness is opposed by a direction away from it. This version of the ideal-real distinction, which takes seriously both the continuing goodness of creation and the pervasive effects of the fall, was to prove pivotal in the neo-Calvinist attitude to culture, allowing it to oppose, for example, the perversions of modern technology, science and art, without rejecting these phenomena as such. Bavinck puts it as follows:

> The assertion that modern culture is in conflict with Christianity is thus a meaningless phrase. Who ventures to assert that marriage and family, state and society, art and science, trade and industry as such are condemned and opposed by Christianity? At the most such an assertion may be made as to the manner and the direction in which these institutions and activities at the present time are developing or are carried on.[21]

It is the telltale phrase "as such" which here indicates, as so often, an awareness that the creational structure of something is not obliterated by its religious direction.

Scope

It follows from what we have said about the law-subject correlation that creation in neo-Calvinism is very broad in scope. God's ordinances apply to everything, therefore everything but God is creational. Consider the following quotation from Kuyper:

What now does the Calvinist mean by his faith in the ordinances of God? Nothing less than the firmly rooted conviction that all of life has been first in the *thoughts* of God, before it came to be realized in *Creation*. Hence all created life necessarily bears in itself a law for its existence, instituted by God himself.... Consequently there are ordinances of God for our bodies, for the blood that courses through our arteries and veins, and for our lungs as the organs of respiration. And even so are there ordinances of God in logic, to regulate our thoughts; ordinances of God for our imagination, in the domain of aesthetics; and so also, strict ordinances of God for the whole of human life in the *domain of morals*.[22]

As our earlier quotes have already demonstrated, creation in this understanding includes the institutions of society and culture. There is a remarkable convergence here with the idea of cosmic order in the civilizations of the ancient Near East, including that of Israel, which did not know the modern dichotomy between nature and culture, between fact and value. Creation is a comprehensive category; in the terminology of the early Vollenhoven, who made a distinction between the two Dutch words for "reality," the spatio-temporal world or *werkelijkheid* is only part of the created world or *realiteit*.[23]

It is therefore common for the neo-Calvinists to speak of "created life," for example in a discussion of economics, in order to express their conviction that underlying all human cultural activity is a substrate of created reality which both makes possible that activity and sets normative standards for it. It is in that sense also that Bavinck can say that "science is itself a creature,"[24] or in general that societal and political life, as well as art and science, are the "works of [God's] hands."[25]

Dynamism

Creation, understood in terms of God laying down the law, is a dynamic reality, an active force. The law of creation asserts itself, it makes itself felt in a variety of ways. For one thing, the order imposed by God in creation restrains evil and promotes the good. Creational law is "in force," it impinges on its creaturely subjects. In this sense it is closely allied to the notion of "common grace" (or "conserving grace").

This is a point which is already clear in the writings of Guillaume Groen van Prinsterer, the statesman and historian who is one of the earliest representatives of neo-Calvinism. As Harry Van Dyke writes in his recent study of Groen's classic *Unbelief and Revolution*, it is not true that Groen reduces everything in history to the religious ideas of its actors. Historical causality has a deeper dimension:

Most fundamental to Groen's causal analysis is the role in history of the moral world-order. For this is what restrains the revolutionary doctrines from running their logical course to the very end....[26]

Groen uses a number of different terms for this restraining order, including "the ordinances of God," "the universal principles of Justice and Right," and the "immutable laws which the Maker and Sustainer of all things prescribes for his creatures and subjects."[27] It is the restraining power of the created order which curbs and checks sin and its effects in the world.

The same point is made repeatedly by Kuyper and Bavinck, especially in the former's three volume work on common grace, and the latter's rectoral oration on the same topic.[28] The emphasis is no different in the writings of Dooyeweerd.[29]

Knowledge

Another way in which creation shows its active character is the way it manifests itself to human cognition. Creation makes itself known; there is a revelation in and through the created order. This is what the theological tradition has called "general revelation": a revelation of God and his attributes in nature. In neo-Calvinism this revelation is associated with human knowledge in general, including the knowledge acquired in the sciences. As Bavinck puts it: "To acquire knowledge, the Scriptures refer man not to his own reason, but to the revelation of God in all his works."[30] Or again:

> [God's] thoughts and words speak to us out of the whole world, even out of the world of plants and animals. When botany and zoology trace out these thoughts, these sciences, as indeed the natural sciences in general, are glorious sciences, which no man, certainly no Christian, may despise.[31]

Kuyper went so far as to say that a Christian university, in being bound to the word of God, is bound in the first place to the word of God in creation. Consider the following passage from his *Band aan het Woord*:

> ... It is undeniable that a *word of God* also comes to us in that which God created, or did, and still does.... From what God did and does there always proceeds a kind of *speech* (*eene sprake*—allusion to Psalm 19:3 in the Dutch *Statenvertaling*). There is a speech of God in nature, a thought of God is spoken forth in history, there is a word of God in our reason, there is a speaking of God in our inner consciousness of God.... And so it is firmly established that every one who fears God, and binds himself and his striving to the word of God, must immediately take into account the all-sided speech of God which goes out to us in Nature.... This has always been the confession of the Reformed Churches; Article 2 of the Belgic Confession says: "We know God by two means, namely (not first from Scripture, but) *first* by the creation, preservation, and government of the universe, since that universe is before our eyes like a beautiful book in which all creatures, great and small, are as letters to make us ponder the invisible things of God." Already from this it is apparent that to say without further qualification, "I am bound to Scripture,"

is a highly incomplete formula. We must even begin by referring to that quite different word, to the speech of God in Nature....[32]

A few pages later in the same publication Kuyper goes on to say the following:

> The University too must be bound to the *word* of God, in every way in which God makes known to us his word: in nature, in history, in our own heart, and in his Scriptural revelation. Do not forget that the University does not only have a Theological faculty, but also investigates nature, history, the juridical sphere and so much more. It is therefore not enough to say that it is bound to Scripture. Wherever and however God speaks, the University must always give ear and follow. Materially, therefore, there is no difference of opinion: the University must be bound to God and to God alone, whenever and wherever God makes manifest his Wisdom, his Will, and his Ordinance, or renders them knowable through investigation and research.[33]

It should be stressed that while scientific knowledge is dependent on creational revelation, the same is true of human knowledge in general, including the intuitive knowledge of the child and the artist. It is not only to rational apprehension that creation manifests itself.

Constancy

The creation order is immutable, not subject to the flux of history. In this sense it is a bulwark against all historicism and relativism. We thus hear Groen van Prinsterer speak of "eternal and unshakable principles," "immutable laws," and "unchangeable ordinances of God."[34] For Groen, as for Kuyper and Bavinck, this immutability was conceived in neo-Platonic terms: the changelessness of creational ordinances was that of metaphysical principles which participate in the eternity of the ideas in the mind of God.[35]

In the thought of Vollenhoven and Dooyeweerd, the immutability of creational law is dissociated from the long tradition of Christian Logos-speculation, and is grounded directly in the faithfulness of God, who does not abandon the works of his hands. For them it is more appropriate to speak of the *constancy* of the created order, since "constancy" is an ethical rather than a metaphysical concept. Dooyeweerd still speaks of "supra- arbitrary principles" that are given with creation, and that are not subject to history, but this is no longer a matter of rational necessity, but of reliable steadiness grounded in the faithfulness of God. This shift in emphasis comes clearly to the fore in the way Dooyeweerd speaks of "natural law." In 1925, in an essay entitled *Calvinism and Natural Law*, he still uses the term "natural law" to describe his own conception, but in his mature thought he vigorously opposes the notion of natural law as a metaphysical construct.[36] This is somewhat misleading, since Dooyeweerd's own emphasis on constant normative principles given with creation clearly stands in continuity with essential aspects of the classical Christian conception of natural law.

History

On the basis of what we have said above about the distinction between principle and positivization, and of the dynamic nature of creation, it is clear that neo-Calvinism does not see a contradiction between the idea of a constant cosmic order and that of historical development. In fact, it views creation as the indispensable *condition* of historical development. As Bavinck writes in connection with the theory of evolution: "But development is not opposed to creation, but is possible only on the basis of the latter."[37] It becomes one of the distinctive features of neo-Calvinism that it conceives of history as the unfolding of creation, the carrying out of a task contained in the ordinances of creation.

One of the clearest ways in which this comes to the fore is in the neo-Calvinist conception of what is termed "the cultural mandate," the command given by God to Adam and Eve to multiply and "subdue the earth" (Gen. 1:28). As Bavinck puts it:

> All culture, that is, all work which man undertakes in order to subdue the earth, whether agriculture, stock breeding, commerce, industry, science, or the rest, is all the fulfilment of a single Divine calling.[38]

The connection between creation and cultural mandate is so close that some neo-Calvinists have preferred to speak of the "creation mandate" instead. Culture, and indeed all of history, is the bringing forth, through human responsible action, of the riches latent in God's good creation.

All of this is put in a broad redemptive-historical context. From the beginning of human life on earth, the human race is mandated to work toward a great future goal: the development of creation in accordance with God's design. That development has been disrupted, but not annulled, by the fall into sin, and is reaffirmed in salvation. The goal toward which history moves is therefore not a return to the garden of Eden, but an eschatological fulfilment of creation pictured as the New Jerusalem, into which the glory and honour of the nations will be brought (Rev. 21:26). The movement from the primordial garden to the eschatological city embraces history, and is from first to last a struggle for the manifestation of the riches and goodness of creation.

Differentiation

For the neo-Calvinists there is also a close association between creation and the idea of separation and differentiation. To create is not only to bring into existence, but also to bring into existence different kinds of things, kinds which are ontologically separate from each other, each with its own creationally guaranteed nature. This theme is rooted in the creation story of Genesis 1, which speaks of repeated separations, and about the creation of living things "after their kind,"[39] but it is applied more generally to the created order as a whole. Bavinck, for example, writes:

The world is a unity, but that unity manifests itself in the most magnificent and beautiful diversity. Heaven and earth were distinct from the very beginning; sun and moon and stars each received their own task; plant and animal and man each have their own nature. Everything is created by God with a nature of its own, and exists and lives according to a law of its own.[40]

This general theme is worked out by Kuyper in his principle of "sphere sovereignty," the principle that different spheres in society (such as family, state, and church) have their jurisdiction limited by their created nature. Coupled with the notion of historical development, this led to the concept of societal *differentiation*, a process whereby creationally distinct spheres gradually disengage themselves, as part of the overall unfolding of creation, in the course of time.

It was Kuyper who first emphasized (going beyond Groen) that sphere sovereignty should be understood as a *creational* principle,[41] and it was Dooyeweerd who expanded the notion of sphere sovereignty to mean ontological irreducibility in general, including the irreducibility of such modal aspects as faith and feeling. Ontological diversity, whether sociological or modal, was grounded in creation and creational law, and provided a criterion for criticizing various kinds of societal totalitarianism and theoretical reductionism.

It is striking that Hendrikus Berkhof, in his *Christian Faith*, also discerns a connection between creation and separation, notes how this theme has been made fruitful in the work of Dooyeweerd and Vollenhoven:

> The merit of the much-disputed *Philosophy of the Cosmonomic Idea* of the philosophers Dooyeweerd and Vollenhoven (Free University) is that, from the perspective of the idea of creation, it puts such a strong emphasis on the variety and plurality of the various levels of existence, and points out the confusion that results from the failure to discern the laws which hold for those different levels.[42]

The connection between creation and the diversity of kinds is very strong in Dooyeweerd, so that his appeals to let the "creation motive" have its effect in Christian theorizing are in fact exhortations to recognize the given diversity of kinds.[43] He himself puts the matter quite forcefully:

> The creation motive of the Christian religion is engaged in an irreconcilable conflict with the apostate tendency of the human heart to eradicate, level, and erase the boundaries between the peculiar and intrinsic natures that God established in each of the many aspects of reality. For this reason the principle of sphere sovereignty is of powerful, universal significance for one's view of the relation of temporal life to the christian religion.[44]

The themes of historical unfolding and differentiation (worked out in detail in Dooyeweerd's theory of the "opening-up process") have the effect of making neo-Calvinism much more open to historical progression than orthodox Christian movements generally are. Conjoined with the distinction between structure and direction, these themes enabled the neo-Calvinists to adopt a stance of critical openness to much that was new in the modern world, including contemporary academia and technology. The world in its historical unfolding was everywhere fallen, but that same world was everywhere also *creational*.

INTEGRATION INTO A WORLDVIEW

Having completed our survey of the salient features of the neo-Calvinist understanding of creation, it remains for us briefly to point out how creation, thus understood, fits into the overall religious vision of life and the world espoused by neo-Calvinism.

The matter can be put quite simply. Undergirding the neo-Calvinist understanding of biblical religion is the theme which was so often stressed by Herman Bavinck: grace restores nature. That is to say, the meaning of the Christian religion is the restoration of the fallen creation. And because creation was understood in such comprehensive terms, embracing all of history and culture, the neo-Calvinist view of grace, of the Christian religion, and of the kingdom of God, was equally comprehensive. Redemption is a cosmic salvage operation whereby the entire created order is reclaimed by God in Jesus Christ. In this expansive vision of the Christian religion, it is throughout the good creation of God which is at stake in the world-historical drama of salvation, and it is creational normativity which is an ever-present factor in the questions of Christian ethics.

PROMISE AND PERILS

Let me conclude with a few short evaluative comments. In my own personal opinion, probably the greatest merit of the neo-Calvinist worldview is the way it combines a recognition of the pervasive effects of sin with a recognition of the continuing presence of the good creation in a wide range of phenomena. This combination, captured in the distinction between "structure" and "direction," is a useful heuristic guide in avoiding all kinds of practical and theoretical false dilemmas. It should be noted that this distinction has such a wide application only because it is based on a comprehensive concept of creation, a concept which has direct roots in the Scriptures, and is at odds with the regnant ideologies of the secular West.

Furthermore, as I see it, one of the advantages of the neo-Calvinist conception of the created order is its promise to break through the dilemma of Platonism versus historicism. It rejects both the assumption of supra-historical metaphysical entities (in later neo-Calvinism even such entities "in the mind of God") and the relativistic denial of all constants. Instead, it seems to me that there is a promising alternative in the notion of normative principles and positivization, especially as this has been worked out by Dooyeweerd, in legal theory and elsewhere.

In my judgement, the greatest ideological danger to face the Christian church since Gnosticism in the second century is the historicism of the modern world. While recognizing this danger, I consider it a mistake to respond to it by clinging to, or reverting to, the long theo-ontological tradition of Christian orthodoxy, with its *analogia entis* and God as *summum ens*. Faced with the Greek idol of *ousia*, and the modern idol of *Geschichtlichkeit*, I say: a plague on both your houses. As an alternative I would suggest as prime category the biblical idea of *'emet*, "steady faithfulness." The neo-Calvinist concept of creational ordinances, shorn of all neo-Platonist trappings, seems like a good place to start in reforming our categorial frameworks in a more biblical direction.

I also believe that the concomitant idea of creation-as- separation is an effective antidote to the various kinds of reductionism which are so rampant in contemporary academia.

However, I do see two problems with the overall approach to creation which I have sketched, one epistemological and one ethical. I will do no more than name them. The epistemological one is the question of the knowability of creational ordinances, especially the normative ones. Assuming that there are given standards for economics or art, what methodological safeguards can we devise against epistemological subjectivism in establishing what is normative in these areas? How can we decide between "beautiful harmony" (Dooyeweerd) or "allusivity" (Seerveld) as aesthetic norm? Do we have no recourse but to appeal to intuition or self-evidence? (I leave aside here the question of the light of Scripture, which makes the matter both easier and more difficult.) The ethical problem I see is the danger of legalism. A tradition which emphasizes the ubiquity of law, and the broadness of the call to obedience, is in constant danger of losing the joyful spontaneity and the willingness to make or tolerate mistakes which the redeemed life calls for.

Finally, let me note that Herman Bavinck, when he returned to the Netherlands after his visit to Toronto in 1892, spoke of the city as "the centre of Presbyterianism in Canada," and went on to describe it as follows:

> There are in Toronto no fewer than 150 churches, and no more than 75 saloons. The Sunday is observed here even more strictly than in England. No newspapers are published on Sunday. The stores are closed without exception. The streets are deserted. The Puritan ethos is clearly in evidence.[45]

It is difficult to tell from Bavinck's words whether he considered this Torontonian ethos to be an example of the dangers of legalism or of the world-transformative character of Calvinism. In either case, however, I suspect that he saw it as the direct application of a creation ordinance.

Notes

1. See J. Veenhof, *Revelatie en Inspiratie. De Openbarings- en Schriftbeschouwing van Herman Bavinck in vergelijking met die der ethische theologie* (Amsterdam: Buijten & Schipperheijn, 1968) 345-65. This section is available in English translation as J. Veenhof, "Nature and Grace in Bavinck," A. Wolters, trans. (Toronto: ICS Academic Paper).

2. Published in *Alliance of the Reformed Churches holding the Presbyterian System. Proceedings of the fifth General Council, Toronto 1892* (London: Publication Committee of the Presbyterian Church of England, 1892), 48-55.

3. V. Hepp, *Dr. Herman Bavinck* (Amsterdam: Ten Have, 1921), 215.

4. See J. H. Bavinck, *Religieus Besef en Christelijk Geloof* (Kampen: Kok, 1949), 26-38, and idem, *Inleiding in de Zendingswetenschap* (Kampen: Kok, 1954), 248-56.

5. Leo G. Perdue, *Wisdom and Cult: A Critical Analysis of the Views of Cult in the Wisdom Literatures of Israel and the Ancient Near East* (Missoula: Scholars Press, 1977), 19. Cf. C.-J. Bleeker, "L'idée de l'ordre cosmique dans l'ancienne Égypte," *Revue d'histoire et de philosophie religieuses* 42 (1962): 193-200.

6. S. N. Kramer, *The Sumerians* (Chicago: University of Chicago Press, 1963), 116.

7. Perdue, *Wisdom and Cult*, 121, note 3.

8. R. J. Clifford, "The Hebrew Scriptures and the Theology of Creation," *Theological Studies* 46 (1985): 507-23, esp. 509-10.

9. See Leo G. Perdue, "Cosmology and the Social Order in the Wisdom Tradition," in *The Sage in Israel and the Ancient Near East*, John G. Gammie and Leo G. Perdue, eds. (Winona Lake: Eisenbrauns, 1990), 457-78. This entire volume underscores the close ties between ancient Near Eastern wisdom literature and the notion of cosmic order.

10. See G. von Rad, *Wisdom in Israel* (New York: Abingdon Press, 1972), 145-76, and R. E. Murphy, "Wisdom and Creation," *Journal of Biblical Literature* 104 (1985): 3-11.

11. See for example Gen. 34:7 (rape), Deut. 22:21 (fornication), Judg. 19:23 (homosexual relations), 20:6 (rape), 20:10 (rape), 2 Sam. 13:12 (rape), Jer. 29:23 (adultery).

12. See especially his *Wisdom in Israel*. See also the study by von Rad's student Christa Kayatz, *Studien zu Proverbien 1-9* (Neukircher-Vluyn: Neukirchener Verlag, 1966), which makes the connection between creation in the Old Testament and *Ma'at* in Egypt.

13. James Fleming, *Personalities of the Old Testament* (New York: Scribners, 1939), 502.

14. B. Gladigow, *Kosmos und Sophia. Untersuchungen zur Frühgeschichte von sophos und sophie* (Hildesheim, 1965), 140.

15. Cf. the statement by H. Evan Runner in his address "On Being Anti-Revolutionary and Christian Historical: At the Cutting Edge of History, 1979-80" in *Christian Political Options*, C. den Hollander, ed. (The Hague: AR-Partijstichting, 1979), 127: "And central to such an inner reformation must be an explicit orienta-

tion to two realities which the Scriptures consistently teach and which 20th century humanism consistently ignores: the reality of constant creational ordinances (structure) and the reality of a spiritual antithesis (direction)."

16. I use the word advisedly.

17. W. Geesink, "Voorwoord" in *Van 's Heeren Ordinantiën*, 2d ed., 3 vols. (Kampen: Kok, 1925).

18. A. Kuyper, *Lectures on Calvinism* (Grand Rapids: Eerdmans, 1961), 53.

19. Translation of John Hendrik de Vries, as found on p. iii of the "Biographical Note" in Kuyper, *Lectures on Calvinism* (1961).

20. H. Bavinck, *The Philosophy of Revelation* (Grand Rapids: Baker, 1979), 265.

21. Bavinck, *Philosophy of Revelation*, 253.

22. Kuyper, *Lectures on Calvinism*, 78.

23. D. H. T. Vollenhoven, "Kentheorie en Natuurwetenschap," *Orgaan der Christelijke Vereeniging van Natuur- en Geneeskundigen in Nederland* (1926): 4.

24. Herman Bavinck, *Our Reasonable Faith: A Survey of Christian Doctrine* (Grand Rapids: Baker, 1956), 164.

25. "Herman Bavinck's 'Common Grace,' A Translation by Raymond C. Van Leeuwen," *Calvin Theological Journal* 24 (1989): 60.

26.. A. J. van Dijk, *Groen van Prinsterer's Lectures on Unbelief and Revolution* (Jordan Station, Ont.: Wedge, 1989), 232.

27. Ibid.

28. A. Kuyper, *De Gemeene Gratie*, 3 vols. (Leiden, 1902-1905), and H. Bavinck, "Common Grace" (see note 25).

29. H. Dooyeweerd, *Roots of Western Culture: Pagan, Secular, and Christian Options* (Toronto: Wedge, 1979), 36-39, 59.

30. Herman Bavinck, *Christelijke Wereldbeschouwing* (Kampen: Kok, 1913), 22 (my translation).

31. Bavinck, *Our Reasonable Faith*, 201.

32. A. Kuyper, *Band aan het Woord* (Amsterdam: Hoveker & Wormser, 1899), 10.

33. Kuyper, *Band aan het Woord*, 34.

34. Quoted in Van Dijk, *Unbelief and Revolution*, 232.

35. For a clear statement of this general position, see Bavinck's *Christelijke Wereldbeschouwing*, esp. 55-57.

36. See for example *A New Critique of Theoretical Thought*, 4 vols. (Philadelphia: Presbyterian & Reformed, 1953-58).

37. Herman Bavinck, *Schepping of Ontwikkeling* (Kampen: Kok, 1901), 39.

38. Bavinck, *Our Reasonable Faith*, 187.

39. See Paul Beauchamp, *Séparation et création. Étude exégétique du chapitre premier de la Genèse* (Paris: Desclée de Brouwer, 1969).

40. Bavinck, *Schepping of Ontwikkeling*, 41-42.

41. See Dooyeweerd, *Roots of Western Culture*, 54.

42. H. Berkhof, *Christian Faith: An Introduction to the Study of the Faith* (Grand Rapids: Eerdmans, 1979), 162.

43. See A. Wolters, "The Intellectual Milieu of Herman Dooyeweerd," in *The Legacy of Herman Dooyeweerd*, C. T. McIntire, ed. (Lanham MD: University Press of America, 1985), 7.

44. Dooyeweerd, *Roots of Western Culture*, 43.

45. Cited in Hepp, *Dr. Herman Bavinck*, 218-19.

Creation Order and Transcendental Philosophy

Response to Albert M. Wolters

Sander Griffioen

The purpose of my response is not so much to express disagreement with Al Wolters' paper, but rather to narrow down the scope of our subject to on one particular theme, viz., the relation between (the idea of) creation order and Reformational philosophy as a *transcendental philosophy*. I shall first dwell on the pioneers, Dooyeweerd and Vollenhoven, then consider briefly the relation of their thought to Calvinism in general. From there we shall move to a discussion started by my colleague Jacob Klapwijk in the mid-1980s, then compare his position with that of J.P.A. Mekkes, and finally draw some conclusions.

As you will notice, this paper places much weight on developments in Holland. This is not to question the originality of North American contributions to Reformational thought, but rather to stress that we are facing common challenges.

Vollenhoven and Dooyeweerd

To introduce my theme I draw on one of Wolters' own distinctions. I recall that in a lecture he gave for my students at the University of Leiden in December, 1981, he distinguished sharply between worldview and philosophy. The lecture was on the nineteenth century roots of Reformational thought. Wolters stressed that on the level of worldviews the breakthrough came much earlier than in philosophy. Kuyper, Bavinck and *commilitones* had a clear picture of the implications of Calvinism "for all areas of life," but in philosophy they remained tied to the old tradition of Logos-speculation.[1] It was only with Vollenhoven and Dooyeweerd that a philosophical breakthrough came about.

With these two pioneers "law" came to play a decisive role. Where previously in epistemology arguments from Logos-speculation had served to bridge the gap between subject and object, now this connection was sought in God's law as a law-word holding for both the knowing subject and for reality.

To understand the connection between law and creation, one important element needs to be added: Dooyeweerd's transcendental turn.[2] In Vollenhoven law primarily serves as a boundary between God and the world. For Dooyeweerd this is important, too. However, at the same time he placed considerable emphasis on the transcendental significance of the law order, i.e., as the foundation for the possibility of experience, of the intelligibility things have—in fact, of their very being. Present research in Dooyeweerd's earliest philosophical writings shows that once he had taken this course, the connection between law and creation was soon to follow: law-order then became identified with creation order.[3]

Transcendental as used here has as its backdrop Kant's idea of a transcendental philosophy, viz., an inquiry into the apriori conditions of knowledge. Instead of "apriori conditions" we may read, as Dooyeweerd does, universally valid conditions on which the possibility of something else depends.[4] However, at least two differences obtain between a Kantian and a Dooyeweerdian use of "transcendental." In the first place, Dooyeweerd gave the notion of "transcendental" a broader meaning, since his interest was not only in the conditions of knowledge, but in the conditions of experience in general. A second difference vis-a-vis Kant is that transcendental does not function as the last horizon. Here Dooyeweerd's distinction between transcendental and transcendent obtains. Characteristic of transcendental is the assumption of a necessary connection between conditions and what is conditioned by these. Dooyeweerd uses the verb "to require" to qualify this link: conditions which make theoretical thought possible, he states, are *"required by the immanent structure of this thought itself"* (*New Critique of Theoretical Thought*, vol 1, 37). Therefore, he would never speak of creation as being a necessary condition for thought, experience, or reality in general. He would have objected to turning the confession "Who has created heaven and earth" into a formulation of a necessary condition. In its full sense "creation" transcends philosophical knowledge. Yet a link remains. Creation belief, in the Dooyeweerdian perspective, although itself pertaining to a transcendent order, answers problems formulated at a transcendental plane. In this sense I would maintain that the idea of creation had gained prominence within Dooyeweerd's philosophy because of the transcendental approach.

It is important to understand that Vollenhoven's thought did not take such a turn. Interestingly enough, this difference has an immediate bearing on my theme. In his Ph.D. thesis on the early Vollenhoven, John Kok concludes that up to about 1928 one finds next to nothing on creational ordinances.[5] Creation (in the sense of *creatura*) is placed under the law. It is only within that setting that creation arguments play a certain role.[6] Dooyeweerd, on the other hand, interprets creation order as a manifestation of divine law.

Beyond Calvinism?

What prompted Dooyeweerd to take a transcendental turn? Above all it was a concern for the universal. In this sense he remained in line with classical metaphysics. Hence his antipathy towards nineteenth century historicism which—relativistic (Dilthey) or not (Hegel)—sought to link philosophy to the spirit of a time or nation (*Zeitgeist, Volksgeist*) or, for that matter, to a historically conditioned worldview (*Weltanschauung*). Viewed in this light, one easily understands that from the late 1930s on he became increasingly uneasy with the designation "Calvinistic philosophy": it simply smacked too much of particularism. Nor need it surprise us that Vollenhoven did not have similar problems with the term "Calvinism." As Wolters explained in his contribution to the volume *Stained Glass*, he kept using a worldview-yields-philosophy model, and hence continued to see his own philosophy as an expression of neo-Calvinism as a worldview. For Dooyeweerd, on the other hand, "Calvinism-as-worldview" no longer defined the character of philosophy, so that Dooyeweerd (unlike Vollenhoven) henceforth preferred to speak of his philosophy as being simply "Christian," instead of "Calvinistic."[7]

What am I driving at? My point is not that it has been unfortunate that eventually Dooyeweerd, and not Vollenhoven, became the influential reformational philosopher. I am sympathetic to the transcendental approach of Dooyeweerd, because I don't see any other way to develop a philosophy which *qua intent* is both Christian and universal. Klapwijk raised the same point in his response to the paper from which I just quoted:

An expressivist idea of philosophy, or the "worldview-yields-philosophy" approach, such as we find in Kuyper and Vollenhoven, as well as in Professor Wolters himself, is not be recommended for various reasons. Probably the most important is that it leads to Romantic particularism and Christian isolationism.... A transcendental critical idea of philosophy, as we find in Dooyeweerd, is a stronger position than an expressivist one because it seeks to rescue philosophy's claim to universality....[8]

However, for a transcendental turn a price has to be paid. Klapwijk himself stressed on various occasions that Vollenhoven's philosophy remained closer to biblical language. The explanation lies in the aforesaid: through the worldview as medium it remained linked to biblical moorings. I would like to add another point. In relation to the conference theme, "An ethos of compassion and the integrity of creation," it is easily assumed that whatever Calvinism may be missing in other respects, at least it has an emphasis on creation as its distinctive trait. In fact, as became apparent, Vollenhoven placed much greater stress on law than on created order. In this respect he remained closer than Dooyeweerd to what I would suggest is the real hallmark of Calvinism: a deep respect for the God who commands, who through his law-words calls things into being: in brief, a deep respect for God's sovereignty.

In reading a biography of Martin Lloyd-Jones, the great Calvinistic preacher, it has struck me that here one finds next to nothing about creation. What was it then that marked Lloyd-Jones's type of Calvinism? No doubt, it was the confession of the sovereignty of God. As he explained: "The sovereignty of God means that all that exists and happens does so because He wills it."[9] In retrospect, it is unfortunate that no lasting contacts developed between this theological Calvinism and Calvinistic philosophy.[10] If it had, massive condemnations of philosophy as one finds with Lloyd-Jones would less likely have developed. Clearly, he could not even conceive of the mere possibility of a Christian philosophy: "Human philosophy militates against this doctrine [i.e., God's sovereignty]. Men start with their own ideas and thoughts and do not like the sovereignty of God.... Philosophy is the greatest enemy of Christian truth."[11]

Thus questions remain. Dooyeweerd's philosophy, for all the grandness of its scope, nevertheless runs the risk of losing contact with the concrete faith community within which it came to development. Vollenhoven's philosophy, on the other hand, although less outgoing and even isolationistic vis-a-vis the broader philosophical world, yet remains open towards non-philosophers who have their roots in the same worldview.

Meaning and Suffering

Interestingly enough, Jacob Klapwijk, whom we just met as a defender of Dooyeweerd's transcendentalism, on other occasions has worded grave reservations as to one implication of this thought. Dooyeweerd in his later philosophy, to stress the dynamic character of creation (as *creatura*), came to speak of *meaning* rather than of order. Instead of "creation order," "creation as meaning" was to gain prominence. Klapwijk, although sympathetic to the dynamism of this conception, objects to the notion of all-embracing meaning. At an international conference in 1986 in celebration of fiftieth anniversary of the Association for Calvinistic Philosophy held at Zeist, The Netherlands, in a broad survey lecture Klapwijk criticized the identification of creation and meaning.[12]His concern is that human experience be taken seriously. A philosophy which interprets reality in its entirety as "meaning" cannot be true to the pervasive sense of meaninglessness among the hungry and the lonely around us. Klapwijk said, "There are situations in which God's creatures are so tortured by anxiety, by pain, or by stifling loneliness that the word 'meaning' dies on my lips" (116). Klapwijk continued:

> Thinkers like Dooyeweerd can teach us how transparent the creation is.... On the other hand, thinkers like Dostoevsky or Ricoeur must teach us the extent

to which demoniac evil has penetrated to the basements vaults of human existence (116).

This lecture provoked commentaries from a number of people. The same issue of *Philosophia Reformata* in which his lecture was published contained reactions from A.P. Bos, H.G. Geertsema, G. Groenewoud, and J. van der Hoeven. In the next issue an extensive response by J.D. Dengerink was published.[13] I shall restrict myself to Dengerink's critique since it is most characteristic of the transcendental approach.

"Meaninglessness," Dengerink objects, cannot be the right phrase, for nothing in reality is without meaning. Instead, he thinks, terms like "nonsense" or "anti-meaning" could have been used (8), the prefix "non" or "anti" denoting a (negative) response to pre-given meaning. Sin is a case in point: "Only through the original creation-law we acquire an understanding of sin as rebellion against God" (30). To highlight the transcendental nature of this argument I quote a passage from Dengerink's summary:

> Through these laws the meaning of creatures is determined (defined). As such they are the fundamental horizon for human experience. These laws are implied in God's creative and re-creative (redeeming) work. No creature is able to withdraw from them. God's (creation-)law is universal, i.e., comprehensive and all-pervasive (Ps. 119:94). Klapwijk, however, explicitly rejects the idea of a universal horizon of experience as an enduring, super-arbitrary and at the same time dynamic "framework," which holds for every place and time (30).

It would be good if this discussion were continued. I am convinced the issues at stake are highly important for the concerns of this conference. Klapwijk wants to make place within Reformational philosophy for a "depth hermeneutics" of meaning (Klapwijk, 1987: 115-18). I cordially sympathize with him. Yet I do not know how such a hermeneutics of the concreteness of the *condition humaine* comports with the universalist thrust of a transcendental philosophy.

Dengerink and others have rightly stressed that conceiving the transcendental horizon as meaning does not imply a denial of non-meaning or anti-meaning. To the contrary, meaning in this sense provides the background against which non-meaning becomes identifiable as such. Of course, having said this, one has to face the question about the existential value of such an insight. Is it compassionate to tell someone who feels terribly lonely that loneliness is only possible (identifiable, etc.) because the norms for social life hold also in that situation? It is certainly true that loneliness is a deficient mode of human sociability. But does this insight—important though it be in other respects—give access to the experience of those who suffer? The answer is negative. Philosophical answers as such do not afford consolation, and it is not compassionate to employ them to that end. Yet in a more indirect way such philosophical answers may become very meaningful. They may help us to understand that non-meaning has neither the first nor the last word. M.C. Smit touched on this in an essay on the meaning of history. Speaking about the indelible image of God in humans, he pointed out that being an image means being placed in a relation to God, and that a human being "can never fall from this relation, however deep he indeed may fall, which is to say that man can never lose or escape the meaning of history."[14]

Structures under the Rainbow

One philosopher whom I ought to mention in this respect is J.P.A. Mekkes (1898-1987). His work has the reputation of being inaccessible, and rightly so. Not only has little of his work been translated, but also—just to mention one more reason—*prima facie* the significance of this work is not easy to discern. Mekkes's thought seems to move along Dooyeweerdian tracks. Indeed, it was foreign to him to claim originality for his own contribution. Yet, on closer inspection, the fabric of Dooyeweerdian philosophy in the hands of Mekkes appears to have changed drastically. Klapwijk calls Mekkes the "conspicuous exception" among the first generation of Reformational philosophers, for he was the only one to develop a "creational-*messianic* perspective": "It was Mekkes who wrote," Klapwijk reminds us, quoting Mekkes, " 'To speak of creational ordinances as something in them-selves is ... impossible' and he therefore spoke beautifully of 'structures under the rainbow' " (Klapwijk, 1987: 114).

The page Klapwijk refers to contains an interesting example of what Mekkes means. Creational structures, he holds, do not precede but follow the dynamics of the Kingdom of God.[15] It is the Cross that sustains the world, rather than the other way around. In fact, I think, Mekkes comes close to a *philosophia crucis*. But at this juncture my questions return. If it is the Cross that sustains the created world, can creational structures still have a transcendental significance, even though, as Mek-kes states, "... they follow, rather than precede"? Is such a philosophy still able to articulate universal conditions of human life, universal modes of experience, trans-historical norms, non-arbitrary "structural principles" for societal institutions, etc.? In Mekkes's works one finds little structural analysis. In itself, of course, that does not warrant a negative conclusion. In his own courteous way Mekkes used to express appreciation for such work done by others. Probably he saw this as a division of labour, his own calling being diagnostic rather than thetical. But is that the whole story? I for one am not entirely convinced that his philosophy retained the universal intent that is characteristic of a transcendental philosophy.

Conclusion

It is not my intention to end this contribution with clear-cut conclusions. Ideally Reformational philosophy should be ecumenically universal, yet firmly rooted in historical Calvinism. May the Institute for Christian Studies contribute to this project. Such a philosophy would continue to develop transcendental-structural arguments, not as cheap answers to human suffering, but as pointers towards God's rainbows for a fallen world.

Notes

1. See also Jacob Klapwijk's contribution to *Wetenschap en rekenschap*, a volume published to commemorate the Vrije Universiteit's centennial in 1980 (Amsterdam: VU Press).

2. Those elements had already been connected on the worldview level: see Wolters' lecture re Kuyper on "Creation Ordinances." My point, however, is that the connection was to become more stringent within the context of Dooyeweerdian transcendental philosophy.

3. I owe this information to Roger Henderson, who prepared a Ph.D. thesis on the early Dooyeweed at the Vrije Universiteit (defended in March, 1993). According to Henderson, the theory of modal aspects served as an intermediary. The first traces of the latter theory became visible in 1922.

4. The importance of the apriori-idea for the Kantian tradition of transcendental thought comes out clearly in René Van Woudenberg's Ph.D. thesis, *Transcendentale reflecties* (Amsterdam: Vrije Universiteit Press, 1991).

5. See John Kok, *Vollenhoven: His Early Development* (Dordt College Press, 1992), 230: "During the years that have been our focus up until now, Vollenhoven says little or nothing about a 'creation order' or 'creation ordinances.' "

6. For instance, creation (as *creatio*) is posited as the common origin of subjective and objective rationality; see Kok, 1992, 46-47.

7. Albert M. Wolters, "On The Idea of Worldview and Its Relation to Philosophy," in *Stained Glass: Worldviews and Social Science*, P.A. Marshall, S. Griffioen and R.J. Mouw, eds. (Lanham, MD: University Press of America, 1989), 23.

8. Jacob Klapwijk, "On Worldviews and Philosophy," in *Stained Glass*, 52.

9. Iain H. Murray, *D. Martin Lloyd-Jones, The Fight of Faith 1939-1981* (Edinburgh: Banner of Truth, 1990), 238-39; compare 189-97.

10. In 1948 Lloyd-Jones attended the Calvinistic Congress held at Amsterdam. He must have then met Dutch philosophers. However, he definitely did not feel at home. Interestingly enough, the biography focuses on cultural differences: "After hearing the first lecture in the church where they were meeting, he was about to leave for the scheduled coffee break when he was informed that there was no need to do so. Coffee was to be brough in, said his neighbour, lighting a cigar as he spoke. Others took out pipes and soon the place was as smokey as a saloon. ML-J was disturbed by the feeling that truth was being handled with a detachment which is foreign to the spirit of the New Testament. The whole congress alerted him to a danger which he had not previously met: 'It was a warning to me of an intelectual Calvinism'." (155; see also 196).

11. Op. cit., 239.

12. "Reformational Philosophy on the Boundary between the Past and the Future," *Philosophia Reformata*, 52 (1987): 101-34.

13. J.D. Dengerink, "Een brug te ver. Een antwoord aan J. Klapwijk," *Philosophia Reformata* 53 (1988): 1-32.

14. M.C. Smit, *Writings on God and History*, Harry van Dyke, ed. (Jordan Station, Ontario: Wedge, 1987), 202; see also 263 and 266.

15. See J.P.A. Mekkes, *Tijd der bezinning* (Amsterdam: Buijten en Schipperheijn, 1973): "Structuren hebben haar bevestiging onder de regenboog, maar juist deze wijst naar de dynamisch vervulling. Structuren hebben wel de weg voor de Triomfator voorbereid, doch niet om na Zijn overwinning voor Hem uit te blijven gaan doch om Hem te volgen."

The Doctrine of Creation: Judging Law and Transforming Vision

Response to Albert M. Wolters

Carroll Guen Hart

In beginning my remarks, I must express my gratitude to Dr. Wolters for agreeing to attempt a history of our notion of "creation order." It is good to do a history of this concept, because too often we treat it as if it has no history, as if it just dropped down from heaven with no participation on our part. But, as Dooyeweerd has pointed out, humans give articulation to any normativity to which we make deliberate appeal in our decision-making. In an anniversary year it is appropriate to look critically at the sort of normativity we articulate, at where it comes from and where it might lead us.

So let's look at this history of the notion of creation order. Wolters has argued initially that simply *having* a doctrine of cosmic order is in itself not distinctive but generic to human culture. Anthropologist Mary Douglas would back this up in her discussion of purity and danger. All cultures have frameworks of meaning in which things find meaningful place, and these frameworks determine for us what is acceptable and what is not.

So far so good. But Wolters goes on to specify some of the ways in which cosmic order is distinctive among these other cultures. He locates that distinctiveness in terms of the *creation* of this order by a sovereign and transcendent creator; *law* as organizing metaphor of cosmic order; and an emphasis on maintaining *boundaries* and *distinctions* against (in Dooyeweerd's words) "the apostate tendency of the human heart to eradicate, level, and erase the boundaries between the peculiar and intrinsic natures that God established in each of the many aspects of reality." These aspects, then, are what identify the distinctively Christian, and further, reformation-al understanding of cosmic order as *creation* order. On the basis of this creation order, we make the distinction between *wisdom*—conformity to the created order and *folly*—violation of the created order. The reformational version of this is indeed admirably nuanced, managing to acknowledge the reality of sin while holding onto the good creation.

For the purposes of critical self-reflection appropriate, I believe, to an anniver-sary year, let me suggest a slightly different angle on this history—an outsider's view, as it were. Richard Rorty and John Dewey, both descendants in some fashion of the Christian tradition but both alienated by its notion of order, look at the history of western culture, and in particular at the history of our views of normativity. These thinkers suggest that an articulation of order is normal and important to human cultural activity; however, they insist that we view this articulation of order in relation to an appreciation of change. Thus orderedness is our funded, stability-oriented way of distilling our experience of the world into categories which enable us to cope well and wisely with the world. Such a conception of order does shape our experience, but in the long run is itself shaped by experience. Order in this way is a human framework, articulated for the purpose of acting wisely in the world, in Dewey's phrase, "behaving in deference to the connections of things." It is historical, responsive, and responsible. It is also thoroughly functional, and if at some point it no longer helps us to act wisely, it needs to be critically revised and sometimes radically changed. In these accounts, notions of order serve ethics, and not the other way round.

Both Dewey and Rorty draw the line between generic and distinctive in a slightly different way than Wolters would. They are not convinced that the notions of creator and creation make the important difference that they do for Wolters. A cosmic order, they argue, can be related to a sovereign creator and be just a minor variant on the rationality tradition. What does make the Christian tradition distinc-tive for them is thus not an emphasis on transcendence, law, and boundaries, but, in Rorty's terms, "welcoming the stranger," and in Dewey's terms, the notion of God incarnate in ordinary human life, as an illumination of its ideal possibilities. I should point out that Dewey also valued the Christian tradition precisely for its critical openness to experience, evident in the phrase which provided the organizing motif for his philosophy: "By their fruits shall you know them."

However, order pulled out of relation, hypostatized and absolutized, becomes a great evil, providing us with a tool of criticism and control which is itself invul-nerable to criticism. It then allows us to build our own choices and preferences into an order which is then completely "objective." As Dewey points out, this is the way to philosophical bad faith and inauthenticity. But an absolutized notion of order also results in an authoritarian, law-and-order attitude. To this law-and-order mindset, any challenge is by definition anarchy, a rejection of all authority and normativity. Perhaps the worst result of this conception of normativity is that it makes us fearful and distrustful of contemporary experience as chaotic and unruly, needing to be brought under the yoke by a strong authoritarian normativity. This also gives privileged groups the power to pass experience "under the yoke," or, to use Wolters' term, to "lay down the law to creatures."

Let me envision in more congenial terms what this might mean for a view of creation order. For our purposes I shall focus on the function of creation order as a species of that generic kind that anthropologists and theologians call a purity code. After all, it is in the sense of purity code that creation order can be opposed to compassion, as in the title of our conference. This is not by any means all that there is to creation order, but it is a significant aspect. Walter Brueggeman's work on the tripartite notion of "canon" implies, I think, that Israel's Torah provided a purity code intended to make Israel distinct from other peoples; it provided an ethos around which to build a community. However, the distinctive ethical focus of this purity code is its emphasis on "slave memory." Both the creation story and the purity codes are relative to the exodus from Egypt; they articulate Yahweh's intent to establish a culture in which freed slaves may ensure that slaves may continually be set free. "Shalom" denotes the all-encompassing cultural reality which is to be realized out of our common slave memory. Both creation order and purity codes exist in order to help us realize shalom, and not the other way round; as Jesus put it later, the sabbath exists for humans and not humans for the sabbath.

Whenever the current order becomes too settled and too unresponsive to the "new word of the Lord" from those underneath, it is time to look critically at these articulations, as the prophets among us have done and continue to do. This is a difficult and uncomfortable process, for the established order vested in cultural institutions and power has far more weight than the cries of pain and anger from those who do not matter. It is important for us to remember, however, that Jesus deliberately crossed every boundary present in his own religious culture. He ate with tax collectors, sinners, and prostitutes. He took as his examples of faith a bleeding woman, a Roman soldier, an unclean Samaritan, a prostitute. The son who broke all the rules and ate alongside the pigs was welcomed alongside the son who had followed all the rules. And later on a vision convinced Peter that he should "call no human unclean." In Jesus, God's love extends to all of us, transcending our current purity codes and notions of creation order. The only purity code that Jesus recognized involved whatever caused us to do good or evil to our neighbour.

I am not saying that we should thereby do away with purity codes and notions of creation order. Quite the opposite. For these are indispensable tools for building and maintaining a vital Christian community. What I am suggesting is that we need to make sure that our purity codes serve our central ethical focus—to love God by loving our neighbour. Like all communities, it is easy for us to think that the purity code is an end in itself. We then run the risk of allowing it to serve some end other than shalom. I suggest that a notion of creation order which serves shalom will continue to draw lines between right and wrong, acceptable and unacceptable. But—and this is the crucial part—it will also build into this order an openness to Yahweh's working in our midst. If I may put it this way, it is a creation order with a built-in obsolescence, looking not simply back to an original purity, but also forward to the revolutionary, overturning love of Yahweh in Jesus. Redemptive creation order will not shut out people—like women and gays—who cross our current boundaries. Redemptive creation order will create institutions and practices which ensure that the slaves and the marginalized will continue to be set free, that the boundaries will continue to be challenged by the love of Yahweh.

In an anniversary year, then, let us ask ourselves this: Which comes first, preserving the integrity of our boundary lines and concepts, or bringing Yahweh's shalom into our very own community? Are we interested in enforcing law and order, or in transforming our culture so that it shows forth the love and justice of Yahweh? And let me ask this: Whose interest is the notion of creation order serving? The interests of a conservative established majority, or the interests of shalom in which those who were far may be brought near?

In conclusion, let me suggest that we try viewing creation as a vision to be worked toward rather than as a finished reality. Creation would then be, in Rorty's words, an "act of social faith," a way of coming to view all reality as "creatures," as created with the possibility of incarnating shalom. For this possibility is not a positivist fact, something we could see on the surface of things, but something we hold onto in faith. Creation as a transforming vision then becomes a way of opening up and enlarging our sense of the possibilities of things and persons, rather than as a way of closing them down. We look at the present in light of God's future rather than limiting the possibilities of transformation to our current categories and assumptions. In this context, our articulated notion of creation order becomes not something dropped from heaven, but a human artifact intended to help us in our struggle to realize shalom in our time and in our culture. It can be a cumulative deposit of the wisdom we have acquired by living in God's world. A notion of creation order then becomes open to the experienced consequences of life; it if does not succeed in helping us realize shalom, then it must be changed. Period.

It is unfortunate that Elaine Botha, who had accepted our invitation to respond to Wolters' paper, could not be with us, for she belongs to a community which has struggled far more than most of us with the notion of creation order. For in recent times the Dutch Reformed Church of South Africa has struggled deeply with the meaning of apartheid. I think that there has been no conception which has been more firmly built into the creation order than this notion. And yet the Dutch Reformed Church, after decades of struggle, has acknowledged, painfully and with deep shame, that its cherished notion of apartheid is indeed sin. Many South Africans continue to view this as a capitulation to modernity and secularism, and a breakdown of God-given law and order. But most of us, I believe, thank God for a deeply wise and courageous decision. We too must be willing to question our most deeply held assumptions, particularly when people within our own community show us the pain we have caused them by excluding them. On behalf of the women, the gay people, and whoever else is marginalized and impure in our very own community, let us be humble enough to place our cherished and justly important notion of creation order within the context of our own vision of shalom. Let us be willing to question our most cherished categories in the interests of inclusiveness, justice, and human flourishing. For only then, I suggest, will our notion of creation order not be a tool of oppression but an instrument of shalom.

Points of Unease with the Creation Order Tradition

Response to Albert M. Wolters

Nicholas Wolterstorff

Every Sunday, in the company of my fellow believers, I confess that God is the Creator. So do most people who read this. Yet my guess is that Al Wolters' paper on the role of the notion of *creation order* in the neo-Calvinist tradition made most of us feel uncomfortable. Probably a few of us who were reared in this tradition felt smug—this is the old-time religion. Perhaps a few of us who were not reared in this tradition but in a more soteriologically oriented tradition of Christianity found what Wolters had to say intriguing, maybe even liberating. But most of us felt uncomfortable.

Why did we feel uncomfortable? Not because he got things wrong; Wolters' account is admirably accurate, lucid, and economical. Could it be that our heart is not really in it when we confess on Sundays that God is the Creator, and that our discomfort comes from being confronted with our unbelief? I doubt it. One of the deepest features of the Calvinist tradition is a peculiar Yes and No dialectic: a Yes to the world and ourselves as such, and a No to a great deal of what we human beings have done to the world and ourselves; a Yes to most cultural domains as such, and a No to much of what we human beings do within those domains.

One has understood much of the Calvinist tradition when one has understood how this dialectic works. A Yes to music as such but a No to many of the ways in people engage in the practices of music. A Yes to tobacco smoking as such but a No to many of the ways in which people engage in tobacco smoking! I do not say that this dialectic is absent from other traditions of Christianity, only that it is characteristic of the Calvinist. Max Weber classified world religions into world-affirming religions and world-rejecting; he located Christianity among the world-rejecting. To do so is to miss entirely the Yes and No dialectic.

Now I find this dialectic deeply embedded in my own thought; I wouldn't know how to think Christianly without it. Though I have deliberately avoided the word "creation" in presenting it on this occasion, my own view is that the dialectic cannot be articulated—certainly it never has been articulated—without making use of the concept of creation. So No, it's not that I don't really believe that God is the Creator; being confronted with my unbelief was not the source of my discomfort. The belief in God the Creator is fundamental to my thought, not superficial. Yet I feel uncomfortable. Why? Why did you feel uncomfortable, those of you who did?

I want to do my best to answer that question. But before doing so, I want to make a few comments fleshing out the historical account that Wolters has given us. There has been a deep tendency in the main proponents of the neo-Calvinist tradition to play down if not deny antecedents to their thought in pre-Reformation Christian theology and philosophy, and an even stronger tendency to play down if not deny antecedents in nineteenth and early twentieth century secular philosophy. However, the notions of social differentiation and of sovereign value-spheres, which, as Wolters indicates, play so large a role in neo-Calvinism, play so similar a role in the thought of Max Weber that it would, in my judgment, be silly to deny influence—more precisely, to deny common influence. Both are growths from the seedbed of neo-Kantianism.

What I mainly want to call attention to, however, is another strand of influence. I have found the book *Omnipotence, Covenant and Order*, by the intellectual historian Francis Oakley, enormously illuminating. Oakley points out that the dominant world-picture throughout the Middle Ages and on into the early Enlightenment was that of the great chain of being: God expresses Godself in a great scale or chain of being in which there are no possible gradations of being which are not occupied. The vision received its most articulate formulation in Plotinus. Oakley details that at least from Jerome onwards there were those deeply bothered by the necessitarian undertones of this picture. That unease led to the emergence, as a subdominant strand in the medieval tradition, a picture according to which non-divine reality is not a necessary expression of God's being but the consequence of an act of will on God's part, with the result that there is not a continuous chain of being from inanimate objects on up to God, but a sharp divide between God and all else. Almost everybody in this subdominant strand of thought insisted that though the creation was the result of God's will, as is its maintenance, God's will is not arbitrary. God has covenanted with creation, and the faithfulness of the covenanting God means that we can depend on the God-ordained order. In his book Oakley details how this covenantal strand of thought, subdominant throughout the Middle Ages, became dominant among the Reformers. He also shows how it led to the notion of the *law of nature* to which theorists of the new science appealed.

For me it is fascinating to observe that neo-Calvinism is an attempt to blend these two traditions—whether in fact they can be coherently blended is something no one, to the best of my knowledge, has considered in depth. The blend was certainly present in Kuyper and Bavinck; you will have noticed Wolters' reference to the neo-Platonism of their thought. The blend is less obvious in Dooyeweerd and Vollenhoven; they speak more of God's covenant than of God's ideas. Yet Dooyeweerd does speak, in neo-Platonic fashion, of God *expressing* himself. And deep in Dooyeweerd is the neo-Platonic picture of God's simplicity finding its reflection in the differentiating diversity of creatures, all bound together into an ontological unity, each with its own proper place.

But now what is it that makes me feel uncomfortable with the neo-Calvinist way of articulating our belief in God the Creator? Why do I have the sense of having gotten on what seemed the right train and passing familiar landmarks, yet arriving at what doesn't look like the right destination? Let me suggest four points of unease.

There is, for one thing, the legalistic tone of this account of creation—a point mentioned, though only in quick passing, by Wolters. God's creating comes close to being reduced to God's making things for which God lays down laws, including, in the case of us human beings, laws requiring obedience. God the lawgiver almost completely occupies the space of God the Creator. In the writings of John Calvin, quite a different picture comes through. What comes through there is the conviction that creation and its maintenance are an act of love on God's part. Accordingly, Calvin constantly urges that we perceive and receive the world as gift from the hand of God—gift not only for utility but for delight. Creation is to be perceived and received as blessing.

The same note comes through in Calvin's approach to culture. In a famous passage from the *Institutes*, II, ii, 15, Calvin observes that even the works of pagan culture are not the work of the devil but the result of the Spirit of God brooding over humanity. Accordingly, they are to be received gratefully, though also, indeed, discriminatingly, since the humanity over which the Spirit broods is a fallen humanity. In short, what is dominant in Calvin's consciousness as he moves through nature and culture is not the laws for all these things but their gift-quality. There is a sacramental consciousness in Calvin which is lost in neo-Calvinism. For Calvin, gratitude is first, obedience flows from that. In neo-Calvinism obedience is first, and gratitude is something we ought to feel.

What this presupposes is that *creatures* have a standing and a status in Calvin which they lack in neo-Calvinism. Gratitude springs from enjoying and finding beneficial the creatures and creations around you. Our exclamation is not only "Oh, how love I thy law" but also "Oh, how love I thy creatures." This connects in turn with a variety of other themes. It connects with the theme of *rights*. I think it is not accidental that there is little recognition of rights in neo-Calvinism, except insofar as they can be reduced to the obverse of responsibilities. Here I do not have time to argue the point; but it seems to me that rights and responsibilities are two distinct, though indeed interlocking, dimensions of normativity, neither reducible to the other. When my obligations go unfulfilled, I am guilty, morally or otherwise. When my rights are violated, I am morally or otherwise *injured*. Moral injury cannot be reduced to moral obligation. All of us, by virtue of how we have been created, come bearing rights—come bearing legitimate claims to respect and dignity.

In my own thinking I have found it more fruitful to think in terms of shalom than in terms of creation-orders; and that too is connected. For shalom pertains to delight, fulfilment, flourishing of the creatures of the world.

That was the first point: there's more to creation than legality. A second point is that there is more to the fallenness of our world than wrong-directedness on the part of human beings. There is more to which human beings in general, and Christians in particular, appropriately cry out "This should not be" than just the wrongdoing of human beings and the consequences thereof. A great deal of our human pain is connected with such should-not-be's. Disabling long-term diseases, early deaths of promising children—or one which a physician friend of mine had to deal with, feminine persons who find themselves in male bodies and male persons who find themselves in female bodies.

Of course, Calvin was no more successful in coping with this part of our experience than are the neo-Calvinists. He was inclined to place it under the Job-like category of *a trial*. At least, though, he recognized it. Old Israel did better for some of these phenomena, anyway. The category it used for all the things of the world which it regarded as broken was *unclean*. Of course, fundamental in the works and words of Jesus was the message that nothing is unclean. So the category of the unclean cannot simply be taken over by us. But the recognition of *brokenness* which underlies the category must, in my judgment, be regained.

A corollary is that we need guidance, a word from God, in and for our brokenness—under which I include our sinfulness. The tradition of creation order talked a great deal about how God meant things to be in creating them. God didn't mean, for example, that there would be divorce—there shouldn't be divorce. It didn't talk about what we ought to do when immersed in brokenness; it was looking in a different direction. I myself think it is of fundamental importance to keep the cry alive, "This should not be." For that reason I think it's important to keep before us what I think of as creation orders. But it's also indispensable that we have guidance in our brokenness, and guidance in our brokenness is something different from creation orders. One doesn't always say to the divorced person, "Undo your divorce."

A third point of unease is this: Where is Jesus Christ in that picture of creation orders? Did it strike you that Kuyper, in that passage cited by Wolters on our means of knowing God's law, mentioned creation, history, self-awareness and scripture—but not Jesus Christ? There is a strangely deistic cast to it all. Of course the neo-Calvinists are not deists; it became typical of them also to cite Christ as the Word. But still we feel uneasy. The second person of the Trinity has been expressed in the elusively revelatory and revelatory elusive mystery of Jesus of Nazareth. Does God the Creator not wear a different face as a consequence of that?

Lastly, a source of unease which is more philosophical, less theological. There is an overly-heavy dose of essentialism in the way the belief in God the Creator gets articulated in neo-Calvinism. Perhaps one of the lines from Dooyeweerd which Wolters quoted struck you as it did me: "The boundaries between the peculiar and intrinsic natures that God established...." Now I myself don't doubt that plants and animals, persons and minerals, have natures. But I don't believe that cultural artifacts and social practices and institutions have them. Thus I think it misleading to talk, as the neo-Calvinists do, about *the* nature of states, and about *the* norms for states, etc. States are social artifacts. I see no reason to think that the existence of states as we know them today represents the manifestation on the historical scene at long last of natures which God prepared at creation, nor do I think it at all helpful to talk about God-ordained limits and duties of *the* state. Our present-day *concept* of a state has an essence, but it doesn't follow that states do, nor does it follow that we have an obligation to struggle to arrange social reality so that our concept has application. I see no reason not to think that two hundred years from now states as we know them will have disappeared. There may then no longer be political entities having clear criteria for citizenship and sharply differentiated territorial boundaries. And not only may it be the case that entities satisfying our concept of *state* will have disappeared; I see no reason to think that such disappearance would perforce mark a God-defying regression. Our political obligations are to be determined fundamentally by considering what, given the states that we actually have, conduces to shalom, rather than by considering what we will serve to instantiate *the* nature of *the* state and *the* norms supposedly attached to that nature.

Along similar lines, I think it misleading to talk about *the* nature of art and about *the* norms for art. Normative questions about society and culture are to be decided, as I see it, by reference to what serves shalom in our actual situation, not by reference to the duties of, and proper boundaries between, "peculiar and intrinsic natures."

These are some of my points of unease. There are more—I am also made uneasy by the fact that so often appeals to creation order serve as a put-down of one's discussion partner. But these are more than enough for now. Whether they coincide with your points of unease, you will need to tell me. Or perhaps I and I alone was feeling uncomfortable!

Creation Order in our Philosophical Tradition: Critique and Refinement[1]

Hendrik Hart

Diagnosis of Creation Order

Order and the Ethos of Compassion

Compassion is sacrificial love
Ethos is incarnation, a community's response to the spirit which guides it, embodiment of its spiritual self. The New Testament expects the church, body of Christ, to be a community whose ethos is embodied in compassion.[2] Such compassion is not a feeling, but a *divine* act of sacrificial love, *God's* self-giving love towards creation in Christ,[3] who on the cross embodied fully what he began in his shepherding, healing, and feeding of sheep-like crowds without a shepherd: harassed, sick and hungry people.[4] But the New Testament also calls Jesus' *followers* to love their neighbor in the *image* of God's love, calls the *body of Christ* to have the *compassion of God* in Christ.[5] In compassion, stirred in our bowels to suffer along with others, we relieve *their* suffering *through* ours.

Compassion transcends order
Compassion does what law or order cannot accomplish.[6] Its ethos allows us to act redemptively where established ethical order would destructively enforce its authority. In Romans 8 God groans with creation to save it, doing in Christ what no fixed creation order could accomplish. Compassion is a solidarity in suffering so powerful that love shields order from pursuing sin with more condemnation. It frees creation from bondage and gives us the liberty of Gods children to cry *Abba*.[7]

Spiritual freedom to proclaim orders of compassion
In the language of Galatians 3-6: *in* Christ, faith allows God's children to be *like* Christ, God's offspring,[8] spiritually free from any *concretely given* tradition of order which announces *itself* as road to salvation.[9] In an ethos of compassion Jesus'

followers live not by seasons but by the Spirit who makes us cry *Abba*. God's children follow the Spirit in deeds against which there is no law, *to fashion an order* which in the Spirit *embodies compassion*. Creation order and reason, the focus of this paper, are both gifts of God. They are servants whose role depends on how and where God needs them. But they become elemental spirits of destruction whenever and wherever they *themselves* from eternity *determine* our *permanent ethos*.[10] God's Spirit alone sets God's children free, enables Jesus' followers to avoid such an elemental spirit and to embrace a *new order* which is, in Christ, life-giving.[11] Sin remains. Even so, people follow Christ when, rather than seeking redemption in the new order, they bear each other up *in him*, in compassion.[12] Thus sowing in the Spirit, those who cry *Abba* will reap eternal life in the Spirit.

Order as Ethos is Different

A permanent creation order ethos holds compassion captive

To incarnate this ethos of compassion, some Christian traditions, notably the Reformed and the Roman Catholic, need to face a problem with what the Bible calls law. These traditions remain prone to legalism, encouraged by reading the Bible's *political/covenantal* law-metaphor in terms of a realistic metaphysics of eternal *rational* law. Creation order *in the Reformed tradition* became the name for this entry of Western metaphysics into reading creation order in the Bible.[13] In this tradition the law-transcending ethos of compassion is held captive within an a-historical ethos of eternal, apriori, fixed, available order.[14] I submit that unless this heritage is radically reformed, following Christ in this tradition will continually fall short of embodying an ethos of compassion.[15]

A permanent creation order ethos also skews our Bible reading

Creation demonstrates a need for the *light of compassion* in a *darkness* that comes with our *orders,* as we can see for example in the environment, sexual abuse, the abortion and homosexuality debates, women's equality, and global moral-political incommensurability. To bear light in these areas Reformed Christians often find no support in the Bible as they traditionally read it because, placed within *their* creation order, the Bible demands a traditionally *given order* as hermeneutical key. In my church tradition this still is an issue,[16] though it is no longer clear that *such* an appeal to creation order is valid.[17] If the Bible is not obviously a book of doctrines and moral absolutes anchored in a known and unchanging order, but speaks to us more clearly as narrative of divine guidance in history, the traditional message of Scripture changes considerably.[18] Such shifts have, however, instilled fears of relativism, historicism, violating a fixed divine order, and pluralism devoid of truth.[19]

An ethos of order requires critical assessment

Christian communities seriously struggling with such fears obviously seek to avoid arbitrary, individualistic, subjectivistic autonomy. Every significant cultural community today seeks to avoid freedom absolutism.[20] All people, at least for themselves, hope to avoid evil and seek to embody the good. And most of us can recognize an evil we *spell* Hitler. But we find it hard to *tell* Hitler's evil when it still is only a hidden tendency in an ethos of law and order. In conservative communities people protect such an ethos to prevent evil and usually fail to see their ethos leading to the evil spelled Hitler. Hence a critique of an ethos of order is called for. It is too facile to say that postmodern critiques of reason and order destroy a sense of good and evil that is *clear* in Christian tradition. To the contrary, a critical exposure of creation order may help us sort out crises in which the integrity of creation is violated in the name of creation order, and where an ethos of compassion is blocked. For there are connections between *Reformed* creation order and the philosophical traditions *logocentric realism* criticized by postmoderns.

Philosophy and the Ethos of Order

In the Ethos of Order Philosophy Hid the Word of Grace

The philosophical tradition in the West, now under pressure in postmodernism, has given us an ultimate total picture of reality as a *world within the bounds of reason.* In this world faith, knowledge, and truth depend on making reason and rationality ultimate judges of what essential reality is.[21] Philosophy in this manner does for secularism what theology does for Christianity, it rationally articulates the spirit which guides the Western tradition, in which rationality is the fundamental form of autonomy, the guide to emancipation and liberation, the road to secularization, the world seen only as natural-material world without transcendence or revelation. That is: the rule of reason is context, horizon, vocabulary, and conceptual framework for knowledge, experience, culture, truth, and reality. But because this tradition is itself a *spiritual* tradition which articulates a *direction* for a culture, it does not really exterminate faith, religion, transcendence, revelation, or God, but replaces these with substitutes within the bounds of reason. The philosophical tradition is a logocentric ethos. Theology imported that ethos into Christianity. As a result, the Johannine logos of the Word who accomplished in grace what the law could not do, the Word who was truth in the flesh, became compromised in that ethos.[22]

The Philosophical Tradition Now Questioned from Within

Today's secular humanist ethos, however, is shaped less philosophically or theologically and more politically, economically, or artistically.[23] Philosophy still continues as the wisdom of an intellectual Enlightenment community and reason still settles things for Rawlsian liberalism. But the universal law of reason is under attack in the rationality tradition itself.[24] And traditional images of God and revelation in Christianity, originally influenced by a doctrinal/ethical orientation focused on a-historical reason in traditional theology, already undermined by reflections within liberation movements and process theology, now have also—in the wake of secular postmodernism—begun to become unglued.[25] All major Western traditions are reorienting themselves. And rationality is widely admitted to have extra-rational moments in its commitments, vocabularies, and prejudices.[26]

An Ethos of Order must then also be Questioned

A universe enclosed within the bounds of a universal, eternal, immutable, inviolable, rational order, we are beginning to learn, is one only *revealed* to us in the *philosophical* tradition known as realism.[27] Outside of that tradition there is no ground for trusting a creation only within such fixed boundaries. A biblical ethos for dwelling as creatures within creation would encourage trust in God alone.[28] And the images in which *God* becomes known remain *open*. They are never *fixed* or rationally determined.[29] Order can play a role, perhaps at times a central role, but never the role of *permanent center*. The God made known in the history of people and at home in the narrative tradition of the Bible is uniquely made known in Jesus, the incarnation of God's compassion, who is willing to be embodied in the church as living and hence *changing presence of compassion*.[30] These sources don't allow a fixation of God in law or word. In Jesus, the Word that was in the beginning turns out to reveal grace and truth that the law could not reveal.[31]

An Ethos of Order Hides Biblical Themes

The God imaged in an eternal creation order is a close relative of the God of the philosophers and of deism, the God in whom faith *can* be rationally justified, whose revealed authority *must* be so justified,[32] and whose providence is the maintenance of law and order. This God comes into view only where our responsibilities end, by providing a fixed order for which we are not responsible. But the God of Scripture is present in all that happens, at times including evil.[33] *Nothing* happens without God, says Jesus in Matthew.[34] Today only fundamentalists speak that way.[35] This is no longer common faith-language. We more likely use God-language primarily when events transcend our competence, to sanction *our* traditions as *God's own* eternal creation order. But that's metaphysical more than biblical God-language. Only metaphysical ontologies eternally fix identities in immutable essences or norms. In such a philosophical tradition God is Being, an absolutised projection of rational thought,[36] a God whose eternal thoughts are creation's order. But the biblical language of reliance and trust is never a language of ontology, nor is the Bible's wisdom grounded in what we know as rational order.[37]

Creation Order as Ethos has Extra-biblical Elements

The concept of creation order in the Reformed tradition thus shows traces of a non-Christian religious history, namely that of ultimate trust in a rational-conceptual image of reality as the ontological ground and metaphysical boundary of creation.[38] Human rational powers give access to intellectually grasped general structural relations of properties abstracted from time, history, subjectivity, and individuality. When articulated in concepts, propositions, and theories governed by canons of first order logic, these intellectual products are regarded as an order of criteria, natures, essences, universals, norms, and laws of all reality. By ontologizing this order, reason becomes the soul of creation.[39] The concept of creation order imports this ontology into the Bible. It is founded in a visual metaphor, in which the general picture seen by the eye of reason—like a still-photograph of what is the same in different things of the same kind—is rigid and immobile, universality forever fixed on the mind (retina, film).[40] Individuality and change, subjectivity and history, the exceptional and the marginal, are discounted, because that in fact is how concepts are formed, by comparative elimination of what is different and other, of what is not continuous and identical.[41]

The Problems of Creation Order Have Always Been Known

In this way both Reformed creation order and Thomistic eternal law are a species of philosophical realism, of the Platonic heritage inside the Christian tradition.[42] Great minds in the Christian tradition often wrestled with the unbiblical consequences of the resulting rigidity.[43] The Thomas Aquinas of J. P. Reilly is concerned with legitimate exceptions to and changes of the rules: dispensations to make life possible.[44] The John Calvin of William Bouwsma is lost in the labyrinth of realism, though equally anxious in freedom's abyss.[45] The Vrije Universiteit of Kuyper was held captive by God's eternal council until Kuitert gave biblical legitimacy to change in its agenda.[46] For Dooyeweerd the key to dealing with historicism is not to deny the universality of time and relativity, but to find supra-arbitrary criteria. He, in fact, explicitly asserts that principles of order that are eternal and immutable are pagan.[47]

Though We Need Not Deny Order, We Must Relativize It

The road ahead is not, I think, one of denying or ignoring order or reason. To the contrary, the reality of order and its rational detection seem undeniably valuable discoveries of our Western heritage. The history of science taught us to appreciate the institutionalization of rational order-discovery as instrument of power and control through prediction and explanation. The typical Western notions of power and progress through reason were well founded and have resulted in much blessing. Nevertheless, Greek faith in reason as crystallized in the Enlightenment's and liberalism's *autonomous* rational freedom and in the *public-rational* tolerance for religion only when private, is shown by postmodern adherents of the tradition as the merciless *tyranny* of a timeless absolute. Public access to power is denied to whatever does not fit the public-rational consensus. Reason privileges sameness, continuity, and identity.[48] Its frozen general image becomes an immutable universal. When this becomes *the* standard of truth and justice, it ignores what is different and other.[49] When such rationality is thought to reveal—to those who trust it—essential reality, the nature of things, the truth, and true knowledge, the result is that subjectivity is deceptive, that feelings or stories don't tell the truth, that women are irrational, that Jews are too different to belong.[50] Ironically, reason as limit of knowledge and truth has led to a vast loss of wisdom and much loss of control.[51] So the road ahead lies in relativizing reason and order, though not in denying them. But this means that what *we* use to prevent relativism, namely orders of criteria, need to be relativized. Can this be done while remaining responsible before God?

Faith and Reason Can Be Reinterpreted

Instead of dealing with reason in science and faith in religion as two competing forms of belief, through which we gain access to ultimate layers of truth, essential reality, and order, we can also follow more contemporary analyses and understand science/reason as developing instruments of control, and religion/faith as source of trust or surrender.[52] And rational control requires the setting of an ethos founded on trust.[53] To fight over which of these is true makes little sense if we define truth as specifically belonging to only one of these realms and see the other as a deficient form of the chosen one.[54] If truth, on the other hand, is whatever is revealed in the light of our fundamental trust, a disclosure of reality from within our ethos, it should worry us that neither the Christian religion nor secular science have revealed to us the truth of compassion focused on the marginalized other.[55] We have, instead, created a tolerance for a universal Christian doctrine or for public rational knowledge and order at the center, from which others and differents are banned to the margins. Conceptual truth as order of power gives the lie to compassion, thus protecting a world that favors the established powers.[56]

Reason Still Functions in a Legitimate Search for Order

There seems nothing problematic in principle about acknowledging order, reason, necessity, possibility, limit, universality, and principles as structural generalities grasped in logical, analytic, intellectual, conceptual, reasoning behavior. This is the real world's real rationality. But why view rationality as a monarchian over-all framework, enclosing a world with fixed principles of necessity?[57] As agents of freedom in the image of God, Jesus' followers are responsible for creating new order as God's co-workers.[58] And the God in whose presence and under whose guidance we work is not immutable.[59] When in the process of changing, as agents of redemption, we move away from certain practices, convictions, and norms, we do not thereby reject our past, but accept present needs as different enough not to be helped by a past which is the same, by the generalizations and concepts generated in the past.[60] Preserving a past which is the same makes for a past of eternal order which makes concrete, individual, subjective needs, hopes, persons, tastes, or fears relative to an absolute that is designed for control and power. Relatively speaking a culture can accept this, until it leads us to dead ends.[61] Once order as spiritual center is a dead end, we are spiritually free to make it relative to justice, love, peace, and joy, and to reassign it for the inclusion of the marginalized other who is different or has no power. Such change and difference are not departures from truth, nature, or essence and thus relativistic. They only seem so when our criteria for non-arbitrariness have been exclusively rational. The rational criterion demands that we unify behind a lasting and agreed single formulation of a conceptual order. But if reason does not have the last word, relativity seems not only more acceptable but can be a hallmark of authenticity in a world in which we are pilgrims and where we have no lasting home.[62]

Prognosis of People's Compassion and Creation's Integrity

God and People: Compassionate Co-workers

Suppose the argument thus far shows the need for relativizing order and takes care of our fear of arbitrary relativism by exposing it as a fear of the abandonment of reason as idol. How, nevertheless, will we non-arbitrarily pursue the good; especially in a pluralistic world? Without preset rational criteria of order, how will we know how to live? How do we ourselves travel roads that lead to blessing, how do we justify these, and how do we relate to those whose roads seem to us to lead to sorrow? How will God and people be one?

We are free to be God's co-workers

For starters, we can say that the good we seek is not a conceptual abstraction, or a blind following of eternal principles wherever these lead. The good is experienced as God's blessing, as what bears fruit.[63] Evil cannot be simplistically identified as what God clearly forbids in the Bible just because God forbids it. God forbids evil because it destroys, hurts, kills, makes ill, oppresses. But there is not some apriori, ready made, antecedently known, infallibly revealed order which defines and commands the good for all and for ever, as well as identifies and forbids the evil. To the contrary, in Christ we are set free to work out *our own* salvation in fear and trembling.[64] The New Testament gives us responsibility, freedom in the very area of finding our way. Children of God set free in Christ cannot hide their responsibility behind some law. Acts 15, Romans 8, or Galatians expect those who cry *Abba* to spell out in the freedom of the Spirit what good and evil are in our day.[65] Not in a spirit of autonomy, but by accepting *our* responsibility *before God* who is at work *in us.*[66]

We are not Gods

Accepting this responsibility is not like playing God. Or if it is, Christians should acknowledge we already play God when we participate in dealing with abortion and euthanasia, with in-vitro fertilization and extending life beyond its livable margins, with the ozone and the Amazon, with nuclear arms and genetic engineering.[67] Why should we shrink back when, for example, it comes to redefining sexual morality? Why should we not view homosexual relations in the light of Jesus rather than in the context of the specific understanding of a culture that is no longer ours? Why should intimate relations be normed by preserving antecedently known eternal rules? It seems arbitrary in view of the biblical approach to God's authority to say that some rules are made by us (house rules, organisational by-laws, political constitutions) and some by God (church orders, moral laws). To reclaim the world as creation, we must acknowledge God's authority in *all* creation and learn to regard *all* rules, also the ones we now think we make ourselves, as *human* responsibility in the *presence of God.* On what biblical ground do we conclude that some rules God makes alone? What sense does that make of the status of God's children in Christ as God's heirs, co-workers, offspring, images?

The Spirit of God guides us within definite contexts

We articulate norms as children of God, not as Gods. If Westermann is right, Scripture says that God alone truly knows the difference between good and evil.[68] But God's children in Christ are set free to follow where God guides us today.[69] Once we have left behind Greek metaphysics and the notion of an eternal creation order to which it gave rise, what objection is there to accepting the contemporary inspiration of God's children, guided by God's compassionate presence in Christ in whom creation, the Bible, and the story of the church all have their meaning? What can be wrong with continuing the story that has *already begun* in continuity with how it began and how the Spirit guided it? From that continuity we also become aware of *the future* of the Spirit. To reflect on this we have developed theologies of process, of hope, and of liberation. These are not departures from the truth, but only developments beyond where we had gotten. To interpret such developments as departure from the truth seems arbitrary, even though it does depart from what we once said or thought.

We are, *pace* Heidelberg, naturally inclined to seek at least our own good. We all hate pain, sorrow, and death. We all seek joy, peace, and life. We don't get where we seek to go, however, *not* because we are in principle incapable of doing or knowing the good, but because we seek the good outside of God, not in compassion with our neighbor or in the integrity of creation. *Now* we indeed don't know the good. Now we at best know how to avoid evil only when we actually see it, if then; not earlier, because most of us don't see it coming.[70]

We have a real responsibility for order

So instead of rigidly following a tradition of fixed order, or known and unchanging wisdom, or "God says so in the Bible," we have a responsibility to proclaim and live a redemptive *morality for our time.* To take an example from the ever difficult area of our sexual morality, we have a responsibility to tell *why* pregnancy, marriage, and intercourse go together *if* we say they *must.* We need to be able to *show* the force of that "must" by showing the foreseeable *evil* consequences of doing it *differently.* Good arguments may possibly be given for that. But if not, we are free to work out a *new and different* normativity *in Christ.* Romans 8 guarantees us that if in thus doing it differently we do it wrong, we shall not be condemned. We shall just discover the pain of having done it wrong. And Galatians 6 encourages us to bear that pain with one another in compassion.[71]

Order remains, but is relative and changing

This is not freedom to shove aside or ignore creation order, church order, tradition, science, or reason, but a need to understand that they are all relative to visible redemption, to the compassion God seeks to work through Jesus followers. We do *not* stick to a given order and expect *it* to lead us to life, unless by "given" we don't mean "a fixed presence for all times," but simply "gift of God." That given, however, is not incompatible with what we ourselves have fashioned with the help of God, nor with future change. If within a present order in Christ we don't find life, we must seek a new order for life, again in Christ. The apostle says we can't *live* by *any* law. There are no aprioris, no eternal orders, no hallowed traditions.[72] There's only the residue of our groaning and the invitation to try again. The biblical narrative helps us in this with a long term view.[73] It teaches us to see the future of our present in the light of the Alpha and Omega, a future not cast in stone but in compassion.[74]

Reason plays an important role

The role of reason in giving shape to a normative order is important. We deploy our gifts of rationality to detect order, to identify sameness, to articulate continuity, to form shared tools for universal communication. But that order is not an over-all norm, not the boundary within which all exists. It is, rather, a relative, partial cross-section. Faith, our ethos, feelings, traditions of justice, the needs of real people in markets, the rights of women, other races, the poor, people with different sexual orientations, the handicapped, and many others all form boundaries for reason.[75] They all reveal differences that need to be given room, need to be allowed to come into play. Reason cannot be the tolerant guardian over differences, the liberal-Enlightenment's public reason whose central power privatises and thus marginalizes what is different or other. We can indeed construct, and we are free and called and responsible to do so, conceptual frameworks in touch with reality as action guides. But neither these frameworks nor their reality are immutable, nor is it they who make out what we call truth. Nevertheless, the order of things and the rationality of things are the same. The discovery and construction of an order in a changing world is itself a rationally focused endeavor, though not autonomously so. Reason must be guided and directed by compassion and creaturely integrity. Such rationality listens to and respects the world and does not impose its own logical necessity on the world autonomously. The world and the world-of-thought are not identical worlds. We know more than we think. Inside the world of thought we must think logically. That seems to bring the world inside our logic. But, unlike the world-of-thought, the world does not fit inside our logic. Much of what we know of the "real world" should not be sacrificed to our logic, lest we think we did not know what we thought we knew.

Trusting Compassion to Restore Integrity

Justification is possible

But how does a pluralistic world, without the benefit of a public reason, justify the truth of an ethos, when many an incompatible ethos lays claim to such truth. How do we justify the Gospel as truth? The ethos of the church, in this context, is not one of reason, justified by reason. Rather, the measure of its capacity for compassion is the key. The truth of an ethos of compassion is *justified in doing justice* that is mercy. The faith that justifies is our trust in the compassion of God, shown in doing the justice of God in Christ.[76] There is no indication that in the New Testament the church's role is to give doctrines or rules to the world. The Jerusalem synod of Acts 15 resisted exactly that temptation when giving advice to Gentile believers. The unavoidable authoritarianism of the rule of an ethos of doctrinal truth (intellectualism) and moral obedience to rules (legalism) leads to suffering, because the law's only real power is to reveal sin. Compassion reaches out in solidarity to the suffering other and to the groaning creation. This requires that compassion reach out beyond the justification of reason which naturally seeks to legitimate an order of the same with whom we share power rather than of the other who suffers in our margins. The ethos in which the groaning of creation is heard embodies and incarnates God's saving solidarity with creation, God's compassionate presence. The church therefore passes on a Spirit of Freedom.[77] That's an ethos not of subjects obedient to an authority, but of family members, members of the household of God, with a responsibility to set their own house in order.[78]

We need again to relate to God in faith. Faith is not a supernatural clone of the intellect with a revealed conceptual content of doctrinal beliefs or norms. Faith is trust. Faith does not require us to subscribe to a permanent doctrinal content of a sameness which is simply not present in the Bible. Rather, faith is throwing out an anchor, trusting an orientation on a journey.[79] Followers of Jesus, as restored image bearers of God, as children of God, as divine offspring, as co-workers with God are free to create boundaries for life, to be *like* God, *image* bearers. We *trust* that this can be done redemptively, but only in a spirit of compassion, the spirit of Christ.[80]

The embodiment of faith

In our day many people leave the church. In their painful experience the church and its orders and traditions are substitutes for God in which they do not find the freedom or compassion, the life or mercy, the peace or joy promised in the Gospel. The promises the church holds out are not visible *in* the church as *for* the world. The way of compassion is not to preserve the heritage of the church's doctrinal beliefs or moral norms, but to live that compassion visibly, to show faith in God's justice as mercy. God's justification is a matter of setting us free in Christ to do what is just. This transcends the notion that God in Christ holds us guiltless, even though we exist within a framework of order which pronounces us guilty. Only doing what is just can justify an ethos as true. It is time to stop arguing about intellectual beliefs as though our ethos owes an explanation to the philosophical tradition. It is time to have faith, to trust the integrity of creation in God's compassion rather than in its order, the church's order, or any order.[81] To be justified is to have been made just, to have incarnated the doing of justice, and in that incarnation to show that doing justice makes just. If the church needs to convince others of the truth we were given, we can only do this in the embodiment of that truth. And if the church needs to relate to those who in denying the truth—as the church embodies it—suppress God's justice, we can only do that by making visible the darkness of that injustice while we mercifully surround with compassion all who suffer in that darkness.

Notes

1. The text is identical to the original conference text. Notes are largely the same as well, except for needed completions and clarifications. The original notes were given only to conference speakers and were provisional, meant only to give them some background to the text. Where I spoke about Reformed philosophy I limited my attention to reformational philosophers from the Amsterdam school oriented to the thought of D. H. Th. Vollenhoven and H. Dooyeweerd and to Reformed epistemologists Alvin Plantinga and Nicholas Wolterstorff. Where respondents have quoted from my notes I have retained the quoted text.

2. The community whose ethos toward one another is the ethos it has in Christ, see Philippians 2:5-11, Colossians 3:12-17. Ethos is a word which in the Christian tradition would serve to indicate the concrete contours in which the love of God in Christ, available in all ages, takes concrete shape in a given age or culture. So the "summary" or "spirit" of the law in *agape* is here embodied in *splanchnizomai*.

3. See *"splanchnizomai"* in Gerhard Friedrich and Geoffrey W. Bromley, *Theological Dictionary of the New Testament* (Grand Rapids: Eerdmans, 1971) vol. VII, 548-59. See also Andrew Purves, *The Search for Compassion: Spirituality and Ministry* (Louisville, Westminster/John Knox Press, 1989) and Walter Brueggemann, *The Prophetic Imagination* (Philadelphia, Fortress Press, 1978), 82-91. Compassion has an echo of sacrifice in connection with the *splanchna*, the entrails of sacrificial animals. Having compassion (in the synoptic Gospels) is therefore a sacrificial act, not just a feeling. And it is a divine act, relieving those who suffer under the law, manifesting a mercy-love that reaches beyond the law redemptively. But it is also *our* task *in* Jesus. He came to incarnate compassion and to inspire it in his body, the church.

4. Matthew 9:36, 14:14, 15:32; Mark 6:34, 8:2.

5. God's sacrificial love is clearly expected of Jesus' followers. In Luke 10:33 the servants of God who follow the law do not meet the demands of love in the law (see Jeremiah 7), though a Samaritan is seen to express that love in compassion. *We* are called to "do likewise." In Luke 15:20 the compassion of the prodigal son's father comes to *us* as a call from that father. When we do image God's love we do not, of course, thereby become gods. In the reformational tradition in philosophy, especially J. P. A. Mekkes in his 1973 *Tijd der Bezinning* (Amsterdam: Buijten en Schipperheijn) has argued that the centrality of law in that tradition has obscured the biblically required centrality of God's love as shown in the cross.

6. This is a well-known emphasis in Paul. In the face of sin the law can only condemn and cannot make manifest God's love. See for example Galatians 3:1-4:11. That God's compassion accomplishes what the law cannot achieve is clear from Romans 8:3,4. See J. P. A. Mekkes, "Wet en Subject in de Wijsbegeerte der Wetsidee," in *Philosophia Reformata*, 27, 1962: 146. God's compassion shown in Christ enables us to live by the heart of the law—loving God above all and our neighbor as ourselves—in the Spirit. The Good Samaritan, who demonstrates love of neighbor, also clearly acts outside of the rule book, the law, which is obeyed by the priest and the

Levite who live by the book, though not by the Word. See Hendrik Hart, *Setting Our Sights by the Morning Star* (Toronto: Patmos Press, 1989), 157-58. The father in the parable of the Prodigal Son obviously flaunts the traditional order within which his younger son has just expectations. Modern English commonly uses "compassion" in the sense of transcending what the rules allow when we speak of, for example, granting someone compassionate leave of absence.

7. It is hardly possible to overemphasize in this context the importance of the Spirit's enablement to make us cry *Abba*, both in Romans 8:15-17 and in Galatians 4:1-11. We are called, as followers of The Son, to the freedom of being God's offspring. The Child-of-God relationship is not one of immature child and parent, but of members of one family, being of God's generation, image-bearers restored to freedom, heirs, co-workers. (See notes 18, 42, and 50 below.) *Abba*-sayers are doers of divine justice, that is, they "transcend" the law in acts of compassion, possible only in trusting the God who first so acted (see Romans 1:16-17, written under circumstances not unlike those of Habakkuk who is quoted here). Jesus says *Abba* when he faces the cross (Mark 14:36). Justice, which originally would require meeting the demands of the law, now in Christ has clearly become mercy, which accomplishes what the law was intended to do but cannot do in the face of sin. Already in the Old Testament God's seat of judgment on the ark was called mercy seat (Exodus 25:17), referred to in Hebrews as the throne of grace (4:16).

8. See 2 Peter 1:4, Romans 8:12-17, Galatians 3:23-29.

9. Paul's attitude to the law is not unrelated to that of Jesus to the Scriptures (John 5:39) or that of Jeremiah to the law (7:22). Any order tradition is only a historically limited vehicle for the Word and Spirit of God who transcend that vehicle, which is only a carrier, a vessel. Of course, at any given time, any given tradition will always also be a tradition of order.

10. Creation order as ethos is, relatively speaking, acceptable enough. But as available and fixed apriori, its ethos will allow no change in that available order. It may then pass from historical focus to intolerant idol. See notes 14, 19, 28, 56, 57, 62, 72, and 77 below.

11. Neither ethos nor spirit can do *without* order, though both can require a *new* order. Renewable order differs from renewal within fixed order. A *fixed* creation order will not yield to an order of compassion. However, a creation ordered in compassion should differ from a creation ordered in sovereignty. A *historical creation* order is incompatible with an *apriori metaphysical* order.

12. Again, Romans 8, especially the end of verse 17, and Galatians 6:1, 2. The compassion that leads to no condemnation is not a condoning, but a *toleration* of *bearing* one another's burden. So-called "tough love" should not so much be a love that lays down the law, but more a love that bears a cross.

13. A series of articles by A. Troost in *Philosophia Reformata* has direct bearing on this. (See for the first instalment 1992, 3-38.) John H. Kok, in a Ph.D. thesis defended at Amsterdam's Vrije Universiteit (a Christian university in the Reformed tradition, co-sponsor of this conference) on June 12, 1992, deals with the early works of D. H. Th. Vollenhoven (professor of philosophy at the Vrije Universiteit, co-founder of the Amsterdam school of reformational philosophy, the centennial of whose birth was 1992). Kok shows the links between Vollenhoven's later notion of creation order and his earlier metaphysical realism. Thing, substance, idea, and law were more or less identical in the early Vollenhoven of 1918. Later developments after 1926 name and place law differently, though continuity with realism remains. Nothing indicates that there has been an inner transformation. The creation order takes the place of the changeless substratum and is logically accessible. See the "Epilogue" in Kok's *Vollenhoven: His Early Development* (Sioux Center: Dordt College Press, 1992). In early Vollenhoven a thing *is* its law (293, 295). In later Vollenhoven anything's *being subject* to law is in sum what it is before God (292). And law is essentially non-temporal (296). Traces of the early realism remain throughout (302-304). In this, Vollenhoven followed Abraham Kuyper (founder of the Vrije Universiteit), as is clear from Johan Stellingwerff's two volume history of the Vrije Universiteit, *Kuyper en de VU* and *De VU na Kuyper* (Kampen: Kok, 1987). See especially vol. I, 9-10, 17-19, 253-81, and vol. II, 107-27.

14. If we are to obey an eternal creation order, it is necessary that it be known or available. Hence we accept, essentialize, and eternalize known and available order as creation order, and doing so bless the status quo. The traditional Reformed doctrine of creation order is an invitation to conservatism and resists continued radical reformation. Hence the traditional, though otherwise inexplicable, Reformed attitude of wanting to *preserve* a Reformed *heritage*. Once something is accepted as Reformed, it is seen as needing to be reformed no more. Reformed *tradition* in practice then denies the *semper reformanda* of the reformers.

15. Reformed Christians traditionally place strong emphasis on authority, obedience, submission, control, intellectual truth (doctrine), and what's right (moral codes). Love then finds its place *within* this framework, as an element of it. Love is not, at least not operationally speaking, the heart, the core criterion, or transcendental condition for the framework. The apostle Peter learned that not God's law but God's love abides (Acts 10). In Scripture law is more intended as a vehicle moving us to love and love is then the measure of the law. (See note 9 above and notes 31 and 40C below.) Paul's "neither male and female" of Galatians 3:28 echoes Genesis 1:27 and gives redemption priority over creation; see Richard N. Longenecker, *New Testament Social Ethics For Today* (Grand Rapids: Eerdmans, 1984), 74 note and 92 bottom). Herman Ridderbos makes clear that what is finally decisive for Paul's proclamation of being "in Christ" is Christ himself alone; see *Paul: An Outline of His Theology* (Grand Rapids: Eerdmans, 1975), 341. For cautious hints of how this might effect order, hints that, I believe, we can take further than Ridderbos did himself, see 59, 316, 317, 337, 341, 460.)

16. See the report on homosexuality of 1973 in the Christian Reformed Church, 615-16, 621, 623-24, *Acts of Synod,* "Report 42, Committee to Study Homosexuality" (Grand Rapids: Christian Reformed Publishing, 1973), 609-33. Creation order becomes a hermeneutical key to deciding on certain passages. If in their own context they might be read as less damaging to homosexuality, seen in relation to creation order that advantage becomes impermissible. But in this paper I question such use of "creation order," which works with a hermeneutic of the Bible as source of information about the structure of reality, an alternative or a rival to science, giving us revealed universal frameworks. Marten H. Woudstra, late professor of Old Testament at Calvin Seminary in Grand Rapids, Michigan, rejected such a hermeneutic and thought this was quite compatible with his conservative and orthodox approach to theology and Bible scholarship. (Unpublished correspondence and papers.) If creation order is in fact a Reformed version of Thomas's eternal law or of Platonic realism in philosophy, then criticisms of those notions could also affect Reformed appeals to creation order.

17. Theo de Boer, in conversation with Johan van der Hoeven (both are philosophers at the Vrije Universiteit and have roots in the Amsterdam school of reformational philosophy) about the God of the philosophers, remarks that creation order as an indication of what creation might mean is not much more than an interesting antiquated notion. "Vroeger sprak men nog wel...." "Men is er van teruggekomen...." See 175 of "Godsverduistering en Godsdienstfilosofie," in *Philosophia Reformata* 55, 1990: 170-76. The 1992 report "Hermeneutics and Ethics" of the Reformed Ecumenical Council is also significant in this respect. It stresses the confessional character of the Bible and cautions against too facile an adoption of any of its specifically moral or other traditions, on which the Bible does shed the light of faith, but without intending to authoritatively proclaim these traditions as such.

18. It is hard to see how cultures and traditions could provide the sort of context they do provide without "centers" that organise them. In the West reason has been such a center, which is now challenged by postmodernism. Centers need not be permanent. Each period in history will require its own metaphor for the centrality of God. It is plausible that God as the ruler who required obedience and submission was a centering metaphor in Israel, while for Jesus and the apostles *Abba*, who asks us for our love, is arguably their center, given the centrality of God as Father, believers as children and heirs, and similar expressions in the New Testament; see J. van Baal, *Mysterie als Openbaring* (Utrecht: ISOR, 1990), re-issued (with *Boodschap uit de Stilte*, Baarn: Ten Have, 1991/1992.) The new central language is visibly more dominant in the New Testament, though the language of the old center is not absent. Such changes restructure a tradition fundamentally. For though the real center is always God, the metaphor through which we experience God as center both highlights and relativizes dimensions of our experience of God. Our *creaturely* language for *God-as-not-creature* cannot be absolutized. A new central metaphor therefore relativizes former highlights and centers what was more relative before. There is no good ground for us not to de-center reason and order, which in the Reformed Christian and Roman Catholic traditions gave such emphasis to doctrines and norms, if reason no longer manages to speak the Word of Life to our *hearts*. We then need to struggle with the visible effects of such a de-centering. The decentered metaphor is not abandoned, but reassigned. Nevertheless, that can occasion serious discomfort. In our case, the discomfort is called historicism, relativism, and so on. See the section on "An ethos of order must be questioned" below, and also notes 29, 37, 42, 61, and 62.

19. It is curious how a life and universe threatening human intervention in "natural order" such as our depletion of the ozone often seems a matter of no great concern to us, whereas a non-destructive "natural variation" such as homosexuality is almost always perceived by us as very dangerous. The conference discussions demonstrated this very clearly. Behind the scene here lurks a Platonic hermeneutic, in which there is a reading of the Bible, *God's own* reading, which is *the* true reading. Reading the Bible *right* would be to find *this* reading, which does not change. (See note 60 below.) But who has this reading? How can it even be used to measure other readings, if it is not available? (See note 14 above.) Certainly that sort of reading cannot be used as a standard whereby to measure deficiencies of other readings. No reading, including those which pretend to be in touch with this reading, can meet expectations of this sort. Those who claim to have "God's own reading" absolutize the reading of a particular tradition. They are unable to demonstrate either the absence of such absolutization, or why others must share theirs as only true reading. We only have the readings we have. We trust them and usually have good grounds for doing this, just as we sometimes abandon them also on good grounds. But these readings are not arbitrary. They meet standards and expectations we now have, standards we hold dear even though they are not fixed and given by God from eternity. There are examples of Paul's reading of the Old Testament in the New that are part of the inspired Scriptures. Yet no one would recommend such a reading for us today. An example is Galatians 4:21-31. But we can also not hope that the standards whereby we reject such a reading today will remain. Future generations will be puzzled, by their standards, about how we read in our time. The problem of a plurality of truth in our time will at least help our generation to seriously face the lack of impartial access to absolute or universally objective criteria of truth. *Arguing* our way to truth seems less relevant to our age than *living* the truth. Truth of argument and truth that is lived are significantly different. See H. Hart, "Liberalism, Pluralism, and Lived Faith," paper for the Society for Christian Philosophers, Ottawa, June 1993 (unpublished). See also notes 40, 52, 54, 55 below.

20. Enlightenment liberalism is committed to rational autonomy as road to freedom and for that very reason is fearful of irrational approaches to freedom. The freedom of postmoderns has not yet become the ethos of any cultural community outside of disciplines such as philosophy and literary criticism. Besides, in people such as Richard Rorty individual freedom remains limited to private spaces, with substantial shared normativity in place for public and communal life. See his "On Ethnocentrism: A Reply to Clifford Geertz," in *Objectivity, Relativism, and Truth* (Cambridge: Cambridge University Press, 1991), 203-10.

21. Especially Richard Rorty has in the North American context shown the role of reason as cultural superjudge. He identifies the tradition of rationality as the tradition of the logical space of inference and argument. Reason refers, in that tradition, to analysis, to inquiry systematized, controlled, and methodically bound by first order logic; see Rorty, ibid., 95. Reason in that tradition can refer both to that activity and to the order it uncovers. Because reason was *super*-judge, however, "rational" became a name for *all* that is good, orderly, proper, right. So now it also means *whatever* is sound, healthy, sane, civilized, acceptable, responsible, good to someone from the tradition; see Rorty, ibid, 37. In all its guises, however, rational always has an echo of the logical in it, that is, it is non-contradictory, thoughtful, well argued, justified, and so on. Alasdair MacIntyre identifies logicality as the sole constant of the rationality tradition. See his *Whose Justice? Whose Rationality?* (Notre Dame: University of Notre Dame Press, 1988), 4 and 351. Dewey J. Hoitenga, Jr., in his *Faith and Reason from Plato to Plantinga: An Introduction to Reformed Epistemology* (Albany, NY: State University of New York Press, 1991) gives a clear description of the heart of the tradition in the justified-true-belief-strand of it. Reason's truth is changeless, corresponds with reality by representing it, is propositional, and so forth. For contemporary analysis of the philosophical ethos see authors such as Richard Bernstein, John Caputo, Jacques Derrida, Michel Foucault, and Alasdair MacIntyre. The crisis surrounding the postmodern critique of this tradition is well documented and presented in Kenneth Baynes, James Bohman, and Thomas McCarthy, *After Philosophy: End or Transformation?* (Cambridge, MA: MIT Press, 1987). See especially the final essay by Charles Taylor, in which reason is severely criticized but then, since he sees our only choices as either reason or will at the center, maintained as the center nevertheless. See also the analysis of A. Troost mentioned in note 13 above.

22. The Christian tradition has philosopher-theologians as its main early shapers, rather than rulers, artists, land-owners, generals, or other figures with cultural power. That has significantly influenced the appropriation of biblical religion as theological doctrine and ethical code. Christianity is very much a religion of reason and order, of intellectual truth and normativity. Rorty in *Consequences of Pragmatism* (Minneapolis: University of Minnesota Press, 1979) and in *Philosophy and the Mirror of Nature* (Princeton: Princeton University Press, 1979) speaks of Reason as a God-substitute and of its theories as God's-eye-views. I deal with this in its relation to Christianity at length in my discussions with Kai Nielsen in a jointly authored book, *Search for Community in a Withering Tradition* (Lanham, MD: University Press of America, 1990). Inside this ethos of reason-as-the-last-word there is no room for biblical philosophy. If, on the other hand, philosophy is just the rational integration into or within one general theoretical picture of whatever partial rational pictures we have available in various branches of scholarship, philosophy is necessary and to the good of the academy and can well be practised from a biblical perspective. I use "biblical" advisedly here, because within the *Christian* tradition room *has* been made for the philosophical ethos repeatedly, and *vice versa*. Christian and biblical are not to be taken as identical here.

23. By artistically I here mean the literary world, the world of rock music, and the world of television and film, that is, art forms in which a hermeneutic of culture is palpably present.

24. Not only by more radical authors such as Rorty, Derrida, and Foucault, but also by the more moderate Hans-Georg Gadamer and even by Jürgen Habermas, who in other ways holds on to the tradition. Reason is played down, but autonomy is not. In reading Derrida's "irrational" language, one way of understanding him is to see him as dealing with rationality autonomously, i.e., as practising a logocentric but not rulebound hermeneutic.

25. In their own time these images were doubtless liberating and redemptive. Are they still? See John Hick and Brian Hebblethwaite, eds., *Christianity and Other Religions* (Philadelphia: Fortress Press, 1980). Also see John Hick and Paul F. Knitter, eds., *The Myth of Christian Uniqueness: Towards a Pluralistic Theology of Religions* (Maryknoll, NY: Orbis, 1987) and Gavin D'Costa, *Christian Uniqueness Reconsidered: The Myth of a Pluralistic Theology of Religions* (Maryknoll, NY: Orbis, 1990). There is much reflection these days on who God is. The many writings of Walter Brueggemann often deal with new experiences of God. H. Kuitert has just published a book about revisions in our faith, *Het Algemeen Betwijfeld Christelijk Geloof: Een Herziening* (Baarn: Ten Have, 1992); English editions are entitled *I Have My Doubts* (London: SCM and Valley Forge: Trinity Press International, 1993.) For our images of God see also Don Cupitt, *Radicals and the Future of the Church* (London: SCM, 1989); Theo de Boer, *De God Van De Filosofen En De God Van Pascal: Op Het Grensgebied Van Filosofie En Theologie* ('s-Gravenhage: Meinema, 1989); Herman Wiersinga, *Geloven Bij Daglicht: Verlies en Toekomst Van Een Traditie* (Baarn: Ten Have, 1992); J. van Baal, *Mysterie als Openbaring* (Utrecht: ISOR, 1990), re-issued with *Boodschap uit de Stilte* (Baarn: Ten Have, 1991/92); A. van de Beukel, *De Dingen Hebben Hun Geheim* (Baarn: Ten Have, 1990; A. van de Beek, *Wonderen en Wonderverhalen* (Nijkerk: Callenbach, 1991); F. O. van Gennep, *De Terugkeer van de Verloren Vader: Een Theologisch Essay over Vaderschap en Macht in Cultuur en Christendom* (Baarn: Ten Have, 1989).

26. Richard Rorty's notion of a final vocabulary is a good example of reason's respose in a foundation of trust. See *Contingency, Irony, and Solidarity,* (Cambridge: Cambridge University Press, 1989), 73 and *Objectivity, Relativism, and Truth*, note 20 above. The literature of feminist epistemology is very strong in this area. See for example Lorraine Code's *Epistemic Responsibility* (Hanover: University Press of New England, 1987) and *What Can She Know?* (Ithaca, NY: Cornell University Press, 1991).

27. Revelation is here understood as the disclosure of a world in the light of one's fundamental trusts. For a culture deeply trusting a rational center, the revealed world has been a rational world. Literally: a universe within the bounds of reason, where reason is taken as content of rational understanding, or as what can be rationally understood, or as the rational methods and criteria whereby understanding becomes rational. See also A. Troost, referred to in note 13, above.

28. It might be put, for example, in the words of H. Evan Runner (philosopher at Calvin College, co-sponsor of this conference, whose work is also rooted in the Amsterdam school of reformational philosophy), "What is needed for the direction of life is *faith*, ... commitment to the Word that God has given.... For that Word is after all simply God himself...." (In *The Relation of the Bible to Learning* (St. Catharines: Wedge Publishing, fifth edition, 1982), 118. As Thomas Aquinas says it in the *Summa Theologica,* God's law "is not something other" than God. (Q 91, Art. 1, Repl. to Obj. 3.) But in terms of the philosophical tradition, both Thomas's law and Runner's Word become associated with an eternal and immutable rational order *as side of creation.* Herman Dooyeweerd (professor of law at the Vrije Universiteit, co-founder of the Amsterdam school of reformational philosophy with D. H. Th. Vollenhoven) speaks of it as "the temporal world-order rooted in the divine order of creation." See *A New Critique of Theoretical Thought* (Philadelphia: The Presbyterian and Reformed Publishing Company, 1957), vol. III, 169 and many other places. He protests that creation order is very different from metaphysical realism (for example, II, 559), but it is not apparent that there is a real difference. Dooyeweerd did develop a critique of reason that remains, even today, so radical that it can truly be characterized as post-modern. Nevertheless, it seems clear enough that his notion of creation order and metaphysical realism are related interpretations of an underlying "same," as well as that reason has a special connection with both. The principles of creation order are *theoretically* accessible (II, 548). And in his own view the absolutization of *theoretical* reason leads to metaphysical realism. There is no compelling evidence that in Dooyeweerd "the *structure* of reality" differs from "what *theory* investigates." At I, 146, he identifies theoretical universal validity with substitution for creation order. His view of the structure of transcendental theoretical analysis at I, 37 is that it lays bare the order of possibility. His law-subject relation can be interpreted as addressing the problem others approach as form-matter, knowing-being, reason-experience, and many others. In the final analysis, creation order gives divine backing to the results of our own best contemporary analysis of general structures. (See notes 14, 19, above.) A good example of how relative this all is can be found in his analysis of marriage at III, 326-29. This is not to say that Dooyeweerd did not attempt to develop a radically biblical notion of creation order nor that he failed completely in that attempt. All it means is that the reconceived notion remains related to the metaphysical tradition and needs to be further disentangled. See also A. Troost, cited in note 13, above; and notes 38, 39, 47, 50, and 57, below.

29. All images of God, including the Bible's, are creatiomorph. There is no reason to believe that some of them should be so privileged as to be fixed. God then becomes caught inside a humanly privileged order. And certain creaturely realities, such as for example authority or norms, are seen as especially divine or holy. Changes in the images of God will also lead to, of course, changes in our call to be human in God's image, and consequently changes in our view of self. When postmodern critiques of self attempt to de-center a fixed, autonomous, rational self, they open an important space for a biblical view of self as a calling in progress. The God of Abraham is, of course, the same as the God of Jesus. But that sameness is not a rational-conceptual sameness, it is not an identity of essence. "God of so-and-so" is a way to speak of identity linked to uniqueness and individuality. Hence we can also see development in Gods self-revelation between Abraham and Jesus.

30. For embodiment and change see Ephesians 1:9-23. It is enriching to meditate on "the presence" of Jesus in the elements of communion ("this is my body") in relation to that presence as a presence of compassion in "the body" that partakes of the elements.

31. See the Prologue to the Gospel of John. Jesus, of course, in grace fulfilled the law and did not thereby break it. The law was always intended to reveal grace and truth. The point is not only that it did not, but also that it could not do so when confronted with sin. In any case, it would be a mistake to interpret what the Bible calls law too closely in relation to what in Reformed tradition is called creation order. (See also notes 34, 37, 40C, 42, 50, and 57.)

32. The journal of the Society for Christian Philosophers, *Faith and Philosophy,* in 1988 requested articles for a theme issue that would "discuss the 'rationality' (permissibility) of acceptance of the Bible as authoritative."

33. Though neither the Old nor the New Testament would ever suggest that God *sins,* the Old Testament does at times speak of *evil* as coming from God, and also of God as deciding to do evil. See for example Exodus 32:12, Joshua 23:15, Judges 9:23, 1 Samuel 16:14-23; 1 Sam. 18-19; 2 Samuel 24:1, 10.

34. Matthew 10:29. The traditional "will of God" is not in the original text. Language in the Bible that points to overarching relations to creation is not so much language about order as it is language about God. It is God "in whom we live and move and have our being" (Acts 17:28), and "from him and through him and to him are all things" (Romans 11:36) and God "fills all in all" (Ephesians 1:23). If that sort of language enters into creation it applies to Christ (Colossians 1:15-20) and to the church (Ephesians 1:23), who in the name of God become receptacles of God's fulness and who are therefore also all, in and to all (1 Corinthians 9:22, 12:4-6,13; 15:22-28, Ephesians 3:14-19, 4:3-6, Galatians 3:28, Colossians 3:11).

35. The practice of speaking of human decisions in terms of "God wanted me to...."

36. See Herman Dooyeweerd, ibid, vol. I, 71-73, vol. II, 20-21, 25-26, 56-62. If we predicate "is p" of "x" we can also speak of x's "being p." In relation to all things we can speak of their "being" such and such. Vollenhoven spoke of being in this way for all of his career. For him, God, law, and creation all three "resort under" being. See John H. Kok, idem., 303. Dooyeweerd, correctly in my view, calls it an absolutisation or hypostatisation or substantialisation when we move from this feature of the language of thought to the conclusion that there *is* something called being, absolutely in God, in some other way (relatively, analogically) in creatures. For Dooyeweerd the thinking-being relation is a product of thought, a logical "A and not-A" division of reality from the perspective of theory. "Being" is a single name for all that is *Gegenstand* to thought.

37. The Bible can certainly not be regarded as "revealing" any ontology, whether for its own time, another time, or all time. See Gerhard von Rad, *Wisdom in Israel* (Nashville, Abingdon, 1972). If we take seriously von Rad's warnings in the beginning of chapter IX, "The Self-revelation of Creation," that "the texts do not bother to provide the reader with conceptual definitions which appear indispensable to us" and that "the questions with which we approach these texts are not entirely pertinent" we can profitably read that chapter to tell us that the wisdom of creation talked about in Proverbs and Job differs significantly from Greek realistic rational order; see 145-76. See also Roland E. Murphy, "Wisdom and Creation" in *Journal of Biblical Literature,* 104/1, 1985: 3-11. Murphy offers an implicit argument for reading von Rad as not having taken his own warning seriously enough. On the notion of the necessity for an immutable structure in the Bible see Walter Brueggemann, *Israel's Praise: Doxology against Idolatry and Ideology* (Philadelphia: Fortress Press, 1988). See especially the first chapter, "Praise as a Constitutive Act" (1-28). He speaks of a "new post-Enlightenment epistemological situation" in which it is "no longer tenable to imagine that there is a 'given' world... (x)." At the same time he emphasizes that when the Bible calls us to creative activity, "the text will function to discipline, legitimate, and energize that world construction (xi)." This throws interesting light on the creator-creature distinction. Normally Christians would say that, being creatures, humans are not creators. If, however, all that we say about God is creatiomorph speech, the notion of creator is a creaturely notion and hence we could also speak of ourselves as creators. Would that make humans world-makers? Today we might answer: "Yes, as God's co-workers of redemption." (See Reformed epistemologist Nicholas Wolterstorff's "Are Concept-Users World-Makers?" in James E. Tomberlin, ed., *Philosophical Perspectives I: Metaphysics* (Atascadero, California: Ridgeview Publishing Company, 1987). The notions of *concept*-maker and *world*-maker are very close in the world of realism.)

38. Nicholas Wolterstorff, in the "Epilogue" to an older book which was much more "realistic" in outlook than his later developments express, gives a good modern example of such a boundary when he speaks of a structure which "holds for all reality whatsoever—necessarily so.... Nothing is unique in that it falls outside this fundamental structure of reality. God too...." [*On Universals* (Chicago: University of Chicago Press, 1970.)] That he has a law-like structure in mind not only appears from his use of "holds" but also from terms like *"normal, properly formed"* and "determines things" (245, 254), used in the context of discussing certain manifestations of this structure. Trust in such structures in the Western tradition "replaced" faith and revelation. These structures, trusted as eternal ontic realities (an absolutised projection of a theoretical view of reality), originated in Greece as a substitute for faith in myths. Dooyeweerd in his writings is aware of this, yet he would dismiss that the notion of creation order he embraces is a Reformed Christian version of that tradition or in any case a theory with retained traces of the Greek tradition. My own earlier version of Dooyeweerd's theory in *Understanding Our World* (Lanham, MD: University Press of America, 1984) certainly does bear traces of the Greek metaphysical tradition. See also Troost, note 13, above.

39. Dewey Hoitenga, op. cit., makes this all very clear. Herman Dooyeweerd, op.cit., in many places refers to the metaphysical concepts of realism as absolutizations of the theoretical attitude, i.e., of how we see reality when we theorize. See for example vol. I, 92-93, 146, vol. III, 3-5, 7, 10. He does not usually stress that in the theoretical attitude we are preoccupied with what he calls law, structure, principle of possibility, and order. Nevertheless, volume III of his major work opens with a lengthy explanation of why individual, concrete, subjective reality is not accessible to theory. And in volume I he characterizes the transcendentally critical task of theory as an inquiry into universal conditions (37). In many places he refers to law structures as principles or conditions of possibility (for example, III, 108), and connects them with analysis. It is therefore plausible that also in Dooyeweerd the encompassing law gives us a view that primarily derives from theory.

40. Several comments are in order here.

A. Visual imagery plays an important role in the rationality tradition. An idea is something beheld. Evidence is "seen." Understanding is insight. Theory is a view. Descartes takes his starting point in what can be seen clearly and distinctly. Alvin Plantinga somewhere describes self-evidence as literal lucidity, as an aura of light around what one sees. In *Philosophy and the Mirror of Nature* Richard Rorty analyses these visual metaphors in depth and connects them with the representational view of knowledge and with truth as correspondence. Concepts are mental copies and will be true if they correspond to the original. On this see George Lakoff, *Women, Fire, and Dangerous Things: What Categories Reveal about the Mind* (Chicago: University of Chicago Press, 1987). The better they are the more chance that the holder will be called brilliant or bright, that is, glowing with the light reflected by the copies of the real thing. And it is admittedly hard to be wrong in what you see. You just simply see what you see, you can't help seeing what you see. With normal 20-20 vision, how could you not see what in fact you are seeing? The absolutization of the rational order concept is related to this seeing. In theory what is thus seen, what is theoretically grasped, becomes frozen, the abstracted picture is rigid, fixed, still like a photograph. "Reality" is to the view of theory "enclosed" within the categorial order of intellectual conception. What is thus "seen" is thought to be real "outside" of "the mind's eye" just the way it is seen. What is intended in the conceptual grasp is an abstraction, taken out of its temporal coherence and then held rigidly fixed within a logical framework. It is an invisible reality made luminous to the intellect, which in the act of *intelligere* sees the invisible. And once you've "seen" it right, it will ever be that way. (Dooyeweerd early in his career characterized abstraction as fixation, as logical clamping; see John H. Kok, idem., 291-92. He also discusses logical analysis in terms of a lifting of structures out of their coherence and continuity, see for example II, 467-70.) What the intellect thus grasps is capable of being developed dialectically while it remains abstracted, by subjecting the conceptual content to the rules and methods of first order logic. Truth and order then seem immune to history and change.

B. In this tradition truth is mostly a seen as correspondence between the concept and the reality this concept copies or represents. In distinction from this the pragmatic concept of truth is oriented to guidance in action. Truth then is a matter of delivering the goods promised in the concept by acting on the concept. Apart from the religious history of the discovery of reason in Greece, it is hard to see why we would refer to a conceptual image of properties things share as essence or truth. The view of concepts as instruments of control seems more appropriate, but remains partial as well. (Dooyeweerd sees truth more broadly, but retains a logical focus; see I, 153.)

C. Order in the Bible has a very different ring to it. It is heard rather than seen, because it is a ruler's command. The Greek *metaphysical vision* of order is therefore not to be read as the biblical *covenantal* order which is presented as kingly rule. Biblical order is path along which to *move*, while Greek order is *immutable* structure in which all is enclosed. Confusion is easy here, because in Plato the philosopher and the king became united, as well as because the vision of each can be referred to as order and as law. Both can also be without change. But here, again, even the possibility of immutability in either view is different. The fixed resolve in a law of Medes and Persians is a different immutability than metaphysical absence of change. Further, both laws and orders, of course, are also related to words, language. Hence the possibility of (con)fusion exists on many fronts. And there are similarly significant sources of confusion with regard to the notions of truth and revelation in relation to order, semantic realities, and rationality; as well as with regard to faith taken as belief where belief is no more than the assentful holding of a concept; see note 52, below. This goes all the way back to Augustine's view of faith as thinking with assent.

D. Though Dooyeweerd attempted to center creation order in love, it is clear that what he means by law is theoretically discovered general structure. Thus he reads law at least also ontologically in the Bible. See note 28, above.

41. The wisdom of which the Bible speaks in the wisdom literature is precisely geared to guide us with practical advice, rather than with general rules.

42. Not much argument is needed for this it seems. In Reformed epistemologist Alvin Plantinga's *Does God Have a Nature?* (Milwaukee: Marquette University Press, 1980) there is a clear struggle with the tension between this metaphysical order of logical necessity on the one hand and the biblical revelation of God's sovereignty on the other. In *Understanding Our World* my "world-order/ordered world" distinction is oriented to the metaphysical tradition as well. It seems to me there is no harm in using the metaphors of rational world order as an important entry into the meaning of Christian experience. This has had salutory results for many centuries. Though not being the same as Platonic realism, the notion of creation order allowed the believer to be "in the world" in a way that related very closely to the "world" of our world's rationality tradition. But now that attention to foundationalism, logocentrism, and many related versions of the contemporary critique of reason have made us aware of the darker sides of this tradition, it will be equally beneficial to exchange the core metaphors of the West for others, in order to get a new hold on what it means to be in this world. Authority, obedience, and (conceptually) knowing the truth as indications of a privileged image for our relation to God need not permanently occupy center stage. Friendship, childhood, love, and other metaphors can with equal legitimacy occupy center stage for a while, clustering around the *Abba* of Jesus rather than the King of Israel. Such a move creates tensions only if new centers are seen only in relation to old centers, that is, if different notions are placed in tension *as* centers. But where a former center is replaced and given a place off-center, oppositions, dialectics, dilemmas, and other problematic oppositions need not occur.

43. Rigidity was not, of course, the only result. An ethos of order also has significant advantages, especially where its role is to regulate and orient lives in a threatening and confusing world.

44. An interesting reading of St. Thomas's realism along these lines would be that he had no choice, given the intellectual climate, other than to accept the world of Greek metaphysics; while at the same time his writings often did not stress the immutability of that order, but rather the legitimacy of all the exceptions to, changes in, and individual readings of the rules. See James P. Reilly Jr., *Saint Thomas on Law* (Toronto: Pontifical Institute of Medieval Studies, 1988).

45. See the fascinating book *John Calvin: A Sixteenth Century Portrait* by William Bouwsma (Oxford: Oxford University Press, 1988). Bouwsma's thesis is that the sixteenth century gives all of us our identity and that Calvin is the exemplary sixteenth century person, struggling with the metaphysical inheritance of reason and order in relation to our freedom and subjectivity. Herman Dooyeweerd has made the tension between reason and freedom a central theme in his analysis of the humanist view of autonomy, op. cit., vol. I, 61-63, 169-495, 501-505.

46. Stellingwerff, op. cit., vol. II, points to the important role played by the 1962 Ph.D. thesis of H. M. Kuitert on biblical anthropomorphism with regard to God *(De Mensvormigheid Gods,* Kampen: Kok, 1967). Stellingwerff claims that this study broke through the impasse with respect to the immutability of God and of divine decrees and opened the Vrije Universiteit for a radically different development, favorable to change.

47. See op. cit., vol. I, 9, 72, 91-93, 144, 147-48; vol. II, 237-41; vol. III, 5, 14. See also Stellingwerff, op. cit., vol. II, 160. Dooyeweerd's intellectual biographer also notes this; see Marcel E. Verburg, *Herman Dooyeweerd: Leven en werk van een Nederlands christen-wijsgeer* (Baarn: Ten Have, 1989), 124. It is arguable that in various aspects of his work Dooyeweerd anticipates postmodern themes. He is after prevention of arbitrariness and not against relativity or change. In spite of this, however, the available language and the conceptual traditions of his time continued to influence him to favor terms like constant and invariable for order (II:548, 550, 553-54, 557, 559; III: 78-79, 82-83, 94, 106, 147, 158, 170, 268, 272). But given the fact that primitive societies are said to have just such an order (op. cit., III, 82, 94), such constancy can hardly be thought of in terms of metaphysical immutability. See also, for example, what he has to say about the order of marriage (III, 325-29). He does speak, however, of relative constancy (III, 174). Nevertheless, his articulation of his own views was deeply influenced by the available language, perhaps more so than by his deepest intentions, possibly influenced by the controversies surrounding his and Vollenhoven's work in the late 1920s and early 1930s (see Stellingwerff, II, 168, 208, 210, 211, 223, 224, 268, 401). The most blatant example of Platonism in Dooyeweerd is in the discussion with J. Lever in *Philosophia Reformata* in 1959. There he distinguishes between a finished (structure of) creation and a process of becoming in time.

48. Rational inquiry, conceptual examination in the logical space of argumentation, proceeds by comparing entities in order to detect the structure of continuously shared properties, that is, tries to conceive of how things are "the same" as other things, how they are "of one kind." And it regards this conceived structure as law, boundary, condition of possibility, principle of necessity, universal order. When "applied," these discoveries help us *control* the realities we thus have in our (intellectual) grasp, because they give us handles on property relations of all individuals of some kind, allowing us to explain and predict events; see also notes 49, 50, 52 below.

49. Since theoretical concepts are primarily instruments of power and control, a rationally focused society privileges classes, races, sexes, genders, and orientations that seem to constitute "the rule." Those singled out and identified by this "orthodoxy" or truth of understanding also become the powerful, wealthy, and privileged in such societies. They in turn impose rule. A conceptual order tends to preserve the powers that make the present same what is same about it, that is, it preserves identity and power and tends to favor conservatism. Interestingly, in the tension between political liberalism and conservatism, conservatives admittedly are conservers of the status quo who complain that liberals who use principles of criticism are rationalists, while liberals practice a conservatism with respect to their principles of liberalism.

50. There is really no good reason to believe—outside of the revelatory structures of a tradition which religiously favors rationality—that sorting out reality rationally should have the privilege of being perceived as sorting out truth and reality from non-truth and non-reality. It would be better to perceive rational sorting as sorting for power and control, or sorting for sharing and communicating. But other sorting is possible and legitimate. Eggs that fall through a fixed grid are not bad eggs. They would be retained with a different grid. Of course, there is nothing as such wrong with privileging the metaphor of rationality. When Dooyeweerd, for example, has to name the core meaning of reality in its religious sense, he privileges love and then specifies: not in its modal sense (op. cit., vol. II, 140-63.) With this move he makes our call to love central in a way that transcends whatever else we may be called to. The same move plays a role in the project I undertake in this paper. At the same time, Dooyeweerd states that "love" is also just *one* of the *many* aspects of our calling. But in his view, *all* modal special meaning is *one* in the religious *unity* of existence. It would therefore seem just as possible to privilege other aspects, such as intelligibility or being rationally ordered, as the core meaning of reality, rather than love. All that would be needed would be the specification: reason not in its modal sense (op. cit., vol. I, 104-106 and vol. III, 65-69). What becomes objectionable is to eradicate the relativity of the privileging. In the Old Testament there is no doubt a privileging of jural-political metaphors such as rule, sovereignty, and authority on the one hand, and obedience and submission on the other. God is King, we are subjects. (Brueggemann, op. cit., makes a good case for regarding images deriving from kingship in Israel with a sense of their ambiguity.) In the New Testament Jesus relativizes this privileging, as the rulers well understand, by calling God *Abba* and by referring, hence, to us as children. And "children" does not mean "immature dependents," but offspring, heirs, co-workers. It also seems clear, hence

Dooyeweerd's views, that the New Testament itself centers what God requires of us in love. See also notes 7, 18, and 42.

51. Western culture has reaped vast benefits—economic, scientific, technical, medical, and many others—from instruments of control developed by theoretical inquiry. They have made available power for the good: control of illness, control over nature, power of progress. But it is also clear now that our serving of these powers leads to an uncontrolled market, an endangered creation, runaway technology, medicine priced out of reach, and other forces that no longer are within our control. Contemporary feminist epistemology is very instructive on this topic.

52. The modern English word "belief" primarily refers to an accepted or trusted proposition or concept, that is, states of affairs conceptually appropriated with assent. On the history of belief in relation to faith see Wilfred Cantwell Smith, *Faith and Belief* (Princeton: Princeton University Press, 1979, 1987). He argues convincingly that understanding faith in terms of belief has a distorting effect on understanding what the Bible means by faith. Belief has practically no fiduciary content in most modern philosophy. There is today a cautious recovery of faith as trust and reliance, with its own relationship to truth of revelation as dependable spiritual direction. There is also an increasing recognition that reason and science are not so much our primary access to truth (reductionistically taken as well-formed belief in its modern sense), but rather the sources of instruments of power and control in technology and language. *Rule*—discovery—gives access to *regula*-tion, that is, control. See especially the works by Lorraine Code cited earlier. Foucault's analysis of power is also helpful here. And it is instructive to realize that Dooyeweerd, as did Mekkes, referred to the humanist motive of control as the science motive.

53. If we *religiously trust* reason and control, we have a special case and special problems of (con)-fusing faith and reason, because (now hidden trust in) reason makes trust itself suspect to reason. In our culture this has for two thousand years led to the rejection of faith and revelation and to the mistaken view that reason could be self-grounding. The functioning of reason, however, needs a wider context of trust in which reason itself cannot make trust superfluous (see Code). It is refreshing to see someone like Richard Rorty, still within the bounds of the liberal Enlightenment, speak of community "as having no foundation except shared hope and trust created by such sharing..." (*Objectivism, Relativism, and Truth,* 33).

54. If truth primarily characterizes judgment, assertion, claim and belief, then to talk about truth of faith or truth of religion would require us to deal with these as primarily matters of judgment, assertion, claim, and belief. In that case reason would become judge of faith. The biblical meaning of truth is decidedly different. Jesus' saying "I am the truth," for example, would be incomprehensible if we used contemporary philosophical meanings of truth as propositional. Foucault's truth as power would come closer. We are talking here about embodied disclosure of God's hidden presence.

55. By truth here I do not mean a set of beliefs. Truth of "revelation" is what is "brought to light" in terms of experiences rooted in trust. Living a life of trusting compassion "reveals" a reality to us that differs from the truth of conceptual control. See notes 40 and 52 above.

56. When we deal with controversial problems in our culture we may be interested in solutions that are helpful, loving, just, or redemptive. But usually we first of all want to know whether they are "right." And by right we mean: fitting a preconceived immutable order. This rightness is the privileged category of priority and will make us do things that are unhelpful, unloving, unredemptive. And behind it all lies the conviction that we already know what is right. For an illuminating example of what "right order" can do in terms of fundamentally causing harm see Stuart Clark, "Inversion, Misrule, and the Meaning of Witchcraft," in *Past and Present,* no. 87: 98-127.

57. Reason has for religious-cultural reasons had this all-encompassing or, put differently, central place in the West. But rationality (or logical necessity and possibility) is not in principle, necessarily an apriori universal, given prior to all times for all times, nor does it essentially indicate a primary need to be satisfied in all situations. So reason does not reveal a (logically) necessary structure for all reality whatsoever, as Wolterstorff once—though certainly no longer—talked about it (in *On Universals).* It is not a structure of logically necessary eternal truths, nor does such a structure exist as Plantinga talked about it when discussing the nature of God *(Does God Have A Nature?).* Nor is there reason to accept, as Dooyeweerd speaks of it, an overarching order (op. cit., II, 557). We may at most discover that, given the way we think, the logical space of reasons requires us to think in certain ways, perhaps necessarily so. But that does not warrant the leap to an ontology of logical necessity. There is also no need to interpret Scripture as requiring us to subscribe to such an eternal order. There are, of course, orders. Some are long lasting, all provide continuity/identity, all are channels for blessing whenever they come from God. But these orders are just one of the many cross-sections of reality, not the category that *metaphysically* divides all reality into the *logical* disjunction of order and the ordered. This division is an absolutized distinction, one in which we see reality enclosed within categories. Order is what becomes visible to analysis, to theory, to thought. In the work of J. D. Dengerink, *De Zin van de Werkelijkheid* (Amsterdam: VU Uitgeverij, 1986), 5-8, 129-31, and 170-259), of M.D. Stafleu, *Theories at Work* (Lanham: University Press of America, 1987), 232-60 and *De Verborgen Structuur* (Amsterdam: Buijten & Schipperheijn, 1989), 9, 10, 20-39, and of H. van Riessen, *Wijsbegeerte* (Kampen: Kok, 1970), 92-98, 133-65), it appears that students of Dooyeweerd clearly see a privileged relation between universal order on the one hand and theory making on the other. They follow Dooyeweerd in this. But they do not draw the conclusion that I as a follower of Dooyeweerd here draw for the first time, namely that "order" is *no more* than what we see of reality from a logical point of view. I therefore need to relativize the views I once held and discussed in *Understanding Our World* about world order and ordered world. The ability we have of abstracting order does not *divide the world* into two sides, layers, or halves. Hence the universal problem of the place and dual character of the law in reformational philosophy (see Troost, note 13 above). Since it is proper in doing theory to view the world theoretically, that is, from the point of view of general structural relations, it is also theoretically proper to distinguish such structures from all that *is* not such a structure but just *has* it. But there is no reason whatsoever for proclaiming that point of view as the eternal and most basic correlation in reality. The structures of and for thought are not therefore also the one universal structure of all reality.

58. This brings fundamental relativity (though not arbitrariness) into our lives. Whether that is bad depends on whether we once subscribed to a fixed order of reason. Such an order forbids the relativity it calls relativism. But apart from the criteria of that tradition, there is no danger of arbitrary relativism. There is nothing to be feared from abandoning a cultural order of reason which, although it once was a channel for blessing, has become a temptation to curse. Christians have always known that there was a problem with a culture which, by putting its trust in thought, came to distrust trust. There has always been a faith/reason *problem* in the tradition. There can be no harm in the restoration of faith as the more reliable vision of our destiny in hope (see Hebrews 11). What is to be feared is the arbitrariness of freedom in autonomy. But what I here propose is far from that. See notes 62 and 66 below, and Brueggemann, *op. cit.* My proposals will, of course, more easily lead to a critique of the identity of structures of power in our culture. This will cause resistance. But that should not embarrass a *reformational* tradition.

59. John 5 shows that, against the rigidity of the tradition, Jesus presented a God not "all done" as some have expected on the basis of Genesis 1. God is still at work (5:17). A God who is still at work is, consequently, also a God not easily recognized when we fixate that God from within the fixed horizons of the book (5:39). This is a "different" God from what people had come to expect and believe.

60. Truth is not something like: if I am right about something, whoever two centuries from now will also be right about it will have my position. Nor is conceptual truth a matter of how a copy or representation—which a concept is not, just as a work of art is not—corresponds to the real thing. Nor, again, is truth literal. To be literal is simply a mark of that language whose conceptual pole has the widely agreed meaning that is recorded in the dictionary.

61. A culture can, for a time, center itself in order. Since all traditions relativize things to what is central in the tradition, and since a rational center as a historical center is not in principle objectionable at some time, we would only need to de-center reason if faith in God revealed to us the need for a new center. Such a need would arise if in the present center it is difficult for God to become known *as God*. Decentering is dangerous when it is an autonomously human shift in an autonomously human center. It is salutary when it is discovered that a historical center darkens the counsel of God as time moves on.

62. Relativism as arbitrary individualistic subjectivism is no one's view. And the problems relativists are accused of causing seem to exist in practice for non-relativists as well. However, if we reject unitary, universal, eternal, immutable principles, there is no need to panic. We can still count to ten, read the street signs, fry an egg, do a heart transplant, recognize the poor, hate war, and so on. Life without some *traditional* criteria or life with *shifting* criteria is not life *without* criteria. Such a life, of course, does give us some responsibility for the criteria we will live by. They are not ready-made and already revealed by God. As world-makers we not only make airplanes, *in vitro* babies, and resolutions, but we also make criteria, rules. That does not prevent us from saying God gave them to us, just as love-making and pregnancy do not prevent us from saying God gave us our children. God-as-creator remains a creaturely designation of God (see note 18 above). In Dooyeweerd the subject-object relation in human life is essentially a world-making relation, especially if seen in conjunction with the task he sees us have in the positivization of principles.

63. Experienced fruitbearing or blessing is a litmus test of God's goodness. A litmus test is not a criterion or standard, but a way to tell. It is typical for us that in trying to know the good, we Westerners seek for definitions and concepts first of all. We would not tell what the good is by telling a story. But there is no good reason why we might not start telling stories if abstractly finding definitions has proved unfruitful. See Brueggemann, op. cit., 74-85, on the Psalms and experience. Jesus' powerful appeal to experience to reassure John the Baptist that the promises of the prophets were being fulfilled is a key example of experience as litmus test (Matthew 11:2-6). And there are other examples, such as Exodus 16:11-12 (a theme found throughout Ezekiel) and the appeal to experience everywhere in Deuteronomy. J. P. A. Mekkes frequently refers to lived experience and sees it as the seat of revelation (e.g. op. cit., 62 and 86).

64. Philippians 2:12. See also Acts 15:19 and Romans 14:1-9.

65. It is typical for New Testament freedom that the Gentile Christians are expected to find (though not arbitrarily) their own way, even though Jewish Christians need not abandon theirs. That's the significance of Acts 15 for our discussion. Romans 8 encourages us to use that freedom even if it brings along great perplexity (see 7:24, 25), because in Christ our mistakes will not lead to condemnation, but only to the pain that mistakes bring along. In Galatians Paul encourages us to shape our spirituality in freedom, and never again to let it be concretized by being "cast in concrete," but only to let it "be concretely" specific in a given time (5:1-6).

66. Taking such responsibility seriously is not done in a vacuum. We live in a world in which much is known and familiar to us and helps us make our decisions. Christians do this in the context of the church and her history and traditions, seeking wisdom through the Scriptures, and trusting their message that God's Spirit is there to guide us and that the Jesus of the Scriptures is present in the church as a beacon. In this context much reliable knowledge of a God-given order of reality (which need not be construed on a Western-tradition-centering notion of rational immutability) can also be assumed. If there is a fear that my proposed change in perception will make things go wrong we should remember that now, with our present perception, things are also going wrong. We do not now have a perception of things such that nothing goes wrong, nor one which we already know will make things go right. Delusion in principle clings to present order as well as to proposed changes.

67. The state of Oregon in the USA is working on a list of diseases that will be treated in an order of priority, depending on available resources. There will be 708 treatable diseases. In the case of disease 709 it may seem to be arbitrary to cut off medical help, but if treating one person with that disease requires spending the resources for treating hundreds of other seriously ill patients, that decision is made. Exceptional situations will not be used to set or abandon policy.

68. Claus Westermann, *Genesis, I. Teilband Genesis 1-11.* Volume I/1 of *Biblischer Kommentar* (Neukirchen-Vluyn: Neukirchener Verlag, 1974). For comments on Genesis 3:5, "knowing good and evil," see 328-37.

69. As in John 5, to see where God is at work. That does not absolve us from either obedience or order. There is order in reality that comes from God and we will, of course, do well to heed such order.

70. We are still uncomfortably comfortable with telling evil in sex and seem oblivious to telling evil in mega-salaries for stars in sports and entertainment.

71. The Reformed Churches in the Netherlands (GKN) as well as the Presbyterian Church USA have in recent years made efforts to come to terms with our sexual morality in ways the tradition would not foresee. Unfortunately both have done little explicit confessional grounding of their approaches in the biblical text.

72. To say that they exist, though we do not fully know them and can only approximate them, seems a "cop out" because that way there is no knowing what it is that we do or do not approximate either.

73. Such as is portrayed to us in Psalm 73: good and evil, even in terms of their fruits, seemed hard to understand until the poet looked at it in the presence of God and saw what the apparent good fruits of evil would add up to down the road. So the perspective of faith with our eyes fixed on the future (the faith of Habakkuk, of Romans 1, and of Hebrews 11) is necessary to understand good and evil.

74. The rock on which Jesus encourages us to build at the end of Luke 6 is a foundation of mercy, if indeed we may connect that parable with what precedes it. The mission of Jackie Pullinger's St. Stevens Brothers in Hong Kong demonstrates the fruitbearing of a mission not built on rules/orders, but on compassion, by unconditionally taking in those suffering from drug abuse, also when they continue to backslide. If there is any discipline there, it is the discipline of mercy: no condemnation. See her book *Chasing the Dragon* (Eastbourne: Kingsway Publishing, 1987).

75. They would inside a theory play their role via what Wolterstorff, *Reason within the Bounds of Religion* (Grand Rapids: Eerdmans, 1976, 1984), has called control beliefs and via what Dooyeweerd (op. cit.) designates as logical anticipations of other dimensions of experience. Wolterstorff does not hesitate to recommend that in devising strategies for theory making we concentrate on theories that make for justice and peace; *Until Justice and Peace Embrace* (Grand Rapids: Eerdmans, 1983), 162-76.

76. See my article "The Just Shall Live" in *Christian Scholar's Review,* March 1987: 265-82. The truth God reveals in Christ's incarnation is the truth of God's bodily presence. See note 55 above.

77. David's eating of the temple loaves against the rules (Luke 6:1-5), Peter's experience of the sheet that broke into his "hermeneutics" (Acts 10), Paul who tells us "I have no revelation" when he takes responsibility "in the Spirit" to pass on his own advice (1 Corinthians 7), and many other New Testament stories make clear that the role of order in our lives is not one of immutable universality. The *absolute* authority of a *present* order, which in our experience damages creation and human relationships, receives little support in the ministries of Jesus or Paul.

78. I have dealt with this impossibility at length in *Setting Our Sights by the Morning Star.*

79. Faith, as trust, is a link to a solid ground, a chain to an anchor. It does not, unlike understanding, have a content within my grasp, but grasps a lifeline. It is a solid ground *on* which I stand. To see faith as having a content of beliefs makes faith essentially a form of reason, a supernatural form of cognition given content by revelation. This does not mean conceptual beliefs may not be important to faith. But faith is primarily a *holding on* to something, rather than a *holding of* a content. (See notes 40, 52, 55.) The faith of the West has been a holding on to thought as containing the reliable revelation of truth and essential reality. But *having faith while thinking* would be a holding on to something that *guides us in our thinking,* most likely something other than thinking. If we can learn to see the Bible as book of faith and not take that to mean book of beliefs, we will learn to see that the Bible as a whole does not contain any single permanent "same" as a structure of its own that we can discover as its single doctrine. It is helpful to read texts in which belief and faith both occur in English, as texts which only have *pistis* in Greek. See for example Romans 3:22, 4:3 and 11, 14:2, 1 Peter 1:21 and Galatians 3:5-9 in the RSV.

80. That is, in terms of the ethos of key texts such as Philippians 2:5-11 and Colossians 1:15-20.

81. If we wait till we can conceptually grasp this, we will never trust the integrity of creation.

Thinking of Creation Order and an Ethos of Compassion

Response to Hendrik Hart

Atie Th. Brüggemann-Kruijff

It is a pleasure to be able to respond to the paper of professor Hart, whom I have known as a man of outspoken ideas and outstanding philosophical qualities since the beginning of my study in philosophy at the Vrije Universiteit, a long time ago in the roaring sixties.

I found his paper inspiring and his analysis of the notion of "creation order" very much to the point. Your proposal, professor Hart, to switch over from "creation order" as ethos to an "ethos of compassion" as the leading notion in thinking about the integrity of creation made sense to me and I agree with your intentions.

There were some analogies that struck me between your analysis and that of Emmanuel Levinas, the French philosopher inspired by Thora and Talmud, on whom I have done recent research. Levinas too seeks for real humanity transcending the totality of order set by ontology. By ontology I mean a way of philosophizing which fixes meaning solely within the bounds of the correlation between thinking and being. Levinas too finds real humanity in the transcendence of the ethical relation, of *l'un-pour-l'autre*: I am not myself, fixed as being there for myself, but moved in my bowels for my neighbour who has nobody but me. Levinas too plays with the Hebrew words *rekhem* (womb, bowels) and *rukhama* (compassion), working out the incarnation, the embodiment of the inspiration from "the other side" of the correlation of being and thinking, from the Infinite.[1]

It is perhaps because of these analogies that in thinking about your lecture some questions came into my mind. They are questions about faith and reason, about having faith and doing philosophy, or perhaps more precisely, about belonging to a Christian community and being a philosopher.

Therefore, I would like to tell you a story. It really happened, in those roaring sixties I mentioned before, but I will tell it to you as a parable.

Once upon a time, I could not help listening to the conversation between two fellow-students, one of them a male Canadian, my main character. There were lots of Canadians at that time studying philosophy at the Vrije Universiteit. They talked about keeping philosophy going no matter what happened. Both men were married, I believe. The Canadian student said:

"Yesterday, I was at home alone, brooding about some problem in my thesis I could not overcome. I was sitting at the table, still thinking, when my wife came home. I heard her stumbling up the staircase to our apartment. She came in, bags in her arms with food and so on. She had done the shopping and was tired and apparently fed up with it. She saw me sitting at the table and she shouted at me that it was not fair—she was doing all the work and I was doing nothing at all." Both students shook their heads very sadly. They knew and they understood each other: What a pity when your wife does not understand that you are working so hard, even when sitting still at a table, chewing on your pipe.

I heard the story and I was confused. I still am, so to speak. Of course, he *was* working hard. I know the situation myself: ideas come and go, while the world around is only background out of which voices sometimes arise as meaningless noises. But there is the overwhelming feeling that it is indisputably evident that of course philosophy is work of the highest rank! Too high a rank to see the work of the other as work as well and, even worse, unable to see the rightfulness of the accusation at the address of a philosophy that circles around the ego of the philosopher!

At this point in my confusion I will begin exegeting the parable. And please remember that the story deals with my questions about faith and reason in relation to the "creation order" and an ethos of compassion.

Doing philosophy, thinking about any theme whatever, always involves self-reflection, that is, thinking about the relation between the theme and our thinking, about the meaning and task of philosophy and about me, the self who does the thinking. This is, I think, the true dynamic of philosophy without which it would lose its meaning. In this respect there are several messages in this parable.

The Partnership of Modernity

The first reading I propose is that we look at a partnership, the *partnership of modernity* in which she stands for faith, he for philosphy. They are connected, both doing work, that is, they care for the creation order, but they ignore this connection.

Philosophy cannot deal with himself in relation to faith. He shuts her out even though they are partners. And so philosophy thinks about order in reality apart from the dynamic of creation, that is, apart from the fact that the Lord, every day anew, gives us his work as an appeal to our creative loving response. But she too—faith—

holds tightly to the ideas with which she lives, some coming from philosophy, as philosophy likewise depends on her. For they are partners. One of these ideas is that of "creation order," and she holds tightly to that, too. But because she denies its source in philosophy, she proclaims it to be an eternal truth of faith, dictating the way of her being herself.

My question to you, Dr. Hart, in light of this interpretation is this: Is it not the Christian community in the first place, at which your criticism is directed, which is at fault because she deals with the philosophical idea of creation order as a "dead letter," smothering new readings of the scriptures, readings in the living spirit of loving compassion?

Philosophy on this reading of our story is the philosophy of *modernity*. It has to be criticized. But because of its incapacity to listen to Faith, this criticism should take the form of a *philosophical* dialogue in which its self-knowledge can be challenged. Don't you think so?

You are, however, criticizing another philopsophical position, knowing its dependence on faith. This philosophy questions modernity. But how? I will move to a second reading of the parable.

The Dialogue of the Soul with Herself

I propose we now look at our parable as a difficult moment in *the dialogue of the soul with herself*, that is, philosophy as a bond between faith and reason. The dialogue aims at self-knowledge—who am I in relation to God, to the people and world around me.

As I said, this is a difficult moment, for although both recognize their bonding, it is reason that defines the terms of their relationship. "What a pity," he says to the other reasonable guy, "that she does not understand...." *He* understands both her and his position: she embodies the condition on which he can express the meaning of the totality of this order of things. In his way of explaining the situation to himself, he cannot hear this other voice of hers that appeals to him to get up from this table. It's a stumbling dialogue.

Is it the male domination of reason over faith in philosophy that makes Christian philosophy, too, hold tightly to the order of its discourse as if it were always the transcendent creation order?[2] Does it thereby legitimate the status quo of familial and social relationships?

But, Dr. Hart, do you do justice to Dooyeweerd in this respect, the Christian philosopher I know best? Creation order in Dooyeweerd's vision has several dimensions of which the transcendental order of time in which all our understanding is structured refers to a transcendent dimension that in its religious dynamic never can be grasped by reason. But there are indeed tensions. The temporality of human understanding, laid down in the process of disclosure and the task of positivizing norms every time anew in light of the commandment of love, is in conflict with a conception of the task of philosophy to approach a theoretical insight in the "*totality* of meaning."[3]

I think, however, that unless we proclaim the end of philopsophy we have to live with this tension.

Do you not think, with me, that real philosophical self-reflection should reckon both with an ethos of compassion, never grasped, but as a voice from elsewhere inspiring and correcting? And that this other ethos of the philosophical urge for theoretical truth and order, an order that, once reached, also locates compassion, betraying the transcendence of its inspiration?

Emmanuel Levinas speaks of the ongoing need of rearticulation in light of this dynamic in philosophy: the wisdom of love should be a guide for the love for wisdom.[4]

Reflection on the Calling of the Christian Community

As with all parables there are still more readings left. I will try one more, my last one. I propose we look at this marital quarrel as telling us something important about the church, about a *Christian community* and the relation between faith and reason, between trust and theology/philosophy in this community.

In the first interpretation I suggested that the lack of awareness of their mutual dependency left faith with a not entirely proper self-understanding. But are you telling us, Dr. Hart, that she should not deal with reason at all in the process of becoming herself?

"It is time to stop arguing about intellectual beliefs as though our ethos owes an explanation to the philosophical tradition," you said. Within the context of a philosophical dialogue, I cannot imagine not doing this, although it becomes rather dull when we have gotten the idea that nobody is listening. The challenge should be to show that intellectual beliefs in the philosophical tradition itself cannot work without an ethos of compassion.

But in the context of the Christian community there are indeed other priorities. Nevertheless, I would like to argue for a reconciliation of the partners of faith and reason in this bond of the Christian community as well.

This is because a Christian community also needs the ongoing process of self-reflection, and because of the need for thinking about the creation order, about God's commandments in the spirit of compassion.

As for the community in need of self-reflection: for our renewal day by day we have to relate ourselves, our ideas and opinions, to God's appeal to let the weakest, the helpless, come first. And truly philosophy—in the spirit of compassion—can be of help in this self-reflection of the community. Is it not philosophy, aiming at self-knowledge, which can help change entrenched ideas about the relationships in which we should work out this ethos of compassion? Philosophy can be of help in relating the historicity of the scriptures, of which we are more and more aware, to the creation order, culminating in God's commandments of love. And such a philosophy, inspired by the ethos of compassion, cannot do without reason, without analyzing and reflecting. Is it not true that there can be no such thing as a Christian community which refuses to think about its position and task in this world? And in our time, we can not pretend to think just in a naive way. Many philosophies have enriched our Christian heritage.

As for thinking about the creation order in the spirit of compassion, we would then have a philisophy which answers to the task of discerning the spirits. But we shall never have finished this task: there is no fundamental proof at our disposal.

One last question remains: What happened to this young Canadian couple? Well, I have justified reasons to believe that after their reconciliation, they lived happily ever after.

Notes

1. See for instance Emmanuel Levinas *Autrement qu' être ou audelà de l'essence* (Den Haag, 1974), 3-25 and 167-218, and *Humanisme de l' autre homme* (Paris: 1972), the last chapter.
2. About this male domination of reason, see Genevieve Lloyd, *The Man of Reason* (London: Methuen, 1984).
3. See Herman Dooyeweerd, *A New Critique of Theoretical Thought,* vol. I (Amsterdam, 1953), 4.
4. *Autrement qu' être...,* 206, 207.

Too Far the Pendulum Swings

Response to Hendrik Hart

John E. Hare

Dr. Hart's paper is a stimulating proposal of the following point of view. He sees a conflict between two kinds of ethos, an ethos of compassion and an ethos of permanent creation order. He proposes to give the victory in this conflict to the ethos of compassion. I have only a limited space to respond. What I want to do is to look at these two kinds of ethos, starting with the ethos of compassion, and then suggest that it is a faulty view of both of them that leads to the view that they are essentially in conflict with each other.

First, then, what is compassion? Hart says the compassion he is talking about is not a feeling but an act. I tend to think it is a feeling that results in an act. Suppose we say, roughly, that to act is to produce an intentional change in the world. Take the two cases Hart refers to in Luke's gospel.[1] The Good Samaritan is moved by compassion, in the Greek *esplanchnisthe* referring to his bowels, and goes over to the man lying by the side of the road. The father of the prodigal is moved by compassion, *esplanchnisthe* again, and runs to meet his son. The texts suggest that the compassion is something that happens in the bowels, something we might describe as within the person's heart, and the person then acts as a result.[2] But if this is right, it does not mean that the compassion, because it is a feeling, is *merely* passive. Compassion, let us say, takes on suffering from a sufferer; but there is a misleading way of thinking about this. If I put a lump of cream cheese next to some crushed garlic on a shelf, the cream cheese will take on the smell of the garlic; it has no choice in the matter and is merely passive in respect of the change. But human emotions are also active, because they standardly involve assessment.[3] Even relatively simple emotions like anger involve assessing insult or offense. This becomes clearer with emotions like envy or nostalgia. "Assessment" is in one way a misleading term here, because it suggests a quantitative evaluation, as in the assessment of the value of a house. We could say, alternatively, that emotions involve "construal," but this term has its own awkwardness.[4] I will stick with the term "assessment," trying to ignore the implication of measurement. This activity of assessment turns out to be important when we try to understand the relation of compassion to creation order. It does not much matter for the purposes of this response whether compassion is correctly described as an act or as an emotion, once we grant that emotions standardly involve assessment. Acts certainly require assessment, and most feelings do; and this notion of assessment is what I want to use for my critique of Hart.

The assessments we make in our emotional life depend upon the evaluative frameworks within which we live. A framework is a set of qualitative distinctions which structure our evaluations of what is important and what is not.[5] Homer's heroes live in a framework very different from ours, though influencing ours at many points. It may be that most of those living in, let us say, Toronto, in 1992 do not have a single framework within which they live, but parts of several competing ones. I want to put the question behind Hart's paper in terms of the assessment characteristically involved in compassion. If I feel compassion for someone, what kind of assessment am I making, and what kind of framework holds that assessment in place?

Surely, I make the assessment that the other person is suffering? But this is not quite right, for I can be moved by compassion for people who are not now suffering. Jesus, looking out over Jerusalem from the Mount of Olives, was moved by the sense of what its inhabitants were *about* to suffer. It is possible to be moved with compassion for people who are in *danger* of suffering, even if we do not know whether this danger will be realized or not. Finally, it is possible to feel compassion for those who, because of the nature of their defect, cannot experience suffering from the defect at all. Probably the best general account is that when I feel compassion, I make the assessment that another person is in need. But now what framework governs this assessment? Why is it that one thing strikes me as need, and not another thing?

Assessments of need derive from some conception of the human good, and what is necessary in order to attain it. This conception will be given by the framework or frameworks within which a person lives. The assessment of need is an evaluation that some component of the human good, or some necessary means to attaining the human good, is lacking. Compassion involves such an assessment, and it also involves being moved to try to ameliorate the lack of it. On prescriptivist meta-ethical views these are not separate from each other; but if they are separate, compassion involves both of them.[6] Tying compassion to this kind of evaluation helps us see what might be meant by talking of *inappropriate* compassion; it will be inappropriate where this kind of evaluation is at fault.

There can thus be a tension between the assessment internal to the emotion and the assessment by reflective judgement. This is a standard feature not only of compassion, but of most human emotion. We can also see that feeling compassion for someone is not yet the same as legitimating that person's activity. For it is possible to acknowledge that someone is lacking in some component of the human good, or some necessary means to attaining it, and it is possible to be moved towards trying to ameliorate that lack, but not to endorse that person's own response to that lack.

One framework question is whether human needs stay the same or whether they change. My main point in this response is to deny that an ethos of compassion is inconsistent with the evaluative framework within which there is a central core of human needs which stay the same. That is, compassion does not require a framework within which the assessment of what constitute core human needs changes over time. Let me distinguish three schematic positions. First, a completely fixed framework. If we confine needs to constants such as food and company, and we distinguish needing something from merely wanting it, we might say that human needs all stay the same. Second, a completely fluid framework. We might emphasize the psychological role of changing culture, and insist that the descriptions under which humans identify their needs change radically over history. Then we might deny that we can identify any human needs that stay the same. To me the most plausible position, overwhelmingly, is a mixed framework, that some needs change and some needs stay the same. On this position, we can hold not only that some needs stay the same, but that these needs form a core surrounded by the needs which change. We can also say that the needs in the core stay the same, but that the necessary means to meeting some of those needs change with culture. If compassion involves the assessment of need, and if my framework is informed by the mixed position I have just stated, then I can expect that there will be a core of cases in which my compassion is aroused, namely those cases in which I am struck by needs which I assess to be in the core of needs. There will also be cases outside this core where I assess need, and where I am moved by compassion.

I have not argued for a mixed framework. Such an argument could be made, I think, on the basis of our increasing knowledge of the biological or genetic base of human needs, coupled with an acknowledgement of the profound changes in our condition brought about by culture. I have also not said anything about how we are supposed to recognize what belongs in the core, on this picture, and what belongs on the periphery. Even putting the question in terms of core and periphery is misleading, because it suggests an evaluative ranking in degrees of importance. I do not mean to imply this, for on the mixed framework there may be some changing needs which are more important than some stable ones. What I am claiming is that it is possible for a community to have an ethos of compassion *and* think of needs as structured within the mixed framework I have started to describe. If this is right, then we should not think of an ethos of fixed creation order as being in conflict with an ethos of compassion merely because the ethos of creation order acknowledges that there is a *fixed* core to human need. There can indeed be conflict between an ethos of compassion and some particular framework of fixed creation order. Suppose, for example, I hold that creation order establishes that black people are natural slaves, and do not have the need for communal respect that white people have. But the conflict will then be between compassion and the particular framework, not between compassion and the notion of a fixed core in itself.

Now for Hart, "a permanent creation order ethos holds compassion captive," and "a fixed creation order will not yield to an order of compassion."[7] He thinks the two kinds of order are in dispute with each other, and he supports the second against the first. There are, I think, three main reasons he gives for preferring the order of compassion; he gives other reasons, but they derive from these three. He lays three charges against the ethos of fixed creation order; first, it is a kind of legalism, which kills the freedom of the Spirit; second, it is conservative and leads to the evil spelled Hitler; third, it is an alien philosophy from the Greeks, and distorts the reading of Scripture. I want to discuss each of these charges briefly.

First, the freedom of the Spirit. In theological terms, Christ's resurrection has restored to us the freedom of children and heirs of God.[8] We can think of this as the restoration of Adam's place in creation. Adam had the authority to designate or name the character of the created reality which he encountered. Calvin says that in the Fall we lost those names, which captured the natures of what was named by them.[9] Our redemption has restored this authority to us. This does not mean, however, that the Holy Spirit has, as it were, withdrawn authority from the rest of the natural order which confronts us. We have to ask, "What are we free *for*?" The line of interpretation I would argue for, though I cannot do so here, is that we are not freed from the law, but from being *under* the law.[10] Being under the law in this sense means being under a demand which one is unable to meet. The position of the Christian is that he or she is given by grace the means to meet the demand, which comes to lose over the process of sanctification the character of demand and gain the character of welcome guidance. This line of interpretation will be familiar to you.[11] On the mixed framework I have started to describe it will still be possible to condemn legalism; but legalism will not be the acknowledgement of a fixed core of needs as such, but the confusion of fixed needs with changing ones, or with changing means to reach fixed ends. Or we could call "legalism" the failure to make the transition from the sense of demand to the sense of welcome guidance.

Second, conservatism. It has to be admitted that conservatives have often used notions of a fixed creation order to support the *status quo*. But we should also look at the historical record of the ideas behind the evil spelled Hitler. The philosophical romantics have at least as much to answer for as the friends of reason; in fact they have more. Hart puts proponents of a fixed creation order on the side of the philosophers of the Enlightenment, and launches at both of them what he calls the postmodern critique of logocentrism. But we have to be careful with the philosophical use of the term "postmodern." The views Hart attributes to postmodernism are for the most part recapitulations of philosophical romanticism. But postmodernism has as its *raison d'etre* a distinction from modernism; and modernism, as for example Charles Taylor describes it, contains within itself the tension between romanticism and the Enlightenment.[12] We should not simply baptize as postmodernism one half of this tension. In any case, the term "postmodernism" in philosophy has not yet been given a clear sense. The important point is that there have both been lots of romantic conservatives and lots of opponents of the *status quo* who have prophetically held society accountable to created order. My point is that prophets call us back as well as calling us forward. The idea of the lion lying down with the lamb is an idea of restoration, not merely what Hart calls a "new and different normativity in Christ."[13] We are called forward to a new Jerusalem, a city and not a garden. But this does not mean that the order immanent in the garden has been repealed; for the key images describing our first state in Genesis are recapitulated in the description of our new state in the book of Revelation.

Finally, the question of alien philosophy. Hart appeals to Gerhard von Rad to make the point that Wisdom in Scripture differs significantly from Greek realistic rational order. But von Rad's reading of Wisdom is not in fact congenial to Hart. Von Rad sees the "good" person as one who conforms to the pattern of reality which can be discerned in the world. He sees continually in the Wisdom texts the notion of limits within creation, to which the godly person conforms, and which provide the condition for his or her freedom. Hart quotes von Rad's warning that the texts do not give us conceptual definitions; but the point of the contrast, as von Rad goes on immediately to say, is that Israel spoke of *facts* rather than definitions.[14] These facts are, he thinks, what wisdom sees. There are, to be sure, differences between the notions of cosmic order in Proverbs and in Anaxagoras, let us say, or Heraclitus or Plato. It is a significant difference that none of the Greeks had the biblical notion of creation. But I do not see the difference that Hart does, namely that the Greeks held the cosmic order fixed whereas the Bible does not. The psalms, for example, move often between on the one hand the limits God set on the waters and the earth and the seasons and on the other hand the limits violated by the proud and wicked inhabitants of the earth. God upholds both kinds of limit, and the unchanging character of the second is established by comparing it to the first.[15] This at least seems to be the natural reading of the wisdom texts.

I want to conclude by saying something about our access to permanent created order, supposing there is such order. Hart objects to the proposal that there is a fixed order, but we do not fully know it and can only approximate it. He thinks this a "cop out, because that way there is no knowing what it is that we do or do not approximate either."[16] But here again we have a bogus either/or. *Either* access, which is arrogant to claim, *or* a proper epistemic humility. But suppose we try applying the same principle to our knowledge of the physical laws of creation, rather than human need. Suppose I say that I believe there are physical laws, but I do not fully know them; I can only approximate to them in my understanding. Will Hart reply that this is a cop out, because that way there is no knowing what it is that I only imperfectly know? Christian humility requires the admission that now we know only in part; it does not require abandoning the claim to any access at all.

I am very aware that I come as an outsider to this discussion, and there is a history to it within this community that I only dimly understand. What strikes me, however, is that what is going on in Hart's paper is a throwing out of the baby with the bathwater. It sounds to me as though he wants to liberate himself from an ambitious but finally arrogant claim to know the created order. Compassion will recognize that someone in his situation may indeed need freedom. But compassion will, I think, locate this need within a framework of needs. Freedom from the authority of a particular human system of thought should not be identified with freedom from authority period. Hart argues that a spirit of freedom is not the ethos of subjects obedient to an authority, but of family members, members of the household of God, with a responsibility to set their own house in order.[17] But there is a dichotomy here proposed between divine fatherhood and divine kingship.[18] I do not find myself wanting to remove from the gospel the notion of the kingdom, in which we are not simply co-workers with God, but his subjects. I certainly do not think we can legitimately remove this idea in the name of faithfulness to the biblical record.

Notes

1. Luke 10:33 and 15:20.
2. Sometimes compassion will require *not* acting, but this could be accommodated by Hart if he agreed that "acts" could include deliberate refrainings from action.
3. See Allan Gibbard, *Wise Choices, Apt Feelings* (Cambridge: Harvard University Press, 1990). The intentionality or cognitivity of emotion is already seen by Aristotle. See Nancy Sherman, *The Fabric of Character* (Oxford: Clarendon Press, 1989), 165f.
4. See Robert C. Roberts, "What Emotion Is: A Sketch," *Philosophical Review* 97: 183-209.
5. The notion of a framework is analyzed in Charles Taylor, *Sources of the Self* (Cambridge: Harvard University Press, 1989).
6. See John E. Hare and Carey B. Joynt, *Ethics and International Affairs* (London: Macmillan, 1981), 1-23.
7. Hart, op. cit., 78, note 11.
8. I have learned a great deal on this topic from Oliver O'Donovan, *Resurrection and Moral Order* (Grand Rapids: Eerdmans, 1986), 22f.
9. Calvin, *Commentary on Genesis* 2:19.
10. Romans 6:15.
11. What O'Donovan adds, op. cit., 22f., is that we are also given by grace the means to understand and hence "name" the demand. This puts us at once into both an active and a passive mode with respect to creation; passive because we are not the creators, and active because with the mind of Christ we can in principle see through to the nature of what was created. I say "in principle" because sin blocks not merely obedience to the law but seeing it with full clarity.

12. Taylor, op. cit., chap. 25. My view of postmodernism, which I cannot argue for here, is that we need to distinguish within it different reactions against the different tracks followed within modernism.

13. Hart, op. cit., 74.

14. Gerhard von Rad, *Wisdom in Israel* (Nashville: Abingdon 1972), 144-45. This is chapter IX, not chapter XI as Hart says, op. cit., footnote 37.

15. See for example Psalms 65, 74, 89, 104, 124, 144, 146. I am indebted in this discussion to Raymond C. Van Leeuwen; see "Liminality and Worldview in Proverbs 1-9," *Semeia* 50 (1990): 111-44.

16. Hart, op. cit., footnote 72.

17. Hart, op. cit., 76.

18. (Footnote added 17 January 1944) I now think that I have overstated this point. Hart is not suggesting that kingship (or fixed creation order) be removed from the gospel. He is suggesting that an ethos of fixed order (which gives a subordinate role to compassion and fatherhood) be replaced by an ethos of compassion (which gives a subordinate role to fixed order and kingship). Moreover his suggestion is indexed to a particular community, namely to those within the Reformed tradition. Still, my criticism can be rephrased to make essentially the same point. An ethos of compassion will embody, I claim, some characteristic assessment of peoples' needs, whether these needs are seen as fixed or changing or both (in some mixture). Hart may mean that the particular community he is interested in should move from a characteristic assessment which sees the needs as more fixed to one which sees them as more open to change. It is important, however, not to usurp the name "compassion" for one of these characteristic assessments over the others. The same is true, *mutatis mutandis*, with fatherhood. This is important *if* Hart wants to avoid the charge of begging the question against his opponents by his choice of language.

Portrayal of Reformational Philosophy Seems Unfair

Response to Hendrik Hart

Johan van der Hoeven

Hart's paper sparkles with involvement and passion. It is also strongly program-matic. Those qualities appeal to me. I can also join in some of the main accents of his "prognosis." Yet his exposition elicits more than a little criticism on my part.

My response focuses on two major questions. First, is the picture of "our philosophical tradition"—I will give attention chiefly to what Hart calls "reforma-tional philosophers from the Amsterdam school oriented to the thought of D. H. Th. Vollenhoven and H. Dooyeweerd"—sufficiently correct and fair? Second, is Hart's own position sufficiently clear and satisfactory?[1]

Right at the start of my reading I was struck by the term "diagnosis." Is the tradition that upholds the notion of "creation order" to be associated with an illness, a *disease*? Some passages and a certain intonation do give me that impression. Perhaps there are personal traumatic experiences that induced the choice of this term. That seems possible and to a certain degree that would be recognizable. Already an older thinker among the "reformational philosophers," J. P. A. Mekkes, emphatically pointed out the necessity of using the term "law" with "more caution." He even says, "Talk about 'creational orderings' as something in itself is ... impos-sible."[2] Still, when we use the term "diagnosis" we will have an association with a disease or with traumatic experiences, so if we wish to point toward healing, there is a need for special diagnostic carefulness. On that score I am not satisfied. Neither do I believe that this can be excused with the remarks made in note 1. For what is at stake is a philosophical tradition—our tradition—and then carefulness is not a secondary requirement. Moreover, the purport of the paper is "critique and refine-ment." Now, in the picture that Hart draws I do recognize a couple of features. However, on the whole it doesn't seem to me correct and entirely fair.

But before elaborating on this I want to state that I (together with Hart, I think) consider legalism as a permanent threat. This threat has always been present—see the biblical writings, Old and New Testaments—and it will always be there. Ap-parently human beings cannot overcome the temptation to *appropriate* a salutary gift of God (his "law"), instead of marvelling at it and singing of it, and to stagnate the dynamics of guiding the life-journey into a system (or survey) of determinations of a life-area.

However—now again turning to the tradition of "reformational philosophers from the Amsterdam school"—I found it remarkable that Hart virtually restricted himself to references to Dooyeweerd and Vollenhoven and hardly paid attention to what other and subsequent philosophers from this "school" have brought forward with regard to "(creation) order," "law," and "structures." Of course, there is the problem of limited space; still, a reference or two would not have been out of place, especially now that we have the twenty-fifth anniversary of the Institute for Christian Studies.

But even within these limitations the references to Dooyeweerd and Vollen-hoven are not really convincing. I cannot go through all of them. But, for example, the comments on Vollenhoven in note 13 amazed me: no "inner transformation" after 1926, and a creation order that "takes the place of the changeless substratum and is logically accessible"? Hart must know that also in Vollenhoven "knowing" is more and deeper than logical thinking, precisely when the "creation order" is concerned. He must know, too, that Vollenhoven gradually came to see the law of *love* as the heart of law. That's what I read in the Epilogue of John Kok's book which he mentions here. The emphasis on love is recalled, though, in note 50, in connection with Dooyeweerd. But if this emphasis is to be taken seriously and, more accurately speaking, this love is to be understood as the *proper meaning-fulfilment* of "law," then I cannot understand what I read in note 28 about Dooyeweerd: "He protests that creation order is very different from metaphysical realism ..., but it is not apparent that there is real difference." Besides, this statement does not seem to tally with the mentioning—and apparent appreciation—of Dooyeweerd's talk of "... the task ... in the positivization of principles" (note 62).

The other observations in note 28 on Dooyeweerd's views do not give evidence of careful and contextual reading. There is no time now for real checking, and such checking would now also be boring. Only the last reference there (to *NC* vol. III, 326-29, an attempt at structural analysis of the marriage-relation) seems to me to have some relevance. Also in my opinion that piece contains antiquated statements, although Dooyeweerd's observations at that time certainly were not simply conser-vative.

To my mind, the main thing is that Hart shows the tendency to undervalue Dooyeweerd's continual repetition of the term "temporal" and to interpret his view within the scope of an "eternal creation order," a *lex aeterna*. That temporality precisely connotes a *dynamics* ("anticipations," "retrocipations,") a *rhythm* (again of anticipations and retrocipations, and of diverse "correlations"), and a *destination* (disclosure, fulfilment) that we don't come across in the metaphysics that Hart rightly criticizes. I'll get back to that in my more thetical comments.

Now suffice it to refer to Mekkes, mentioned already, who happened to be my own academic mentor. He was keenly aware of certain perils, but he drew a more correct picture, I believe. I already mentioned his recommendation of more caution in our use of the term "law." He also said that now that we have heard of the "fulfilment" of the law and seen what that involved, we should not try to build a conception of cosmic ordering guided by the idea of "creational law." However, and he reminded us of this as well, over against the dominant delusion of "autonomous" thought, the intention of "law-idea" was first of all to point to super-arbitrariness, to human knowledge as being bound to an ordering of knowing which determines its meaning and of which it is held to give an account, implicitly or explicitly. The same super-arbitrary determination was also maintained in the development of the structural investigation. But then, too, Mekkes said, "Right from the beginning reformational philosophy emphasized the dynamic character of creation as being God's first revelation to the creature. That's why it spoke of the ground-*motive* of creation."[3]

Some of Dooyeweerd's statements and formulations may give a different impression, but on the whole there is no doubt that "law" cannot be dissociated from "meaning" and "time."[4]

Does Dooyeweerd speak of an "overarching order" (note 57)? I was not able to find it, at least not on the page mentioned by Hart. Instead I noticed that the argument there results in the notion of the "perspective structure of the horizon of experience."

Insufficient justice is also done to Abraham Kuyper. When I read in note 14: "The traditional Reformed doctrine of creation order is an invitation to conservatism and resists radical reformation," how then should I understand the establishing of the Anti-Revolutionary Party (which was also intended to break through conservatism) and Kuyper's famous performance at the first Social Congress?

Hart's Description of "Law"

As to Hart's description (or indication) of his own position, I address myself to two topics, his idea of "law" and his focusing on "compassion." The latter weighs heavily with him and with this conference. But also in view of this latter one, the first one cannot go entirely undiscussed.

It would be too much to collect and compare all of Hart's statements on "law," "order," etc. When I studied them, I did not succeed in getting a clear and consistent picture. For example, already in note 2 the "universal *agape*" is called the "summary of the law." Who among Christians (and Jews) would contradict this? But in note 3 we read about a "mercy-love that reaches beyond the law." The last expression is sometimes replaced by the phrase that this mercy-love (compassion) "transcends" the law. But how is this to be connected with the first (note 2), or rather, with the biblical word "fulfilment (of the law)"?[5]

Compassion does what law or order cannot accomplish (67). That's true enough. But the law was and is not intended to "accomplish" or even to "do"; it is given with a view to human (and other creatures') doing. As such Paul keeps honoring it, also in the passages mentioned in note 6 (see especially Romans 8:4). The same holds true for Jeremiah.[6]

Further, Hart continues to speak of creation order as a "gift of God" (68). But he also says—again with an eye to Dooyeweerd—that "the concept of creation order imports this ontology [reason as the soul of creation] into the Bible." (70) I do not deny that this has happened and remains a threat. However, for one thing, Dooyeweerd was careful enough not to use the term "concept" here, but to speak of an "idea."[7] Hart might object that the distinction between concept and idea is less relevant to his real point, namely that a "visual metaphor" is dominant (see 70 and the long note 40). There is something to be said for that.[8] Certainly it is important to take into account biblical speaking of "hearing" and "obedience" to a "ruler" and his "commands." This was too much neglected, I would agree. But I get confused when earlier in the paper, in a critical vein, traditional Reformed Christians are characterized by their "strong emphasis on authority, obedience, submission...." (note 15) Later on (note 50) there seems to be an attempt to point out a shift in the Bible itself. But what is said in that note strikes me as unclear and rather sloppy. What about the "kingdom of God" in the New Testament, especially in the Gospels? And on the other side, what about the uniqueness of kingship in Israel (in contrast to the other nations)?

Creation order as "servant" is indeed a biblical expression for all the "decrees" in creation (Psalm 119:91). It is a striking indication of the personal character and the intensity of God's salutary "ruling." To this—because Hart has problems with "constancy"—I have just a minor question: are there also servants with "tenure," and if so, are they less respectable than others? The poet of Psalm 148 did not think so (vss. 1-6), and I could mention more. But indeed, it is not fortuitous that precisely poems—songs for community singing—speak that way (compare also Revelation 4 and 5). If "creation orderings" do no longer stand in the sign of the song, the poem, then they are easily denatured. They are there for our *wonder* (continually), for our *gratitude* (salutary protection against disorientation, darkness and the forces of destruction, chaos—see what happened to the Soviet Union, see Los Angeles), and they are intended for *praise*. Only in this meaning-coherence are they there to be acted upon, a "law-subject correlation" which pervades creation. In a considerable part of Hart's and my common tradition I often hardly recognize James's words about the "royal law," i.e., the "law of freedom." Unfortunately, neither do I in Hart's "critique and refinement."

Second, the passage of Scripture just mentioned brings me to the topic of compassion. For, as you know, the passage ends with the words, "Mercy triumphs over judgment" (James 2:13).

Here Hart makes important, penetrating remarks, remarks with which I can often heartily agree and which I want to take to heart.

Still I keep having questions. A first question again concerns the picture evoked of a traditional Christian community (especially the church) and its contrast with what Hart would like to see. Has it not been so, even during the time of the church as an established power with its dominant "doctrinal" preoccupation, that the *diaconal* service was an essential side of that church community, and isn't that still present, now also with mondial scope? It's true that in that work, too, there were and are all sorts of defects and deformations. Yet it was real and is real, and as "charity" it has been beneficial to Western (and other) nations. Hart does not deny it, but to my knowledge he doesn't mention it either. Again, is that entirely fair?

The second, more thetically pointed question is whether it is right to focus so strongly on "compassion." Surely compassion is necessary in our lives, and we have to disseminate that new life in a world like ours more than ever. But I believe that this world is as much in need of (re)discovering the *praise*, the daily praise or worship of God. The passage mentioned in note 2 (Phil. 2:5-11) ends up with that. The congregation (also) is the vanguard of the doxologists (the entire world).[9] Creation—here is the connection with our first question—exists, despite very, very much, in the sign of *liturgy*. It is this liturgy that has its time-orderings. That's what I recognize in the to and fro, the rhythm of the "anticipations" and "retrocipations," and in their common directedness to the final fulfilment.[10]

I am aware of the fact that in our tradition this more often has remained an undertone than an overtone. But in John Calvin it was vividly present: to the glory, the actual and daily praise of God—that's what drove him. And even in Kuyper, who, as we now know quite well, was not free from activism and triumphalism, I recognize the urge to make room for the sound of that praise; reformation of society under the guidance of the principle of "sphere sovereignty" is (also) to be understood as clearing the way for a range of non-competing institutions, like different parties and instruments in an orchestra.

To emphasize this liturgical dimension does not mean that I want to play it off against compassion. To those who might have that impression (or inclination) I recommend the reading of the seventh chapter, "Justice and Worship," in Wolterstorff's book *Until Justice and Peace Embrace*.

Notes

1. I have considered adding a third question, concerning the reading and use of the Bible. However, this would have made my response too long. In my discussion of the questions raised I will make one or two comments on Hart's Scripture reading, though.

2. "Met meer omzichtigheid." "Spreken over scheppingsordeningen als iets op zichzelf is dus onmogelijk," *Tijd der bezinning* (Amsterdam, 1973), 59-60.

3. *Tijd der bezinning*, 58f. The quotation reads in Dutch: "Van meetaf heeft reformatorische wijsbegeerte nadruk gelegd op het dynamisch karaketer der schepping als immers eerste openbaring Gods aan het schepsel. Daarom sprak zij van het grond*motief* der creatuur...."

4. See also my "In memory of Herman Dooyeweerd: Meaning, Time and Law," *Philosophia Reformata* 43 (1978): 137-44.

5. See Hart's own statement in note 31. By the way, at least in the text to which this note belongs there seems to be an incorrect contrast. John does not mean to say that "the law" did not reveal grace and truth. How could this reader/hearer of Exodus 33-34 possibly have meant this? The grace of Christ was already there in the law of Moses. When Jesus came, it meant "grace upon grace."

6. See the verse that follows the one mentioned in note 9.

7. That Hart does not make this distinction might have to do with his own view on the specific relation of "rational inquiry and conceptual examination" with "law," "boundary," etc.; see note 48. Once more I refer to Mekkes in this connection: speaking of the specific task of a reformational philosophy, he says, "Rejecting every autonomy, she *follows* the structures in the *search* for their meaning, a search not by the light of intellect, but with understanding under the light of integral truth through *faith*"; op. cit., 61.

8. See also H. G. Geertsema, *Horen en zien, Bouwstenen voor een kentheorie*, Inaugural Address at the University of Groningen, 1985.

9. See also Colossians 3:12-17; compare note 2.

10. Elsewhere I have used the image of a procession, gaining density and intensity: "Wijsgerige reflectie op de tijd" in *Aspecten van tijd* (Kampen: Kok, 1991), 119.

Reply to My Respondents

Hendrik Hart

Hare correctly reports that I see a conflict between an ethos of compassion and one of permanent creation order. He then, helpfully, announces his intention to look at these two kinds of ethos. In what follows, however, he seems to have overlooked some aspects of my discussion that were central to my project and therefore ends up more with his own analysis of the relation of compassion to permanent order than with a critical response to my views. In writing his own analysis, nevertheless, he clearly thinks to be engaging my views, hence my reply will concentrate on that.

It is arguable that Hare reads my project as a general philosophical analysis of permanent order and compassion; or, minimally, as written with such an analysis in the background. He himself, at least, is concerned with "the best general account" of compassion. And I see no evidence in his response that he noted my more limited interests in permanent order and compassion. For instead of pursuing a general account, I was interested in these two notions within the bounds of three limitations: their role as ethos-shaping spiritual centers in a community, their historical role in specific communities, and the specific meaning of compassion in the gospels.

Without those limitations in view, Hare does not appear to have given full weight to my distinction between compassion and permanent order on the one hand, and an *ethos* of either one of these on the other. It would never occur to me that order and compassion would, as such, be in conflict. My thesis is that an *ethos* in which one of these is the *central spiritual focus* for a community would be in conflict with an ethos in which the other plays the *same* role. Even then, in either of these communities the item not having the central focus would not be absent, but would play *an important role off-center,* centered by what is the focus. Thus, in a community whose ethos is compassion, order would remain an important concern for that community (indeed, I agree with Hare: even within an ethos of compassion we are "not freed from the law"), but the focus of that order would be on ordering compassion. That, I take it, is the relation of the summary of the law (love) to the law itself (order) in the way Jesus presents it.

If he missed this, Hare then probably also missed that I was not concerned with a general philosophical analysis of how permanent order and compassion relate, but rather with the historical circumstance (in my view) that a prevailing ethos in some Christian communities has been an ethos of permanent order. In such communities compassion has not been absent, but it has not been central either. Given our present world, I think, compassion—as the form God's love took in Jesus—needs to become central. Love, called by Jesus the summary of the law, first revealed by him in his compassion, and finally in his crucifixion, is in my view less central in our life than it is meant to be in relation to the law. That assessment, as well as my conclusions about some undesirable contemporary consequences of living with an ethos of permanent order, thus lead me to recommend that communities with an ethos of permanent order might, to do more justice to the gospel in our time, do well to consider making order less central.

To put the matter as existentially as I can: I was concerned to detect deep cultural undercurrents in the Reformed tradition of creation order that serve as partial foundation for a diagnosis of the current situation in my own church by Nicholas Wolterstorff, as reported in his and my church's weekly periodical *The Banner* (June 8, 1992, 21):

> The Christian Reformed community has habits that threaten to destroy it.... Our fixation on right doctrine is a rampant, destructive disease.... Love goes out the window, resulting in an appalling sense of hatred and an appalling lack of trust. Fundamental fruits of the Spirit are missing along with the faith that the continuance of God's church does not depend on us. Our unrelenting judgmentalism and our own preoccupations leave societal and cultural crises unaddressed. Our tradition is depleted. We need a new way.

I hear echoes of a relation of order to compassion in the following summary of his suggested new way: "Rather than focusing on grasping the levers of power, we need more solidarity with weeping ones. Our litany of pain is a litany of love."

With his reading Hare probably also overlooked that the notion of compassion I was using was the one the gospels attribute to God and Jesus or to people in parables representing God or Jesus; and that the notion of permanent order I was using had specific historical reference. Thus, the compassion I was talking about had indeed, I again agree with Hare, nothing to do with "legitimating" anyone's activity. To the contrary, I was talking about compassion in relation to suffering which is often the result of people's *illegitimate* activity. That's why I said compassion transcends order. I was reading that use of compassion in the light of modern scholarship available on that issue. The prodigal son met with his father's compassion in spite of the illegitimacy of his activity, as he also met with the brother's rejection because this brother "placed" the event in a context of existing order. The good Samaritan threw caution in the wind, had compassion on his neighbor, and did better than the Pharisee and the Levite who obeyed the law.

Similarly, the notion of order I was using was indeed not one of a framework of "human needs which stay the same," but one of an order to which human beings are eternally subject, quite apart from any of their needs, and which then often serves those who have power to keep in check those who cannot help themselves. What Wolterstorff notices is far from unique in the Christian Reformed Church of today. This story can be told over and over again about stages in the Reformed journey. And I see it as linked to too much stress on order and control and too little on trust and love.

Since Hare suggests my paper is a "throwing out of the baby with the bath-water." I take it that he generally understood me as being against order. Just to show that this was not my intention I quote from the paper verbatim. The quotes come from throughout the text and I have added a few words in brackets for the sake of continuity:

> Creation order and reason, the focus of this lecture, are both gifts of God. They are servants whose role depends on how and where God needs them.

> [I have objections, however, to] ... an a-historical ethos of eternal, apriori, fixed, available order.

> The concept of creation order in the Reformed tradition [in so far as it is influenced by such an a-historical ethos] thus shows traces of a non-Christian religious history....

> The road ahead is not, I think, one of denying or ignoring order or reason. To the contrary, the reality of order and its rational detection seem undeniably valuable discoveries of our Western heritage. The history of science taught us to appreciate the institutionalization of rational order-discovery as instrument of power and control through prediction and explanation. The typical Western notions of power and progress through reason were well founded and have resulted in much blessing.

> There seems nothing problematic in principle about acknowledging order, reason, necessity, possibility, limit, universality, and principles as structural generalities grasped in logical, analytic, intellectual, conceptual, reasoning behavior. This is the real world's real rationality.

> Relatively speaking a culture can accept ... [having its spiritual center in an ethos of ahistorical order], until it leads us to dead ends. Once order as spiritual center is a dead end, we are spiritually free to make it relative to justice, love, peace, and joy, and to reassign it for the inclusion of the marginalized other who is different or has no power.

This is not freedom to shove aside or ignore creation order, church order, tradition, science, or reason, but a need to understand that they are all relative to visible redemption, to the compassion God seeks to work through Jesus' followers.

If within a present order in Christ we don't find life, we must seek a new order for life, again in Christ.

The role of reason in giving shape to a normative order is important. We deploy our gifts of rationality to detect order, to identify sameness, to articulate continuity, to form shared tools for universal communication.

So I conclude that the major issue Hare saw between us turns out, in fact, to be an issue on which, in its core, we agree. For if that issue was my apparent project to reject order and Hare's insistence that compassion itself requires order, I can only say that, far from wanting to reject order, I agree with Hare that without order compassion would not get us very far.

A similar point is at issue where Hare sees me as positing a dichotomy between freedom and authority. My intent was only to suggest that different central metaphors have different force in the communities ordered by them. A community of family members is not a community where authority is absent, but one in which it has a different configuration than in a community of armed forces. Authority is legitimately present in families, love is not in principle lacking among soldiers. Nevertheless, I would in the contemporary world prefer a church modeled on an extended family over one modeled on a battalion.

Two lesser points. One point is that I agree that worldviews of fixed order not only engender conservatism, but can also lead to criticism of the status quo. However, I would also observe that the criticism in such a worldview would tend to call for a conservative response to the critical situation, even when a prior conservatism may be the very thing that led to the critical situation to begin with. The other point is that though both the Bible and the Greeks may have used fixed order language, the Bible's confessional language and the Greeks' metaphysical language still make for an immense difference in the meaning and significance of the fixity they talk about.

That leaves one important point, indeed, a point without which my whole project misses its center. This is the point of positing an order of which we say that we do not really know it. What I am doing here is, of course, rejecting realism. I shall limit myself to social order. It is quite clear that throughout history people who are realists with respect to divine order give examples of such order that are often no more than hallowed codes of their own time. And often when they come to appreciate this, but wish to maintain an eternal divine order nevertheless, they posit a deeper or more general order behind or underneath this known order of their time. But that deeper order, I suggest, is a Platonic *projection* of our Western general *concept* of order, an absolutized one at that. There is no evidence in the Bible that behind God's known law there is another, deeper layer of law.

What then makes God's law trustworthy? Nothing but its being God's. But that does not make it eternal. Otherwise the biblical story of the passage from old to new dispensation does not make sense. Hence, speaking of an eternal order which we do not really know is not humility in my view, but a desire to have a fixity and a clarity closer and more reliable than God's faithfulness. It is, in other words, a way of circumventing trust and mystery. To quote Wolterstorff once more, there is " ... a desperate need for the faith to let go and trust God.... We need to live with unanswered questions...."

Van der Hoeven raises two main concerns: the fairness of my rendering of "our philosophical tradition" and the clarity and sufficiency of my own position. As to the first concern, I should clarify what I meant by "our philosophical tradition." Van der Hoeven is correct in apparently assuming that the tradition at least *includes* the Amsterdam school of reformational philosophy. Nevertheless, a possibly significant misunderstanding may play a role here. For I dealt with "our philosophical tradition" as the Western tradition of realism, as it has influenced both Christianity and the Amsterdam school. Furthermore, I dealt with only *one side* of that larger tradition—the absolutized projection of a general rational picture of reality—and was interested primarily to indicate that *traces* of that *one side* were present in the Amsterdam school. In a similar anniversary context, René van Woudenberg seems to have spoken of "our tradition" in the same way, as can be seen from *Philosophia Reformata* (1993): 237.

I did not intend to give a fair, in the sense of full or balanced, treatment of either the Western philosophical tradition or of the Amsterdam school relevant to my topic. But even if my treatment was lacking in this respect this need not obscure the truth of my point that in Dooyeweerd, as J. P. A. Mekkes had begun to point out in various contexts, the Platonic heritage remains present in important elements that need to be critically addressed today. Even then, I did not leave unsaid my appreciation for the ways in which Dooyeweerd did address the Platonic heritage; for example, in the main text on page 71. My problem with Dooyeweerd is that in spite of his own centering of the law in love he did not thereby overcome in his own views the logocentric character of our Western view of order. I see my project in this regard as a continuation of Dooyeweerd's own critique of the autonomy of theoretical thinking, a continuation already begun by Mekkes. Dooyeweerd's law is *said* to be a dynamic law of love, though it *functions* as an immutable general structure of apriori character.

In addition to this general point, however, I need to address the specifics of van der Hoeven's critique. First his complaint that in my view reformational philosophy is possibly ill, based on my use of diagnosis in a heading. But diagnosis, at least in English, can also serve to identify a problem correctly, and not only indicates an illness. Since problems are the life blood of philosophy and I indeed see a problem here, diagnosis is in place.

Van der Hoeven thinks that I do not sufficiently distinguish between Platonic realism and talk of creation order in Vollenhoven and Dooyeweerd. I certainly agree that both philosophers detected serious problems in realism, as well as that they did much to specify the problems and to formulate alternative approaches. But I am far from convinced that in their notion of creation order they have fully excised an *absolutized general concept* of reality. An article by A. Troost on normativity in the first issue of *Philosophia Reformata* of 1992 deals directly with my concern and seems to me to confirm some of my views. Its subtitle is: "Origin and fall of thinking about creation ordinances." And in his view there is direct continuity and relationship between metaphysics of order and creation order.

The doctrine of an immutable layer of or side to reality which universally encloses all of reality and which can be progressively laid bare as the structural states of affairs which theory discloses is, in my view, a doctrine developed through Greek faith in reason, attached to Greek trust in immutability. And this, in my view, is precisely the heart of Platonism: an absolutization of theoretical generalization. Dooyeweerd employs as one of his major strategies an analysis of metaphysical speculation on this point in which, as he sees it, the creation order is reduced to the theoretical *Gegenstand* relation which has been absolutized. It seems not to occur to him that the Western notion of creation order may result from that absolutization, may be an attempt to transform that absolutization without radically changing its character as an order of eternal (rational) principles that are theoretically knowable.

The way to deal with realism is not, in my view, to say that it is a theoretical reduction of what really is creation order. It would be better to relativize the theoretical point of view instead, rather than to further enshrine it in a religious concept of creation order. The originally metaphysical concept cannot be redeemed, in my view, by being linked to the fact that in Israel God's love is revealed in terms of a tradition of law. In the New Testament that tradition is clearly *relativized* by the love it is meant to reveal.

Van der Hoeven, perhaps anticipating a reply in this direction, sees my main shortcoming as not having taken sufficient note of Dooyeweerd's temporalization of the eternal metaphysical order. But I'm not convinced. My analysis of time in Dooyeweerd (available in a *Philosophia Reformata* article of 1973) as well as my own view of time (in *Understanding Our World* [Lanham, MD: University Press of America, 1984]) lead me to conclude that time in Dooyeweerd primarily means medium of diversity. In time, unity, which transcends time, breaks into (coherent) diversity. This meant that Dooyeweerd had serious problems with biologists who struggled with temporal development, as well as with historians who struggled with historical time. In their view Dooyeweerd did not do justice to time. In his view, they returned to scholasticism. And in fact when Dooyeweerd defended his view of time and order against what he perceived as the evolutionism of J. Lever he made it very clear that he had a deeply Platonic view of order which preceded and was apriori to all temporal development *(Philosophia Reformata,* 1959).

Indeed, for Dooyeweerd *time does not* in principle have to *exclude* everduring *immutability and invariance.* When in this context van der Hoeven reminds me that at heart Dooyeweerd was concerned to contrast the law of God on which we depend (as the foundation that lifts us beyond the arbitrary) with the autonomy of thought in which we are sovereign, he is on target as far as I can see. But does he appreciate that for Dooyeweerd the law's not being arbitrary has to do with its being *invariant?* Dooyeweerd's concept of time as medium of diversity could easily tolerate *temporal* principles that were *invariant.* (See in his *A New Critique of Theoretical Thought* I:100, 507; II:548, 550, 553-554, 557, 559; III:78-79, 82-83, 94, 106, 147, 158, 170, 268, 272.) In my view this means Dooyeweerd was not able to overcome the "eternal principle" element in his own view of law, an element he himself rejected. And that element, as I see it, precisely conflicts with what I think temporality is all about. What Dooyeweerd *calls* temporal, in other words, *is not* really temporal in my view.

I have no objection to temporal *constancy,* but then in the sense of God's *standing with* us *in* time, which I think need not imply ontically immutable invariance at all. H. Geertsema appears to agree *(Philosophia Reformata* (1993): 145). So, as I see it, the standing of God with the creature in the law, not the law's invariance, is what lifts the law beyond arbitrariness. God's standing with us in the law gives the law a con-stancy which is not incompatible with temporal relativity in that same law. Even the language used by the biblical poets about God's everlasting decrees is compatible with that, since their language is meant to be read confessionally rather than metaphysically. They want to say that the law can be trusted, not that it is ontically immutable. Only if change, one of God's good creatures, is not trustworthy in someone's view does reliability become associated with immutability. If van der Hoeven wants to suggest that Dooyeweerd's deepest intentions moved him away from ontic immutability, I am inclined to agree. Nevertheless, it would not be fair not to acknowledge another side in Dooyeweerd, nor is it clear which side is stronger.

I was not a little amazed to see van der Hoeven struggle with my characterization of creation order as "overarching order" in Dooyeweerd. For in that very paragraph van der Hoeven himself refers to Dooyeweerd's *horizon.* One thing a horizon can be seen to do is form *a dome.* A horizon of order, seen as a dome of order, overarches. It is a horizon of totality. Mekkes called it the intelligibility dome of the Western tradition, which he considered still present in Dooyeweerd's views *(Radix, Tijd en Kennen,* 127). Dooyeweerd himself clearly thinks of it in this way. That may not have been clear on the page to which I referred, II:557. But it certainly is clear on pages close to the cited one, where he uses terms like overarching, enclosing, and encompassing (I:99, II:548, 551, 552, 554, 560). Troost, in the above mentioned article, speaks of cosmic order as "all encompassing" (25). One can find the same language in van Riessen, Dengerink, and Geertsema. It is not impossible that van der Hoeven reads too much of his own predilection for a certain side in Dooyeweerd into the entire text.

I find support (both for my reading of Dooyeweerd, and for the trust that a rejection of fixed eternal order need not conflict with the continuity of reformational thinking) in Bob Goudzwaard's remarks at the 1987 Lusaka Conference of the International Council for the Promotion of Christian Higher Education. He mentions "rationalistic constructivism" as the shadow side of Dutch neo-Calvinism (244) and observed that the shedding of that side is "not a denial of its own past" but much rather "a fruit of still standing in the heart of that original revivalistic movement..." (*Rainbow in a Fallen World* [Sioux Center: Dordt Press, 1990], 245).

I come now to van der Hoeven's second main concern, the adequacy of my own views. He has two problems here, namely my views of law and of compassion. He has trouble reconciling my acknowledgement of love as summary of the law and of compassion as transcending the law. One key to this is his different reading of John 1:17. He sees no contrast there between the law of Moses and the grace and truth of Jesus and I do. In the light of his objection I could also state my view as follows: love, grace and truth were indeed *intended* from the beginning to be the meaning revealed in the law. Here I agree. The law, however, did not *in fact become* a vehicle of love in the life of Israel. Faced with sin, the law condemned. But Jesus did reveal the intended love fully, by giving his life in love. And in that sense there is a contrast in the text, an important contrast I maintain. J. P. A. Mekkes made a very similar observation in relation to Romans 8:3 in *Philosophia Reformata,* (1962): 146.

How do I construe this as love (or compassion) *transcending* the law? Certainly not in any temporal sense, that is, as transcending time. But in at least two ways the term "transcend" can be used here. One is that love *goes farther* than the law ever did, goes beyond the law. The other is that though the law was intended as *vehicle* of love, that is not a matter of love being *limited by* the law. There are other vehicles, the cross being the most dramatic one. That Scripture also refers to law in relation to the cross seems to me more a matter of communication in the context of a certain tradition than an indication of the law's predominant priority. Law as limit reaches its own limit when we go beyond the law in transgressing it. Only love can still reach us there, if indeed love is not limited to and by the law.

In addition, however, there is the Dooyeweerdian meaning of a unity which transcends any diversity. Love as summary of the law also transcends the law in that sense. It is not so much another law, but more what comes to expression in the law, though it reaches beyond any and all law. That I spoke of "what the law cannot do" in this context possibly seemed strange to van der Hoeven through the medium of the Dutch language. But I was only quoting Romans 8:3 here. The Greek *adunaton* is translated as "could not do" in the KJV, the RSV, and the Good News versions of the Bible, as "could never do" in the NEB, as "was unable to do" in the Jerusalem version, and as "was powerless to do" in the NIV. It is in us, children of the Spirit and thus of love, that the requirements of the law (that we love one another) can be met says the next verse. In addition to the article by Mekkes I have just mentioned, A. Troost also refers to this in *Philosophia Reformata*, 50 (1993): 229.

When van der Hoeven suggests that I am onesided in not mentioning examples of compassion in the traditional Christian community I can only respond that I had no intention of painting a fair and allround image of the church. I only wanted to highlight the damaging consequences of a strong law, order, and orthodoxy tradition, without in the least even wanting to suggest that in that image the life of the church or even of that tradition can be considered to have been exhausted. It is unfortunate that he did not make a case for my seeing it wrongly, or for the relative unimportance of the point I made, rather my failure to point out what, as I strongly believe as well, is also visible. In my experience a stress on balance and fairness too often results in losing sight of negative or critical points that need to be made about one side in the balance. I have been concerned only to point out that among the many sides there are to the appreciation of creation order, one side places a central stress on it, which results in a centralization of authority, obedience, submission, and power in ways that are detrimental to our future. I have also been concerned to make the point that this side is not only present in much of the Reformed tradition, but also in the tradition of reformational philosophy. And in so far as that emphasis is present, it needs to be reformed in ways that can only appear to be quite radical to many sympathizers.

Van der Hoeven's final question is: "Is it right to focus so strongly on compassion?" Obviously I think so. I think that a church in the late twentieth century looking for an ethos and coming up with an ethos of praise runs the risk of being dismissed as irrelevant by all those who die in darkness. Should the church not praise God and work at making that praise as empowering as possible? But of course. That praise, however, seems to me to be primarily a moment of empowerment for being in this world. But being in this world requires, in my view, an ethos of compassion.

Brüggemann-Kruijff appears to have noted my central point: a "switch over" in the focus of an ethos. Because she appreciates this move there is nothing in her response that indicates problems in this regard. I can therefore be a bit more brief in my response to her. She concentrates on the role of philosophy and theology on the one hand and of faith on the other. She seems particularly concerned that I not despair over a legitimate role for philosophy and theology, even when she agrees that the shaping of our faith by a particular philosophical/theological tradition may need critical (self)reflection.

In her first reading of her parable, which stands in for the relation between faith and reason, I take her to be suggesting that in some respects the two have been isolated from one another in modernity. Then she points out that I may be too concerned here with a critique of a Christian faith that has not been sufficiently critical of undetected philosophical-theological influences, and not concerned enough with an internal philosophical dialogue with modernity. In fact, in this context I did not concern myself with that internal dialogue, because philosophical modernity was not represented at this conference. But I acknowledge the need for and legitimacy of such internal dialogue and can point to Kai Nielsen's and my *Search for Community in a Withering Tradition* (Lanham, MD: University Press of America, 1990) as an example of my taking this task seriously. In this paper, however, I have taken for granted the many legitimate contributions by the post-modern critique of modernity, and have concentrated on how the legacy of modernity and its roots in Greek speculative metaphysics need to be critically engaged in the Christian community.

Brüggemann-Kruijff then shifts to what she detects as my accusation that in reformational philosophy faith has also been too much overshadowed by reason. Here she wonders if I have done enough justice to Dooyeweerd's placing of an element of creation order beyond the grasp of reason. She acknowledges that there are unresolved tensions in Dooyeweerd here, but wonders if they are resolvable so long as we continue to think philosophy is legitimate. But I think there may be more of a way out here than she seems prepared to accept at this point. That way out would be precisely to acknowledge that if philosophy deals with totality at all—and even that may need to be critically challenged—then it can perhaps at best deal with "totality in general" and not "totality in total." For it is indeed the "overarching" claims of reason that I contest in my paper, not the legitimacy of its task as such. "In general" has, in my view, been too much mistaken for "in total." I think this particular tension we can do without. I am more comfortable with totalities, horizons, ultimates, and finalities that come to us in faith and that we can with integrity give space to in-form our philosophy.

Finally, Brüggemann-Kruijff is concerned that I allow for a legitimate role for philosophy within the Christian community. Her concern here seems inspired by my "it is time to stop arguing," by which I meant to refer more to another tradition, in which faith needs to justify itself before the high court of reason. In this context I am made suspicious of philosophy when, as Albert Wolters once suggested, it is itself no more than the secular equivalent of Christian faith. I think Wolters' suggestion has real merit. I think a reading of the Western philosophical tradition as itself a faith-in-reason-tradition makes cooperation between Christian faith and philosophy a dubious enterprise. If, however, philosophy is limited to the general integration of theoretical thought oriented by totality visions that anticipate and are thus spawned by faith, then I would be much in favor of allowing philosophy to have an important voice in a culture in which theory remains as important as it is in ours. Christians need to be thoughtful. And being thoughtful in our times includes being philosophically aware.

In conclusion I make the following more general reply to my critics. It is now common to call the rationality tradition our dominant Western intellectual tradition. Its discourses have especially shaped modernity, but much else in our history as well. Alasdair MacIntyre has described it from Aristotle till now in *Whose Justice? Which Rationality?*, Richard Rorty has called attention to it in *Philosophy and the Mirror of Nature,* postmodernism speaks of it as the logocentric tradition, Nicholas Wolterstorff refers to it as foundationalism, many philosophers speak of realism, and culturally it is widely acknowledged as the (unprejudiced) autonomy of reason embedded in enlightenment liberalism.

An important element of this tradition is a metaphysical concept of immutable, neutral, universal order. This picture of the general structure of reality originated in Greece with the rise to prominence of the rational analysis of reality. From its inception this ascendancy of rational analysis had religious importance. In terms of reading reality, rational discourse became a leading discourse, setting direction for human culture. Its authority undermined the authority of religion, faith, and revelation and reduced our experience of reality.

Religiously speaking the metaphysical picture of reality tries to account for our worlds being meaningful and reliable, a cosmos rather than a chaos, orderly rather than disorderly. It addresses concerns also addressed in the Bible, but not in the same way. This metaphysical tradition ontologizes *theory's* view of reality. It posits (as an absolutization and rigidification of the theoretical vision) an immutable order behind, beneath, above our experienced appearances of changing order. The Bible also speaks of order, but does so politically rather than rationally. Its order is the direction-setting law of a ruler. It is never more than the covenant-order we actually experience. Its reliability is not dependent on the immutability of a deeper order, but on its being a gift of God. Ontic immutability as ground of religious dependence is foreign to the Bible. It is, rather, a Greek notion. The fear of shifting appearances made the metaphysical tradition look for reliance in mathematical order, characterized by the absence of change and hence called immutable. As such, of course, mathematical relations lack not only change, but also extension, color, sweetness, scarcity, justice and a host of other qualities. The attachment of *religious* significance to the *absence* of certain other characteristics of creation in its mathematical realm is adequately explainable in this context only when understood as a form of idolatry. Indeed, Dooyeweerd already early in his career spoke of eternal principles as pagan.

The above does not mean we should object to seeing the world as ordered, nor to accepting in faith that good order is God's gift. That the world is ordered needs no argument. And Christians trust that whatever order leads to blessing came from God. But "came from God" means the same when we say that our children also came to us as God's gift. "Came from God" does not as such mean: so we had nothing to do with it; or, it is now from eternity and will ever be as is. I see no harm in saying that what we acknowledge as order is rational, a (hidden) feature of reality we dis-cover by rational reflection. I can see no objection either to ascribing per-manence or con-stancy to order as evidence of God's enduring presence in it, so long as these words are not translated as immutable, beyond time, eternal.

However, some crucial mistakes are to be avoided. *One* would be to regard truth and reality as having their "essential nature" in the order of reality. If truth is primarily disclosure of God's presence in creation (Jesus *as* the truth, our *standing in* the truth), then the truth and reality of order as rationally discovered is the truth and reality of conceptual instruments that are widely applicable (universality) and relatively durable (continuity) *handles* on the world. They give us a measure of control. They pick out what is "continually the same" in things. We can benefit from that. But if they privilege our sense of truth and the real we will miss the truth and reality of individuality, difference, subjectivity, and much else.

A *second* mistake would be to take rationally disclosed order as immutable. That would link our view of order too closely to a religious origin not acceptable to Christians, primarily based on invariant mathematical or exceptionally durable physical order, and discounting the historical structuring of physical reality, of organic evolution, of animal genetics, and of human development. Immutable order essentially freezes the theoretical view of what is same and continuous.

Third, I think it is misleading to view order as an overarching reality within which all else that is real is enclosed, order as the universal condition of all possibility and necessity. We would be able to do more justice to other dimensions of the world if we saw them next to and equal with the dimension of order, rather than as dimensions *of* or *within* order. I trust the biblical message that God is the only all-surrounding, all-penetrating, all-transcending reality in creation.

I see a *fourth* mistake in the permanent centering of our experience in order. People, cultures, institutions, traditions, systems, and many other wholes or totalities require a certain "centering" for their identity. We may see such centering as Dooyeweerd's religious agency, as his unity and totality of meaning, or along the lines of his qualifying functions. In Calvinism we may say that "sovereignty" is a centering notion for our experience of God. As a result I also believe that in Calvinism obedience, or "ordering our lives," is a central notion for living. As unavoidable as such centering may be, it should not be permanent, because it can always only partially place us *vis à vis* what is total.

Centers are ways of con-centrating on the presence of God. We choose centers that bring God to us as light into our darkness. If our choice of center replaces God (the Old Testament temple), it eventually begins to cause darkness itself. It is then time to de-center the current center and to re-center ourselves in other ways. De-centering and re-centering involve discomfort. People feel lost without the old center and experience it as gone, even though the old center is only reassigned a place around a new center and continues to play a role. People also have difficulty reading other realities in terms of the new center, wonder about the meaning of the new center as center, and may experience arbitrary relativism.

I do not believe these problems can be avoided, certainly not by a balance of all meaning without any center. The center indicates the core of our experience of God. That's why we cannot do without it and why it, as creaturely image, cannot be permanent. It does not, of course, have to be called center. We can call it unity, focus, goal, or foundation. People have their identity in con-centrating on God, whose image they are. They have an open and developing identity, depending on the particular way the calling of God is disclosed.

A *fifth* mistake to be avoided would be to say the Bible's talk about order is the same as Greece's talk about order. The Bible simply talks about what people concretely experience as the ordering God does in their lives and in the world as their faithful ruler, by covenantal decrees that set direction. Thus, if it is at all biblical to talk about "creation order," that could never simply be taken as the Bible's talk about *the general structure* of creation, the way philosophy would deal with it.

A *sixth* problem would be to miss the Bible's centering of all order (whatever it means in the Bible) in love. This love is interpreted already in the Old Testament as mercy, grace, and forgiveness. Jesus "centers" the law in love of God and neighbor and incarnates it as compassion. Thus Dooyeweerd places love centrally in his conception of creation order and calls it transcendent to the temporal order. "Transcendent" seems useful to express the fact that love as the core of all the law is not to be found as such in a particular law. Love is not one element next to others, but rather what all the law pursues. Obedience to law is meant as road to love. But not in such a way that whenever we obey we love. Rather, whenever our obedience falls short of love or wherever the law requires an action that is unloving, we are called "to love God more." Jeremiah 7 and the parable of the Good Samaritan show this. The priest and the Levite are "obedient." But in being obedient they are "on the other side" of where they needed to be. When Jesus interprets the law as "in sum" God's call for love, I take that to mean that love is the proto-call in the law. The law is therefore relative to love. Whatever requirement does not lead to love cannot be God's law. Love is the "test" of any law. In the same way that justice is not exhausted in and thus goes beyond what is legal, so love goes beyond what is lawful. Isaiah (chap. 56) saw that the law's exclusion of eunuch and stranger somehow did not do justice to God's love.

Love does not replace law or is not contrasted with law. Love tells us what law is and is always more than law. Law condemns transgression, love covers it. Transgression exists as transgression of law. No law prohibits love nor is love against any law. Love also does not condemn. Order which does not channel love is disorder and love is not as such dependent on order as its overarching limit. No order, in fact, is sufficient to express the love that is called mercy, grace, and compassion. Love is supremely expressed when it accepts our own death as a consequence of resisting evil on behalf of the beloved. All these realities make clear that love "transcends" order. It is impossible to understand, on the one hand, giving our life for someone as the greatest expression of love, and on the other hand to understand it as obedience to a universal command. The former goes farther than the latter. Love is greater than faith and hope.

It may now be clear why for the past decade, as a result of reflecting on Dooyeweerd's critique of the autonomy of reason and in keeping with his centering of order in love, I have been preoccupied with the Reformed tradition's con-centration on obedience, law, authority, and God's sovereignty. There is evidence of con-fusing Greek realism and God's faithfulness in talking about creation order. Hence I have continued to reflect reformationally on this conceptual cluster. The need for this was not only an *intellectual* concern about conceiving faith along the lines of accepting orthodox doctrine and obeying rules (intellectualism and moralism), but also a *pastoral* one related to the mounting evidence that rigid authoritarianism is doing much damage among Reformed and many other orthodox Christian believers, as well as that criticism of our intellectual heritage meets with much intimidation.

There is evidence of the con-fusing of Greek metaphysics with biblical order also in Dooyeweerd's views about creation order. On the one hand he had a radical reformation of the tradition in view with his critique of reason and his temporalising and relativising of the order of creation. He himself saw Greek metaphysics as an absolutisation of the theoretical view of reality. His own desire was to see law as limiting arbitrariness, not as an eternal, immutable, rigid frame. But three elements in his views contributed to his not taking the radical reformation far enough. One was his concern to guard against historicism and its relativisation of principles of order. Another was his view of time, in which change was not an especially important characteristic and in which not all of temporality was fully historical. A third was that he did not consistently see the theoretical attitude as a rational investigation of order (as do van Riessen, Stafleu, and Dengerink), but as an abstract splitting up of the unity and totality of meaning, taking distance in thought from the temporal coherence of creation's diversity. Yet when he characterizes philosophical thought he sees it as laying bare structural conditions. All of this combined contributed to Dooyeweerd's seeing creation order as unchanging in time and as enclosing all of temporal reality.

Biblical Hermeneutics and a Medical Ethos of Compassion

Allen D. Verhey

I have been asked to address a topic that has been on the agenda of the Institute for Christian Studies for a very long time: hermeneutics and the Christian life. This topic, of course, is on the agenda of every reflective Christian, for every Christian longs to live in ways that are faithful to Scripture.

The Reformed Christian community has had—perhaps because of Calvin's appreciation for the so-called "third use of the law"—a special interest in the relevance of Scripture to ethics. And I think sometimes that Dutch Reformed Christians have this interest in their genes somehow.

I don't know whether the trait is dominant or recessive, but a case can be made that it's genetic. The evidence is anecdotal, I admit—and no researcher on the genome problem has so far confirmed it; but the stories are striking. There is a story, for example, of my great-great-grandfather in the Netherlands—and perhaps of everyone's great-great-grandfather in the Netherlands. Great-great-grandpa was famous for his piety. He could, the story goes, recite a verse of Scripture appropriate to any occasion. It was quite a remarkable gift, and villagers would frequently consult him on the occasion of a funeral or a wedding or the birth of a calf. Unfortunately, great-great-grandpa was also infamous as a horsetrader, and none of the villagers would have much more to do with him than to consult him for the appropriate Scripture. He was reduced to taking advantage of strangers. Once a stranger's horse went lame, and needing a horse to return home, the stranger paid great-great-grandpa four times what an old nag was worth. Great-great-grandma heard the transaction, and she gave great-great-grandpa a little nag of her own, "You know what the villagers say," she said. "Your reputation suffers more every time you do something like this." To that great-great-grandpa quickly retorted, "But great-great-grandma" (she is always called great-great-grandma in the family stories), "I did it by the command of the Lord. I saw a stranger and I 'took him in.' "

Great-great-grandpa's reading of Scripture was flawed, of course, and one of the great passages of Matthew was used to rationalize self-interest rather than to evoke compassion and hospitality. However, the story does suggest that the need to relate Scripture to conduct may be in the genes of Dutch Reformed types like me.

Even if it's not in our genes, it is a part of our inheritance. Perhaps a better case could be made that we come to this interest by training, by nurture rather than by nature. I remember occasions—a sermon, a Sunday school, or that best of schools, a Sunday dinner discussion—when someone—a preacher, a teacher, or a parent—would struggle to connect the reading of Scripture to the life I lived. I remember vividly one episode of my college training. Dr. Tiemersma of Calvin's English Department was my professor. Dr. Tiemersma delighted in humbling young men who could be identified as "pre-sem" (and there were then no young women). It was the beginning of class, and when he had gathered everyone's attention, he looked at me and said, "Verhey, I understand you're going to be a pastor some day." I nodded, worried about what was coming next. "Well," he said, "one day you will find yourself counseling a married couple. Suppose the issue is whether to have more children. The wife says she is worn out by the three they already have and would like to go back to her career when the youngest goes to school. The husband, however, wants more children, and he says to you, 'But pastor, it says in Scripture, "Happy is the man that has his quiver full." ' And what would you say, Verhey?" I responded quickly, "Um ... well ... um." The class was silent, and with the part of my mind that I could spare just then, I wondered whether it was silent sympathy or silent glee at my embarrassment. Tiemersma meanwhile was counting the "ums" and judging the blush of my rising embarrassment, and when at long last they reached full measure, he said, "Verhey, has it never occurred to you that quivers come in different sizes?"

Today, thanks to the invitation to give this lecture, I have another chance to struggle to say something moderately intelligent about the reading and understanding of Scripture in a world of new medical powers.

Some Misgivings about Hermeneutics and Compassion

My remarks are entitled "Biblical Hermeneutics and a Medical Ethos of Compassion" in the program for this conference. I have some misgivings about that title. It's not just that it seems a pretentious title for my modest remarks about reading Scripture and medical care; it is rather that I have some misgivings about "hermeneutics" and about "compassion."

When I say I have some misgivings about hermeneutics, I do not mean to license an undisciplined reading of Scripture or to provide backing for the conservatives who insist Genesis 1 contradicts an evolutionary account of origins or that 1 Timothy

2 contravenes the ordination of women. I mean simply to question some long-standing assumptions in hermeneutics.

It may be argued that hermeneutics was born with the Protestant Reformation and grew up in the Enlightenment. The Reformation wrestled control over the Scripture away from the hierarchy, who claimed that they alone were competent to interpret it. And then they used Scripture against the church's hierarchy and traditions. There were gains there, to be sure, but also losses and problems. When Scripture is used against the church, who will govern the reading of Scripture? When Scripture is used against tradition, how shall we stand in continuity with the church's past, which includes Scripture?

Luther and Calvin did not advocate anything like a "right of private judgment" in the interpretation of Scripture, but many of their successors did. The fragmentation of Protestantism into various voluntary associations of a religious sort may be regarded as a cause or as an effect of this hermeneutical individualism, but its coherence with the diminished significance of church and tradition for understanding Scripture cannot be denied.

It was the Enlightenment that sanctioned and sustained the "right of private judgment." The peace and security of the state, public order, was regarded by the Enlightenment as founded on rational and universal principles, not on the particular traditions of specific communities. Part of that order, of course, was the guarantee of freedom of choice in things "publicly indifferent." The interpretation of the Bible was regarded by the Enlightenment as one such publicly indifferent thing, and individuals were authorized to interpret it in a publicly indifferent way, that is, as addressed to the "inward man" about the inward man[1] or as a naive and mythic account of a morality that the "enlightened" now recognized as simply rational.[2]

The task of governing the interpretation of Scripture was given over to the enlightened philosophers, transcending tradition by the demonstration of universal rational principles and speaking for the peace and order provided by a powerful state.[3]

The Reformers did not advocate an undisciplined reading of Scripture—and neither did their successors. Calvin and Luther insisted that the "literal meaning" (or "historical meaning" or "plain meaning") of the text be found and followed. They rejected allegorical, moral, and anagogical meanings as a license to read into the text whatever an interpreter wanted to. They were confident that the literal meaning would provide the spiritual significance, for Scripture witnessed to faith and faith rested on history. To find the literal meaning one disciplined the reading of Scripture by the grammatical and historical methods current in "humanistic" study of classical literature in the universities of the day. That social location for interpretation—namely, the university—had enormous and enduring consequences when the universities got "enlightened." The grammatical and historical disciplines for understanding Scripture required objectivity and neutrality; they required that Scripture be treated like any other text; and they required that the interest in any text be its witness to the historical situation(s) about which it wrote or in which it was written. The literal or "historical" meaning was no longer quite so confidently to be identified with the spiritual meaning. The historians' methods provided results—to be sure, very helpful and interesting results—in the reconstruction of the history of Israel and Jesus and the church, in the reconstruction of the historical situation of each text and in the recognition of the distinctiveness and diversity of the texts. But the methods and the results of the enlightenment historian fragmented the canon and drove a wedge between the literal sense and the spiritual significance. The gap between the historical text and its present significance opened up to an "ugly ditch."[4]

It could hardly be otherwise. The university had displaced the community of faith as the context for interpretation. Unqualified reason had displaced tradition as the test for interpretation. And it had been the community and a tradition that linked that past to the present. The task of governing interpretation of any text—including Scripture—was given over to the "secular" university and its historians—and they conscientiously refused to judge the religious significance of those texts.

The hermeneutical enterprise has been nearly monopolized by the question of the distinctions between the text and the historian's reconstruction on the one hand and between the historian's reconstruction and religious significance on the other. Some insist that the text provides an objective sacred history, the truth of which the historian cannot test or prove. Some claim the historian's reconstruction of what really happened (of the historical Jesus, for example), is what is religiously significant. Some pietists read the texts as a subjective sacred history, as an expression of the author's experience to which a historian qua historian has no access but which believers may wondrously and warmly share. And some read the text as historians in order to identify the literary units that express a mode of subjectivity called "faith," an authentic self-understanding. My misgivings about hermeneutics extend, then, to the options we might call conservative, liberal, pietist, and de-mythologizing.[5]

There are signs that the monopoly may be broken in regarding the text as narrative,[6] and as itself tradition,[7] and in regarding Scripture as a correlative of community.[8] Those signs point beyond my misgivings about a right to private interpretation, disciplined only by the interests of the state and the historian, toward recovery of the community of faith and its traditions as the context for interpreting Scripture and toward the formation and reformation of identity and community as the interest in interpretation.[9]

I hope in what follows to display such a model for interpretation and the way it evokes care for patients, but first I must report my misgivings about the other part of the title: "compassion."

When I say I have some misgivings about compassion, I do not mean to license apathy or hard-heartedness. I mean simply to say that compassion is, if not quite an empty moral notion, at best an open one. All kinds of things, including some morally outrageous things, are done by people who are moved by compassion to do _something_. Compassion feels the pain of another's suffering and is moved to do *something*, but compassion doesn't tell us what exactly to do.[10] I see no reason to doubt the reports that the parents of Baby Doe were compassionate; and Dr. Jack Kevorkian is surely a compassionate man. But Baby Doe and Janet Adkins are dead. When compassion is exercised in a context of a parenting which is charged with the awesome responsibility of making perfect children and making children perfect, then compassionate parents end up killing the child who doesn't measure up, the child who cannot achieve the American ideal of the good life.[11] And when compassion is exercised in the context of a medicine which is regarded as a marketplace commodity, as value-free skills with which to do the bidding of the one who pays, and when medicine is charged with the awesome task of eliminating human suffering and our vulnerability to it, then the compassionate physicians end up as killers. Compassion needs other virtues in order to be virtuous; it needs a fuller account of the moral life in order to know *what* to do. If all we needed to live morally was to be moved to do what we already know we should do, then compassion would be all we need. But I judge that the problem is deeper, and that compassion is not sufficient.[12]

So much for my misgivings about the title. Let me finally proceed to the paper itself, to some remarks about Scripture and medical ethics.

The Case of Coles' Friend

Since this is a paper that is related to medical ethics, no one should be surprised that it starts with a case. I want to use this case of a compassionate chaplain visiting a dying patient, first, simply to claim that in Christian reflection about medical ethics, Scripture should be used *somehow*. I want to use it also to make a modest proposal concerning *how* Scripture should be used in medical ethics. Finally, I want to use the case at least to hint at the shape of care where Scripture is read in ways disciplined by the community of faith and its practice.[13]

Consider the following case:

In his *Harvard Diary* Robert Coles tells the story of a Catholic friend of his, a physician who knows his cancer is not likely to be beaten back, a Christian who knows the final triumph belongs to the risen Christ.[14]

He was visited by a hospital chaplain, who asked how he was "coping." "Fine,: he said, in the fashion of all those replies by which people indicate that they are doing reasonably well given their circumstances, *and* that they would rather not elaborate just now on what those circumstances are.

But this chaplain was unwilling to accept such a reply. He inquired again. Relentlessly he pressed on to questions about denial and anger and acceptance. But finally he gave up and left.

Then Coles' friend did get angry, not so much about his circumstances or his dying, but about the chaplain. The chaplain, he said, was a psycho-babbling fool. And Robert Coles, the eminent Harvard psychiatrist, agreed. What his friend needed and wanted, Coles says, was someone with whom to attend to God and to

God's word, not someone who dwelt upon the stages of dying as though they were "Stations of the Cross."

Coles' friend was not finished with the chaplain. He invited him to return, put his Bible out, set the bookmark to Psalm 69, and simply asked the chaplain to read.

As Coles points out, Psalm 69 is a lament, a cry of anguish and a call for help: "Save me, O God, ... I have come into the deep waters...." Coles does not mention, however, that it is an imprecatory psalm, a cry of anguish that vents its anger on those who fail to comfort, a cry for help that asks not just for rescue but revenge: "I looked for sympathy, but there was none; for comforters, but I found none. They put gall in my food, and gave me vinegar for my thirst."[15]

Coles' friend was not, of course, complaining about hospital food. He was complaining about a chaplain who had emptied his role of the practice of piety, who neglected prayer and Scripture, and who filled his visits to the sick with the practices of psychotherapy.

Now just imagine that this chaplain had not been trained as a psychological counselor. Suppose he had been trained as a medical ethicist. Perhaps he had been enlisted on the hospital ethics committee and there taught a little Mill and a little Kant, taught to respect and protect a patient's autonomy, taught to regard human relationships as contracts between self-interested and autonomous individuals, taught to speak a form of moral "Esperanto."

The chaplain now is anxious not so much with psychological states and stages as with not interfering with the patient's rights, including, of course, the right to be left alone. His enthusiasm for a generic moral language, for the kind of "Esperanto" medical ethicists like to speak, will make him hesitate to speak in a distinctively Christian voice, hesitate to use and to offer the gifts of prayer and Scripture when people are dying or suffering and face hard medical and moral decisions.

If you can imagine all of that, then you can also imagine that, after visit of such a chaplain Coles' friend might complain no less bitterly about gall in his food and curse the ethicist no less legitimately. He still needs and wants someone with whom to talk of God and the ways of God. He has decisions to make, to be sure, but he wants to make them oriented to God by the gifts of God, by the practices of piety, and not just with impartial rationality.

Now imagine something more: Imagine that the chaplain turned ethicist is stung by Psalm 69, chastened by this angry rebuke, and that he resolves to visit Coles' friend one more time, this time to read a little Scripture.

Imagine, moreover, that we go with him. Before we arrive, however, we grow a little anxious. We remember some stories of the use of Scripture in medical care, and we are anxious not to repeat them.

There is the story of the heart patient who opened his Bible to Psalm 51 and laid his finger on verse 10: "Create in me a clean heart, O God." He told his physician of this remarkable event, and insisted it was a sign that he should receive a Jarvik VII, an artificial heart. The physician tried to explain that a Jarvik VII is probably not what the psalmist had in mind, at least the U.S. Food and Drug Administration seems not to think so. The physician refused to take Psalm 51:10 as an indication of a need for a Jarvik VII or any other artificial heart transplant, and as she left, she put her finger on the still open Bible, on the page before Psalm 51, on Psalm 50 verse 9, and she read the words, "I will accept no bull from your house."

That sort of "bull" is probably not what the psalmist had in mind either, we think to ourselves, but the problem is whether we can read Scripture as relevant to sickness and to the care of the sick without falling into it.

Some Problems of Scripture as Normative for Medical Ethics

So as we enter the room of Coles' friend, we resolve to point out some problems in reading Scripture as relevant to medicine and medical ethics and to ask him just why reading Scripture is so important to him.

"We have come to read some Scripture," we say, "but let's admit there are some problems reading Scripture in this 'world come of age' called a hospital."

"Problems?" he says, "I don't know what you mean."

"Then let us explain," we say and begin to list some.

"One problem is the silence of Scripture. Scripture simply does not deal with new powers of medicine or with the new moral problems they pose. No law code of Israel attempted a statutory definition of death in response to technology that could keep the heart beating and the lungs pumping. No sage ever commented on the wisdom of *in vitro* fertilization or on the prudence of another round of chemotherapy and radiation in what looks like a losing battle against cancer. The prophets who beat against injustice with their words never mentioned the allocation of medical resources. No scribe ever asked Jesus about withholding artificial nutrition and hydration. Nor did any early Christian community ask Paul about medical experimentation. The creatures of Revelation may seem to a contemporary reader the result of a failed adventure in genetic modification, but the author does not address the issue of genetic control.

"The Bible simply does not answer many of the questions which new medical powers have forced us to ask; the authors, even the most visionary of them, never dreamt of these new powers of medicine. To use *any* passage of Scripture to answer directly any of the particular problems posed by these new powers is likely to be no less anachronistic and no more plausible than to use Psalm 51:10 to support a Jarvik VII."

Coles' friend is clearly perplexed by this last reference, but we do not pause to tell the story. Instead we press on to the next problem.

"The silence of Scripture is not the only reason—or the main reason—to be reticent about relating Scripture and medicine. Besides the silence of Scripture, there is the strangeness of Scripture. When Scripture does speak about sickness and the power to heal, its words are, well, quaint.

"The world of sickness in Scripture is strange and alien to us. When King Asa is chided by the Chronicler, for example, for consulting physicians about his diseased feet (2 Chron. 16:12), it is a strange world of sickness of which we read. When the sick cry out in anguish and join to their lament a confession of their sins, as though their sicknesses are divine punishment for their sins, then it is a strange world of sickness of which we read. And when a person with a chronic skin disease, characterized by red patches covered with white scales, is declared ritually impure by the priests and instructed to cry 'Unclean, Unclean' to any who pass by (Lev. 13:45), it is a strange world of sickness of which we read. I mean, talk about the 'heartbreak of psoriasis.'[16]

"It is not difficult to multiply examples; much of what we read in Scripture about sickness and healing is alien to us, and honest Christians are driven to admit that the words of Scripture are human words, words we may not simply identify with timeless truths dropped from heaven or repeat without qualification as Christian counsel for providing or utilizing medical care today."

Coles' friend is nodding in agreement. We hasten on.

"Scripture is sometimes silent, sometimes strange—and usually diverse. That's the third problem. Scripture does not speak with one voice about sickness and healing.

"The lament of the psalmist and the curse of Psalm 69 clearly assume that sickness and suffering are God's punishment for sins, but Job raised his voice against that assumption, rejecting the conventional wisdom of his friends. In the midst of suffering and *in spite* of it, he insisted upon his own innocence and brought suit against the Lord (for divine malpractice, presumably). The Philistines learned at Ashdod, where Dagon fell before the ark, that their tumors (which according to one scholar were probably hemorrhoids)[17] did not happen 'by chance,' that it was God's 'hand that struck us' (1 Sam. 6:9). But other voices could tell of natural causes at work in sickness and in healing, and still other voices spoke of demons or the dominion of death as the cause of sickness.[18]

"The diversity of Scripture on these matters might give us pause before we attempt to relate the practice of reading Scripture and the practice of medicine today."

Coles' friend is patient with us. "Is there anything else?" he asks.

"Yes," we say, "as a matter of fact there is. It must simply be admitted that appeals to Scripture have sometimes done a great deal of harm. When Genesis 3:16, 'in pain you shall bring forth children,' was quoted to oppose pain relief for women in labor,[19] a great deal of harm was done. When the Bible was pointed to by those who said that AIDS was God's punishment for homosexual behavior,[20] a great deal of harm was done. When children are denied transfusions because of a curious reading of a curious set of texts about blood,[21] a great deal of harm is done. When some Dutch Calvinists, the 'Old Reformed,' refused to have their children immunized against polio because Jesus said, 'those who are well have no need of a physician' (Matt. 9:12),[22] then a great deal of harm was done. It may be said—and I think rightly said—that these uses of Scripture are all abuses of Scripture, but patients have nevertheless been harmed, notably, usually women and children and marginalized patients, seldom 'righteous' adult males who need care.

"Episodes of the abuse of Scripture and episodes of the abuse of patients by reading Scripture should make us hesitate before we attempt to connect this 'infallible rule' to medical ethics."

Coles' friend is evidently collecting his thoughts to make response. The moment's quiet is interrupted by our words summarizing the problems and attempting to clench the argument.

"The silence of Scripture, the strangeness of Scripture, the diversity of Scripture, and the abuse of Scripture all seem to hint that there might be wisdom in simply rejecting an attempt to relate the practice of reading Scripture to the practice of medicine. And if there are things about Scripture which seem to hint that such is wisdom, there are things about medical practice and medical ethics which seem to shout it.

"Modern medicine is a thoroughly secular enterprise. It attends to the body, not the spirit; to cells, not the soul.

"And it is a pluralistic society, after all. Public discourse about medical practice seem to require arguments based on universal and generic moral principles or on legal precedents within a society and on an impartial and objective point of view, and such are the arguments one typically finds in the literature on medical ethics.

"It is little wonder that in medical ethics even those trained as theologians sound more like followers of Mill or Kant or John Rawls than like disciples of Jesus. It is little wonder that even those who know Scripture hesitate to quote it."

Sonehow . . . a Relation Between Scripture and Medical Ethics

Coles' friend can restrain himself no longer. "It is little wonder," he says, "but it is nevertheless lamentable."[23]

"It is lamentable," he says, "because a genuinely pluralistic society presumably profits from the candid articulation and vigorous defense of particular points of view. The particular views of identifiable communities serve to remind pluralistic societies not only of the moral necessity of some minimal moral requirements for people to live together and die together peaceably,[24] but also that such requirements are, indeed, *minimal*. If society ignores or denies the richer voices of particular moral traditions, it will be finally unable to nurture any character besides the rational self-interested individual, unable to sustain any community other than that based on the contracts entered by such individuals, and unable even to ask seriously 'what should be decided?' and not just 'who should decide?' "

"The failure to attend to Scripture is lamentable, moreover," he says, "because the practice of medicine is not 'religionless.' The extraordinary human events to which medicine ordinarily attends, giving birth and suffering and dying, have an inalienably religious character.[25] And the care with which we attend to them is no less ineluctably religious.

"Finally, however," Coles' friend says, "it is lamentable for me. When people who know Scripture fail to consider its bearing on medical care, it is lamentable for me—and for people like me.

"Faithful members of Christian community long to live and to die faithfully. If we must suffer while we live or as we die, we want to suffer with Christian integrity—not just impartial rationality. If we are called to care for the suffering (and we are), we want to care with integrity—not just with impartial rationality.

"This longing of faith and of the faithful for Christian integrity is not served by ignoring the resources of the tradition or by silencing the peculiar voices of Scripture.

"In Christian community the tradition, including Scripture, does not merely exist as an archaic relic in an age of science and reason. In Christian community Scripture exists as that which continues to evoke loyalties and to form and reform character and conduct into dispositions and deeds 'worthy of the gospel' (Phil. 1:27)."

"I take it then," we say rather lamely, "that Scripture is important to you."

I'll delete the expletive of his response. He got a little excited then. When he calmed down a little, he said, " 'Important' hardly covers it. It is the Word of God, after all, and 'profitable for teaching, for reproof, for correction, and for training in righteousness' (2 Tim. 3:16)."

"That seems a long way from where we began," we say and remind him that he was nodding in agreement when we talked about the silence and strangeness of Scripture.

"I do not deny that these words are human words," he said, "and I do not claim that we may simply repeat them as Christian counsel about medical practice and medical ethics today. But these words are also the Word of God, our faith reminds us, and they may not simply be discredited at our convenience."

There was a pause, and then he said to us, "You like problems evidently. Let me give you one: There is no Christian life that is not tied *somehow* to Scripture. There is no Christian ethic that is not formed and informed *somehow* by Scripture. Yet, as you say, the world of sickness and healing in Scripture is sometimes strange and alien, and a Christian medical ethic will not simply be identical with it, but *somehow* informed by it.[26] The problem is *not* whether to relate Scripture and medicine, for there is no Christian moral reflection which is not tied *somehow* to Scripture. The problem is not *whether*—but how—to relate them."

There was another pause, but finally we agree and ask the question we had earlier resolved to ask, "So why—or how—is Scripture so important to you?"

How Scripture Is Relevant to Medical Ethics

"Scripture is important to me," he says, "because Article Seven of the Belgic Confession of Faith calls it an 'infallible rule.' " Well, okay, probably not; he is a Catholic after all, but he is no more likely to have said, "Scripture is important to me because the Second Vatican Council calls it 'the supreme rule of faith.' "[27] He has not learned of Scripture and its significance from a confession or a creed but from participation in the practice of reading it with the people of God.

This is what he says: "Scripture is important to me because reading Scripture is what Alasdair MacIntyre called a 'practice.' " OK, he probably didn't say that either. He has probably never read *After Virtue*, and if he had, he would be no more likely to remember MacIntyre's definition of a practice than you are.[28] He is not a philosopher, after all.

But he is a Christian, and he has learned in Christian community the practice of reading Scripture, even if he has never learned MacIntyre's account of what a practice is. He has learned to read Scripture in Christian community. And in learning to read Scripture, he has learned as well the good that belongs to reading Scripture, the good "internal to that form of activity." He has learned, that is, to remember.[29]

And he has learned it not only intellectually. That is to say, he has learned not just a mental process of recollection, not just disinterested recall of objective historical facts. He has learned to own a past as his own, and to own it as constitutive of identity and determinative for discernment. Without remembering there is no identity. In amnesia one loses oneself. In memory one finds an identity. And without common remembering there is no community. It is little wonder that the church sustains this practice of piety, and is herself sustained by it and again and again made new by reading Scripture and remembering.

Coles' friend may never have read MacIntyre, but he has read John Bunyan's wonderful allegory *Pilgrim's Progress*, and he knows what Great Heart knew. He knows what that marvelous helper and guide said to the son of Christian as he pointed ahead to a place called "Forgetful Green." "That place," he said, "is the most dangerous place in all these parts."[30] Coles' friend knows that a pilgrim's progress comes by remembering. "That's why Scripture is important to me," he says.

In learning to read Scripture in Christian community he has learned that the art of remembering among God's people has always involved story-telling. The remedy for forgetfulness has always been a wonderful and lively story. Story after story was told generation after generation. Sometimes on Forgetful Greens the people forgot the stories—or forgot to tell them. And sometimes in Forgetful Straits the people nearly lost their memory—and their identity. But the remedy for forgetfulness was always to tell the old, old story, and a new generation would remember and own the story as their story and God as their God.

In learning to read Scripture in Christian community he has learned as well not only that remembering involved story-telling, but also that remembering took the shape of obedience. To remember that God rescued you from Pharaoh's oppression took the shape of freeing a hired hand from your own oppression, no longer cheating him of a living or of rest. To remember that God gave manna, enough for all to share, took the shape of leaving the edge of the field unharvested for the poor. To remember Jesus took the shape of discipleship.

Coles' friend has learned no theory of memory from reading Scripture,[31] but he has learned to remember. "That's why—and how—Scripture is important to me," he says. "I know the temptation to forgetfulness in the Forgetful Green of health and in the great medical powers to heal. I know the temptation to forgetfulness in the Forgetful Straits of pain and suffering and in the final powerlessness of medicine. I fear amnesia in this 'world come of age' called a hospital and in this 'religionless' world called medicine. That's why I lament so deeply the failure of some medical ethicists who know Scripture to remind me of it. That's why I long so deeply to connect the remembrance that belongs to the practice of reading Scripture with the suffering and care for the suffering that belong to medicine."

"There are problems," we say, ready to rehearse again the silence and strangeness and diversity and abuse of Scripture, but they do not seem quite so overwhelming now, for we recognize that in learning to read Scripture he has learned not only the good that belongs to this practice—remembrance—but also some standards of excellence "appropriate to" reading Scripture and "partially definitive of" this practice of piety.

He has learned, that is, both holiness and sanctification, both fidelity and creativity, both discipline and discernment—three pairs of virtues for reading Scripture.

Holiness is the standard of excellence in reading Scripture that not only sets these writings apart from others but that is ready to set apart a time and a place to read them and to remember, ready to set aside a time and a place and to protect that time and place from the tendencies of "the world" and of our obligations within the world to render our lives "profane," to reduce them to something "religionless."[32]

Sanctification is the standard of excellence in reading Scripture that is ready to set the remembered story alongside all the stories of our suffering and our dying, alongside the stories of our healing and our caring,[33] until *all* the times and *all* the spaces of our lives are made new by the power of God, made to fit remembrance, made worthy of the gospel.

Our practice here is sometimes better than our theology. Our theology tends to construe God's relation to Scripture and to us through Scripture simply as "revealer." Then the content of Scripture can simply be identified with revelation, and the theological task becomes simply to systematize and republish timeless biblical ideas or doctrines or principles or "laws."

In the practice of reading Scripture in Christian community, however, we learn, I think, to construe God's relation to Scripture and surely to us through Scripture as "sanctifier."[34] Then what one understands when one understands Scripture in remembrance is the creative and re-creative power of God to renew life, to transform identities, to create a people and a world for God's own glory and for their flourishing.

Remembrance takes place in holiness and calls for sanctification. It takes place in a context set aside and set apart, and it makes place for the grace and power of

God to touch all of life with remembrance and to orient all of life to God's cause, hoped for because remembered, and present now in memory and in hope.

Besides both holiness and sanctification the practice of reading Scripture also requires both fidelity and creativity.

Remembrance provides identity, and fidelity is simply the standard of excellence that is ready to live with integrity in that identity, ready to be faithful to the memory the church has owned as her own; but fidelity requires a process of continual change, of creativity.[35] Remembrance requires creativity, for the past is past, and we do not live in it, even if we remember it. We do not live in Asa's court or in the Jerusalem of Pontius Pilate. And creativity is the standard of excellence in reading Scripture that refuses to reduce fidelity to an anachronistic, if amiable, eccentricity.

Nicholas Lash makes the point quite nicely with respect to the traditions and ecclesiastical dress of the Franciscans. "If, in thirteenth-century Italy, you wandered around in a course brown gown," he said, "... your dress said you were one of the poor. If, in twentieth-century Cambridge, you wander around in a course brown gown, ... your dress now says, not that you are one of the poor, but that you are some kind of oddity in the business of 'religion.' "[36] Fidelity to a tradition of solidarity with the poor requires creativity and change.

Fidelity to the identity provided by remembrance must never be confused with anachronistic, if amiable, eccentricity. The practice of reading Scripture and the good of remembrance that belongs to it require both fidelity and creativity.

Again the practice of reading Scripture is sometimes better than our theology for it. There are some theologians who insist on continuity, who are suspicious of creativity, and who think of themselves as embattled defenders of a tradition threatened by change. These stand ready to accuse others of "accommodation."[37] There are other theologians (or philosophical theists) who insist on change, who minimize the significance of continuity, and who stand ready to accuse others of "irrational conservativism."[38] But the practice of reading Scripture rejects both extremes; it insists on both fidelity and creativity, on both continuity and change.

Then to treat Scripture as a revealed medical text or as a timeless moral code for medicine is a corruption of the practice of reading Scripture. It confuses fidelity with an anachronistic—and sometimes less than amiable—eccentricity. And to treat Scripture as simply dated and as irrelevant to contemporary medical practice and medical ethics is also a corruption of the practice. It turns remembrance to an archivist's recollection, and runs the risk of alienating the Christian community from its own moral tradition and from its own moral identity. It invites amnesia.

A pilgrim's progress still comes by way of remembering, by the practice of reading Scripture—whether the pilgrim is a physician or a patient—and the narrow path between anachronism and amnesia requires both discipline and discernment.

Discipline is the standard of excellence for reading Scripture that is ready to be a disciple, ready to follow the one of whom the story is told, ready to order one's life and one's common life to fit the story. It is the readiness to read Scripture "over-against ourselves" and not just "for ourselves,"[39] "over-against" our lives, in judgment upon them and not just in self-serving defense of them, "over-against" even our conventional reading of biblical texts, subverting our own efforts to use Scripture to boast about our own righteousness or to protect our own status and power. It is the humility of submission. The remedy for forgetfulness is still to tell the old, old story, and remembrance still takes the shape of obedience. A costly discipleship tests character and conduct by the truth of the story we love to tell.

But the shape of that story and of lives formed to it requires discernment. Discernment is the ability to recognize "fittingness."[40] In reading Scripture discernment is the ability to recognize the plot of the story, to see the wholeness of Scripture, and to order the interpretation of any part toward that whole. It is to recognize how a statute or a psalm or a story "fits" the whole. And in reading Scripture as "profitable ... for training in righteousness," discernment is the ability to plot our lives to "fit" the whole of Scripture, to order every part of our lives—including our medicine—toward that whole. It is to recognize how doing one thing rather than another or doing nothing rather than something may "fit" the story we love to hear and long to live.

Moral discernment is a complex but practical wisdom. It does not rely on spontaneous intuition nor on the simple application of general principles (whether of hermeneutics or of ethics) to particular cases by neutral and rational agents. As there is no theory of memory in Scripture, neither is there any theory of discernment there. There is no checklist, no flow chart for decisions. But as there is remembering in Scripture and in the community that reads it, so is there discernment in Scripture and in the community that struggles to live it.

Discernment regards decision as the recognition of what is fitting, coherent, to the kind of person one is and hopes to become. It asks not just "What should a rational person do in a case like this one?" but "What should *I* do in this case?" It recognizes that serious moral questions are always asked in the first person, and it insists on the moral significance of the question "Who am I?" The practice of reading Scripture and the good of remembrance that belongs to it give us identity and forms our character and conduct into something fitting to it.

Discernment regards decision as the recognition of what is fitting or coherent to the circumstances, to what is going on. It recognizes that the meaning of circumstances is not exhausted by objective observation or public inspection. There is no label for life like a can of peas that tells us what the ingredients are. But reading Scripture trains us to see the religious significance of events, to read the signs of the times in the things that are happening about us,[41] and to locate events and circumstances—as well as our selves—in a story of God's power and grace. Reading Scripture trains us to answer the question "What is going on?" with reference to the remembered story, fitting the parts of our lives into the whole of Scripture.

Discernment is learned and tested in the community gathered around the Scripture, and it involves the diversity of gifts present in the congregation. Some are gifted with the scholarly tools of historical and literary and social scientific investigation. Some are gifted with moral imagination and sensitivity. Some are gifted with a passion for justice; some, with a sweet reasonableness. Some are gifted with intellectual clarity; some, with simple purity. Some are gifted with courage; some, with patience. But all are gifted with their own experience, and each is gifted with the Spirit that brings remembrance (John 14:26).

To be sure, in the community some are blinded by fear, and some are blinded by duty, and the perception of each is abridged by investments in their culture or in their class. To be sure, sometimes whole communities are blinded by idolatrous loyalties to their race or to their social standing or to their power. Witness, for example, the "German Christians" or the white Dutch Reformed Church of South Africa. And to be sure, the practice of reading Scripture is corrupted then. Such communities stand at risk of forgetfulness, even if they treat Scripture as an icon.[42] The remedy for forgetfulness is still to hear and to tell the old, old story, but to hear it now and then from saints[43] and now and then from strangers for whom Christ also died.[44] Remembrance is served in a community of discernment, reading Scripture with those whose experience is different from ours and whose experience of Scripture is different from ours. We may learn in such discourse with saints and strangers that our reading of Scripture does not yet "fit" Scripture itself, and that our lives and our communities do not yet "fit" the story we love to tell and long to live. Then discernment is joined to discipline again, and the recognition of a more fitting way to tell the story and to live it prepares the way for humble submission and discipleship.

Once again, the practice is sometimes better than our theology for it. The slogan *sola scriptura* is sometimes used to deny or ignore the relevance of other voices and other sources, to discount natural science or "natural" morality.[45] And talk of the "authority" of Scripture is sometimes used to end discussion as though we could beat into silence and submission those who speak from some other experience or for some other source.

The practice can become corrupt, we said, but it can also sometimes be better than our theology. Discernment, or the perception of what is fitting, cannot demand that people violate what they know they know in other ways. It cannot demand that they violate either the experience of oppression or the assured results of science or the rational standards of justice. Of course, there can be disagreements—and discussion—about how to read and interpret one's experience or the "assured results" of science or some minimal notion of justice as there can be disagreements—and discussion—about how to read and interpret Scripture.

Where remembrance takes the shape of obedience, the practice of reading Scripture engages the community in discernment. Together they plot the story of Scripture. Together they talk and argue about how to interpret and shape their lives in remembrance. In that dialogue people must listen to Scripture and to each other—and to what each has experienced or knows—muting neither each other nor Scripture. In that communal discernment and mutual discipline, the authority of Scripture is "non-violent."[46] The moment of recognition of Scripture's wholeness and truthfulness comes before the moment of submission to any part of it and prepares the way for it.

In the struggle against forgetfulness both holiness and sanctification, both fidelity and creativity, both discipline and discernment are required. "That's why— and how—Scripture is important to me," Coles' friend says.

We are ready at last to read some Scripture with Coles' friend.

Just then, however, our friend's doctor comes in the room. "She's still trying to talk me into another round of chemotherapy," our friend says to us with more than a hint of impatience.

We politely offer to return another time, but each seems eager to enlist us as an ally in the struggle with the other. The doctor expects us to define our role (as chaplain or as ethicist) in terms of the therapeutic ambitions of the medical establishment, and Coles' friend hopes we will be an advocate of the patient's perspective. We are happy enough to be able to report that we came to read Scripture, to remember the story, and not simply to be defenders of either the authority of physicians or the autonomy of patients.

Coles' friend tells his doctor to sit down for a moment, and she does. He hands us his Bible. It is still marked at Psalm 69 with its curses on the enemy.

We suggest a different text, perhaps the word of Jesus, "Love your enemies ..., bless those who curse you, pray for those who abuse you" (Luke 6:27-28).

Coles' friend insists that he did not intend that we read Psalm 69 again. But he has been reminded by our words—by Jesus' word, actually—of the story of an Armenian Christian woman.

The woman, it seems, was kept for a time by a Turkish officer who had raided her home and killed her aged parents. After she escaped she trained to be a nurse. Some time later, when this officer became gravely ill, she happened to be his nurse. Exceptional nursing care was required, and exceptional care was given. When finally the officer recovered, his doctor pointed to the nurse and told the man that the credit for his recovery belonged to her. When he looked at her, he said, "We have met before, haven't we?" And when he recognized her, he asked, "Why did you provide such care for me?"

Her reply was simply this: "I am a follower of the one who said 'Love your enemies.' "[47]

Our friend's doctor was evidently touched by the story. "It makes me a little ashamed," she said, "of the way I treated the patient I just left. I think I'll look in on him again in a few minutes."

Our friend smiled at that, thinking, perhaps, that there may be hope for this physician yet. And then he said, "That woman was a saint, one of the company of those to whom we must listen when we would read Scripture for the moral life and the medical life. How do you think she read Scripture? She appealed to a command, to be sure, but not as though Scripture were to be regarded as 'a system of divine laws.'[48] She described herself as a 'follower' of Christ. The command to 'love the enemy' coheres with a story, not with some eternal code. Scripture does not give us a moral handbook; it gives us a story we own as our own. It is a story we may love to remember and tell and must struggle to practice and live even when we are dying or caring for the dying. And the plot of the story climaxes in the resurrection of Jesus of Nazareth. There was the *final* revelation, and the reading of Scripture and the practice of medicine must both be made to fit with that final disclosure of God's cause and purpose.[49]

"Jesus came announcing that the good future of God was 'at hand' and already made its power felt in his works of healing and in his words of blessing. He suffered for the sake of God's cause in the world, but when death and doom had done their damnedest, God raised him up. So, we read all Scripture in remembrance of Jesus and in hope of God's final triumph. And reading Scripture, we learn to practice medicine in remembrance of the same Jesus and in the same hope."

It was a discerning judgment, we thought to ourselves, and we began to see for ourselves how—and why—the practice of reading Scripture (in spite of the problems) might form and inform the practices of medicine.

An Illustration of Scripture's Formation of Medical Ethics

We do read some Scripture that day—perhaps a story of Jesus' works of healing, of his victory over death and sickness, over Satan and his hosts, over sin, or perhaps a story of his words of blessing, of "good news to the poor," or perhaps a story of his death. We do not have time to suggest all the implication of reading all Scripture for medicine, but we must at the end at least attend to reading of his death.

There is no remembrance of Jesus if we neglect the story of his death. The Jesus who was raised was a *wounded* healer, and his wounds were raised with him. He "suffered under Pontius Pilate, was crucified, dead, and buried." The story of his passion is remembered by each of the evangelists. Indeed, the gospels decisively tie the memories of Jesus as healer and as teacher to the story of his cross.

Apart from it the church is always at risk of distorting the good news of the gospel into a pollyanna triumphalism and then of self-deceptively ignoring or denying the sad truth about our world—and the sad truth about Coles' friend. Apart from the story of the cross our culture is always at risk of distorting the good news of some medical breakthrough into a pollyanna medical triumphalism, and then of self-deceptively ignoring or denying the sad truth that there is no medical technology to rescue the human condition from finitude or mortality or its vulnerability to suffering.

Jesus has been raised. God has established God's own good future when death shall be no more, neither will there be mourning nor crying nor pain any more (Rev. 21:4). But we live under the sign of the cross, and that promised age of God's unchallenged sovereignty is not yet, *still not yet.*

Yet, already, the story of the wounded healer sheds its light on our sicknesses and on our care for the sick.

To those who suffer, the story of Jesus is a glad story indeed, but a glad story which does not deny the sad truth about our world. The gospel of Jesus and his suffering and his way to death, does not announce here and now an end to our pains or an avoidance of our death, but it does provide an unshakable assurance that we do not suffer alone, that we are not and will not be abandoned, that Jesus suffers with us, that God cares. The glad story of Jesus is indeed a hard reminder that in a world like this one, however righteous and repentant we are, we cannot expect to be spared pain and sorrow. Certainly health and life are goods which I may and must seek, but they are not the greatest goods, and if "a disciple is not above his teacher" (Mt. 10:24), then one's own survival and one's own ease may not become the law of one's own being. In our sad stories we keep good company. That's a part of the good news—and this: that beyond the cross is the resurrection, the triumph of God over diseases and death.

The stories of Jesus and his cross do not "fit" the story sometimes told by medical practice to patients (and sometimes told by patients to medical practice) that death is the ultimate enemy and the worst evil, to be put off by any means. And if people then sometimes blame the physicians for keeping them alive beyond all reason, the stories of Jesus and his cross do not "fit" the story told by Jack Kevorkian and the Hemlock Society that life is the enemy; and that physicians may become killers.

The story of a wounded healer can form not only the dispositions of those who suffer but also the practice of those who would care for them. It is a call to those who would follow Jesus to minister to the sick as though to care for them were to care for Christ. He said as much, of course: inasmuch "as you did it to the one of the least of these ..., you did it unto me" (Mt. 25:40).

Reading Scripture is like putting on glasses ("spectacles," Calvin said) which correct our vision, enabling the physician to see in those who hurt not only manipulable nature but the very image of Christ the Lord.

Called by a story of a wounded healer to minister to the sick, the physician may delight in her tools as gifts of God, celebrating scientific advances and technological breakthroughs for the powers they give to intervene in the sad stories people tell with and of their bodies.

But the glasses of Scripture also correct her vision if she regards her technology as the faithful savior and relies on it to remedy the human condition, to provide the happy ending finally, or to sustain either her patients or her care for them in the face of their suffering.

It is God who will bring in the good future when pain and death will be no more, not technology. With corrected vision the physician may use technology to give some small token of God's good future without extravagant expectations of her tools.

It is God who suffers with us and for us, not technology. And with corrected vision the physician will be less tempted by the techno-logic that, if we can, we must, and may be enabled to give some small token of God's presence to the patient by her own presence, listening to the patient's sighs as well as to his chest, touching the patient in a way that signals simple human compassion and not just medical probing, talking with a patient to share some wisdom about life in a mortal body.

The glasses of Scripture can form the vision of physicians until they learn to see even themselves in a new way—as followers of a wounded healer, as disciples of one who shared the lament of the sick and dying, as imitators of one who knew our pain and did not abandon us to our hurt.

That new vision might nurture and sustain an old vision of medicine, that medical practice has at its heart and center the extraordinary commitment to *care* for the sick. That old vision seeks and celebrates the competence to cure if one can, but it also insists, when one cannot cure, on practicing presence to those in pain, on being the "good company" even the dying may keep, and on never abandoning the one who hurts even when medicine cannot heal. It will refuse to eliminate suffering by eliminating the sufferer.

That old vision of medical practice may not be sustainable in our culture. The tendency to reduce the practice to a technological control over manipulable nature may not be turned back. The tendency in another direction to reduce the practice to skills available on the marketplace to be purchased by presumably autonomous consumers may be irresistible.

But in our culture some Christians still gather to remember Jesus and to attend to God. They read Scripture and pray, and those practices of piety form virtues and visions for both the sick and those who care for them. They form character and finally conduct into something fitting to the gospel.

It is not my claim that the practice of reading Scripture will settle the dispute between Coles' friend and his doctor—or between any patient and any physician. I am not suggesting that the right text will magically resolve medical and moral dilemmas—which are, after all, sometimes the genuine conflict of genuine goods.

I am saying that for Christian patients these decisions are not merely "private" decisions and that for Christian physicians these decisions are not merely "professional" decisions. They ought to be made with Christian integrity. That is to say, they can and sometimes are and surely should be made in the context of the Christian community's attention to God and common memory. That is to say, they can and sometimes are and surely should be made in performance of the story we love to tell.

Attention to God and remembrance can support both the art of dying and the practice of medicine. The church which practices piety may never abandon care for the sick and dying to the medical profession, but neither may it abandon the physician or the nurse to science or to the marketplace.

The practices of piety are not undertaken for the sake of medicine, but the best hope for a morally worthy practice of medicine may finally be the practices of piety. That is my claim, and this: that if we remember Jesus in Scripture, then our own strange world of medicine may be healed a little.

Notes

1. Thomas Hobbes, *Leviathan* (Harmondsworth: Penguin, 1968), Part IV, ch. 47, 710-11.

2. Immanuel Kant, *Religion Within the Limits of Reason Alone* (New York: Harper Torchbooks, 1960), bk. 3.

3. See further John Milbank, *Theology and Social Theory: Beyond Secular Reason* (Oxford: Basil Blackwell, 1990), 17-20.

4. See further David H. Kelsey, "Protestant Attitudes Regarding Methods of Biblical Interpretation," in Frederick E. Greenspahn, ed., *Scripture in the Jewish and Christian Traditions: Authority, Interpretation, Relevance* (Nashville: Abingdon, 1982), 135-51.

5. See further Kelsey, ibid., 151-57.

6. See especially the work of Hans Frei, *The Eclipse of Biblical Narrative* (New Haven: Yale University Press, 1974) and *The Identity of Jesus Christ* (Philadelphia: Fortress, 1975).

7. See further Allen Verhey, *The Great Reversal* (Grand Rapids: Eerdmans, 1984), 171-72.

8. See especially the work of David H. Kelsey, *The Uses of Scripture in Recent Theology* (Philadelphia: Fortress, 1975), 89-112.

9. One promising recent book along these lines is Stephen E. Fowl and L. Gregory Jones, *Reading in Communion: Scripture and Ethics in Christian Life* (Grand Rapids: Eerdmans, 1991).

10. See Oliver O'Donovan, *Begotten or Made?* (Oxford: Oxford University Press, 1984), 10-12.

11. See further Allen Verhey, "The Death of Infant Doe: Jesus and the Neonates," in Stephen E. Lammers and Allen D. Verhey, eds., *On Moral Medicine: Theological Perspectives in Medical Ethics* (Grand Rapids: Eerdmans, 1987), 489-94.

12. I have tried to argue in a forthcoming essay "Compassion: Beyond the Standard Account" in *Second Opinion* that compassion should be armed with wisdom and piety as well as artifice.

13. The remainder of this paper is an abridged edition of the lecture given in honor of Henry Stob. See further Allen Verhey, *The Practice of Piety and the Practice of Medicine: Prayer, Scripture, and Medical Ethics* (Calvin College and Seminary: The Stob Lectures Endowment, 1992), 29-63.

14. Robert Coles, "Psychiatric Stations of the Cross," *Harvard Diary: Reflections on the Sacred and the Profane* (New York: Crossroad Publishing Company, 1990), 10-12; see also 92-94.

15. These citations of Psalm 69:1, 2, 20-22, are from the NIV. All other references are to the RSV.

16. The disease was probably not modern leprosy, or Hansen's bacillus. See Klaus Seybold and Ulrich B. Meuller, *Sickness and Healing*, Douglas W. Stott, trans., (Nashville: Abingdon, 1981), 67-74. The identification of the disorder called *sara'at* as psoriasis is given at 69.

17. D. W. Amundsen and G. B. Ferngren, "Medicine and Religion: Pre-Christian Antiquity," in Martin Marty and Kenneth Vaux, eds., *Health/Medicine and the Faith Traditions* (Philadelphia: Fortress Press, 1982), 53-92, at 62.

18. See Klaus Seybold and Ulrich Meuller, *Sickness and Healing*, 112-14.

19. See Ronald L. Numbers and Ronald C. Sawyer, "Medicine and Christianity in the Modern World," in Martin Marty and Kenneth Vaux, eds., *Health/Medicine and the Faith Traditions*, 133-60, at 134. Numbers and Sawyer also observe, however, that Scripture was also cited to justify the use of anesthetics, notably Gen. 2:21, where God mercifully caused "a deep sleep to fall upon Adam" before removing his rib, 136.

20. According to a 1988 Gallup poll of registered voters 42.5 percent of those surveyed agreed with the statement that AIDS is God's punishment for immoral behaviors (*Newsweek*, 1 Feb. 1988: 7).

21. On the Jehovah's Witness position prohibiting blood transfusions on the basis of Genesis 9:4, Leviticus 17:13-14, Acts 15:29, etc., see W. H. Cumberland, "The Jehovah's Witness Tradition," in R. L. Numbers and D. W. Amundsen, eds., *Caring and Curing: Health and Medicine in the Western Religious Traditions* (New York: Macmillan, 1986), 468-85.

22. See Richard Mouw, "Biblical Revelation and Medical Decisions," in Stanley Hauerwas and Alasdair MacIntryre, eds., *Revisions: Changing Perspectives in Moral Philosophy* (Notre Dame: University of Notre Dame Press, 1983), 182-202, at 197-98. Mouw puts the best possible face of this foolishness, construing in as resistance against the tendency to reduce the human struggle with suffering to the medical model for that struggle.

23. See further Allen Verhey, "Talking of God—But With Whom?" *Hastings Center Report* 20:4, Special Supplement, "Theology, Religious Traditions, and Bioethics," 21-24.

24. H. Tristam Englehardt, "Bioethics in Pluralist Societies," *Perspectives in Biology and Medicine*, 26:1 (1982): 64-77.

25. See, for example, the wonderful essay by William F. May, "The Sacral Power of Death in Contemporary Experience," *Social Research* 39 (1972): 463-88.

26. See the "important two-part consensus" identified by Bruce Birch and Larry Rasmussen that "Christian ethics is not synonymous with biblical ethics" and that "for Christian ethics the Bible is somehow normative." Bruce Birch and Larry Rasmussen, *Bible and Ethics in the Christian Life* (Minneapolis: Augsburg, 1976), 45-46. The same claims are found in the revised edition (Minneapolis: Augsburg, 1989), 189. See also Allen Verhey, *The Great Reversal: Ethics and the New Testament* (Grand Rapids: Eerdmans, 1984), 153-97.

27. "Dogmatic Constitution on Divine Revelation," in Walter M. Abbott, S. J., ed., *The Documents of Vatican II*, (New York: Guild Press, 1966), 111-28, at 125.

28. Alasdair MacIntrye defined a practice as a "form of socially established cooperative human activity through which goods internal to that form of activity are realized in the course of trying to achieve those standards of excellence which are appropriate to, and partially definitive of, that form of activity with the result that human powers to achieve excellence and human conceptions of the ends and goods involved are systematically extended." Alasdair MacIntrye, *After Virtue: A Study in Moral Theory* (Notre Dame: University of Notre Dame Press, 1981), 175. On the notion of "practice" see also Jeffrey Stout, *Ethics After Babel: The Languages of Moral and Their Discontents*, 267-76.

29. For the notion of remembrance as "the good" of reading Scripture (and for much besides), I am indebted to Stanley Hauerwas. See his essay "The Moral Authority of Scripture: The Politics and Ethics of Remembering," *A Community of Character* (Notre Dame: University of Notre Dame Press, 1981), 53-71. See also Hans Frei, *The Eclipse of the Biblical Narrative* (New Haven: Yale University Press, 1974).

30. John Bunyan, *The Pilgrim's Progress* (New York: Washington Square Press, 1957), 234. (It was originally published in 1678.)

31. There is nothing in Scripture to compare, for example, with Aristotle's treatise *De Memoria*.

32. Stephen E. Fowl and L. Gregory Jones, *Reading in Communion: Scripture and Ethics in Christian Life* (Grand Rapids: Eerdmans, 1990), 31-33.

33. See, for example, Stanley Hauerwas, *Naming the Silences: God, Medicine, and the Problem of Suffering* (Grand Rapids: Eerdmans, 1990), 34-147.

34. See further Allen Verhey, *The Great Reversal*, 180-81, and David Kelsey, "The Bible and Christian Theology," *The Journal of the American Academy of Religion* 68, no.3 (1980): 385-402.

35. Continuity and change are marks of any living tradition. They mark Scripture itself, and they mark the tradition and practice of reading Scripture as a guide for faith and life in the church. See Nicholas Lash, *Theology on the Way to Emmaus* (London: SCM Press, 1986); at 55 Lash says, "Fidelity to tradition, in action and speech, is a risky business because it entails active engagement in a process of continual change."

36. Nicholas Lash, *Theology on the Way to Emmaus*, 54.

37. Franklin E. Payne, *Biblical/Medical Ethics* (Milford, MI: Mott Media, 1985), an unnumbered page in the Introduction. Similarly John M. Frame, *Medical Ethics: Principles, Persons, and Problems* (Phillipsburg, NJ: Presbyterian and Reformed, 1988), 2, says "Scripture says it, we believe it, and that settles it."

38. For example, Charles Hartshorne, "Scientific and Religious Aspects of Bioethics," in E. E. Shelp, ed., *Theology and Bioethics: Exploring the Foundations and the Frontiers* (Dordrecht: Kluwer Academic Press, 1985), 27-44, at 28.

39. Dietrich Bonhoeffer, *No Rusty Swords*, E. H. Robertson and John Bowden, trans. (New York: Harper and Row, 1965), 185; see also 308-25. One might regard Richard Mouw's contrast between a "priestly" reading of Scripture and a "prophetic" reading of Scripture to be analogous to Bonhoeffer's contrast; see "Biblical Revelation and Medical decisions," 196.

40. On discernment see especially the work of James Gustafson, "Moral Discernment in the Christian Life," in Gene H. Outka and Paul Ramsey, eds., *Norm and Context in Christian Ethics* (New York: Charles Scribner's Sons, 1968), 17-36; and

William C. Spohn, S. J., "The Reasoning Heart: An Approach to Christian Discernment," in *Theological Studies* 44 (March, 1983), 30-52.

41. H. Richard Niebuhr, *The Meaning of Revelation* (New York: Macmillan, 1974), 109: "What concerns us at this point is not the fact that the revelatory moment shines by its own light but rather that it illumines other events and enables us to understand them. What ever else revelation means it does mean an event in our history which brings rationality and wholeness into the confused joys and sorrows of personal existence and allows us to discern order in the brawl of communal histories."

42. Witness the report of the Dutch Reformed Church's 1974 General Synod, *Human Relations and the South African Scene in the Light of Scripture* (Cape Town-Pretoria: Dutch Reformed Church Publishers, 1974). It appeals to Scripture to justify apartheid. It has been properly subjected to strong criticism in John de Gruchy and Charles Villa-Vicencia, eds., *Apartheid is a Heresy* (Grand Rapids: Eerdmans, 1983); see especially 94-113. Witness also the appeals to Scripture in Margaret Atwood's powerful novel *The Handmaid's Tale* (New York: Faucett Crest, 1985).

43. Stephen E. Fowl and L. Gregory Jones, *Reading in Communion: Scripture and Ethics in the Christian Life*, 62-63. They quote Athanasius, *The Incarnation of the Word of God* (New York: Macmillan, 1946), 96: "Anyone who wishes to understand the mind of the sacred writers must first cleanse his own life, and approach the saints by copying their deeds."

44. See further Stephen E. Fowl and L. Gregory Jones, *Reading in Communion: Scripture and Ethics in the Christian Life*, 110-34.

45. On the relevance of other sources see further Allen Verhey, *The Great Reversal*, 187-96.

46. Paul Ricour, *Essays on Biblical Interpretation*, L. S. Mudge, ed. (Philadelphia: Fortress Press, 1980), 95. See also Margaret Farley, "Feminist Consciousness and the Interpretation of Scripture" in *Feminist Interpretation of the Bible*, Letty M. Russell, ed. (Philadelphia: Westminster Press, 1985), 41-51, at 43-44.

47. The story is told in Geoffrey Wainwright, *Doxology* (London: Epworth Press, 1980), 434, and in Stephen E. Fowl and L. Gregory Jones, *Reading in Communion*, 79-80.

48. Against John M. Frame, *Medical Ethics: Principles, Persons, and Problems*, 10. By this judgment about the wholeness of Scripture, Frame provides backing for his appeals to Scripture as a moral code to answer directly questions about conduct. But many theologians, no less convinced of the authority of Scripture, would argue that such an account of the wholeness of Scripture is not a discerning reading of Scripture, that it is wrong, and that therefore the use of Scripture in ways coherent with it (as moral code) is flawed. I count myself among that number.

49. For resurrection as the key to Scripture see Allen Verhey, *The Great Reversal*, 181-83; David Kelsey, "The Bible and Christian Theology," *Journal of the American Academy of Religion* 68, no.3 (1980): 385-402, especially 398-402; and the essay by Oliver O'Donovan, "Keeping Body and Soul Together," in *Covenants of Life:*

Contemporary Medical Ethics in Light of the Thought of Paul Ramsey, Kenneth Vaux, ed., (Champaign: University of Illinois Press, 1991).

Aspects of Scripture and Medical Ethics

Response to Allen D. Verhey

John Cooper

Introduction

I am grateful to professor Verhey for his interesting, insightful, and imaginative approach to biblical hermeneutics and an ethos of compassion from the standpoint of medical ethics. Since I admire and agree with the substance of his presentation, my response will not consist of a debate with its specific contents. Instead I will focus on some issues which I regard as crucial and foundational to the topic of biblical hermeneutics and ethics in general which I think Verhey presupposes, implies, or mentions but does not explicitly address. I hope he will agree with my attempt to explicate and supplement the framework of his paper.

Verhey is surely correct that in spite of modern developments in biblical hermeneutics and the challenges of applying Scripture to the complex ethical questions raised by contemporary medicine, the Bible is relevant to the formation of medical ethics. Furthermore, it seems right that this formation takes place through the pious communal practice of reading Scripture by Christians—care-givers, patients, and support community—who find themselves involved in health care.

What is not altogether clearly explicated in his paper is the nature of the ethical content of Scripture and how that content gives normative shape to faithful Bible readers. What Verhey seems to highlight are themes important in contemporary narrative and virtue ethics: how communities' stories shape the character and dispositions of their members. This of course is a valuable and fully biblical theme.

But it is not the only one. Two other important themes familiar to Reformed Christians immediately spring to mind: natural law or creation order; and God's revealed law or divine commands. While creation order is not even mentioned by Verhey and the law gets but a nod in passing, I believe these themes are required by his project and are actually involved in it even if they are not named. And that is to be expected. For Verhey deeply desires the Christian community to be shaped by the whole of Scripture authentically appropriated within the context of tradition. Surely creation order and God's law are essential in the Reformed tradition's— Verhey's tradition's—authentic reading and responding to Scripture.

Discussing these issues is important, I think, both because of current debates regarding the foundations of theological ethics and because of the topic of this conference.

The Import of Scripture for Medical Ethics

Let me begin addressing the ethical content of Scripture by sharing Verhey's misgiving about compassion. "Compassion needs other virtues in order to be virtuous; it needs a fuller account of the moral life in order to know what to do" (133). The question I have is whether one has provided the fuller account of the moral life merely by pointing to other virtues in addition to compassion. In other words, is a set of virtues all that the reading of Scripture provides for ethical guidance, or does the fuller account of the moral life also require reference to norms and standards found in the structure of creation and in divine commands?

When elaborating how Scripture shapes us ethically, Verhey repeatedly speaks of the identity, loyalties, character, dispositions, and virtues formed by its stories. Even the criteria considered for properly reading Scripture are a set of reader-qualities forged by this practice: holiness and sanctification, fidelity, creativity, discipline, and discernment. He also speaks of deeds, practices, obedience, and discipleship, but not clearly in a way which has them shaped by anything but the character or behavioral patterns created in us by the faithful reading of biblical narratives. All this might lead the inattentive listener to suppose that Verhey is proposing an exclusive or foundational narrative-virtue ethical approach to the way Scripture shapes medical ethics.

But this is not the case. When Verhey illustrates Scripture's formation of medical ethics, the scope is broader. To be sure, character and disposition are shaped. Doctors who follow Jesus, the wounded healer, are less prone to triumphalism about the saving power of medicine and they are more empathetic and compassionate in their care for the sick. And patients who follow the crucified and resurrected Lord are thereby enabled to endure their suffering in hope.

But there is more. Reading Scripture, says Verhey (146), enables the physician to see in those who hurt not only manipulable nature but the very image of Christ the Lord. What is ethically important here is not primarily the disposition of the doctor but the nature of the patient. Here Scripture shapes by teaching that human beings are the created, fallen, and redeemed images of God. We have a nature, a value, and a destiny which obligate us. We need this knowledge of our nature before God in the biblical drama for proper guidance in difficult medical situations. We need to know that human life is precious to God and that our lives belong to him, not to ourselves or to the medical establishment. God holds the power of life and death. The commandment sanctioning the lives of God's human images is as abiding as the love it expresses: "You shall not kill." All of the above, and not just the narratives of Jesus and his cross, reveal why the story told by Jack Kevorkian and the Hemlock Society is perverse fiction and why physicians may not become killers (146). Verhey's illustrations of how Scripture shapes medical ethics are inextricably connected with the Bible's teaching about human nature and its disclosure of divine law.

This is true also for Coles' friend. He must decide about continuing unpromising cancer treatment. Having all the virtues and right dispositions will not tell him what to do. It is knowing that, although his life is not his own, as an image of God he is its steward, responsible for facing death as much as for living life. It is knowing that Jesus suffered, died, and rose again so that he might suffer, die, and rise again. These biblical teachings, too, augment the fuller account of morality required to help Coles, his doctor, and his friends act with integrity and compassion in this difficult situation. In being assured of these things by the practice of reading Scripture, Coles' friend could with Christian integrity decide that all things considered the faithful thing to do is not to continue pointless treatment but to die in the Lord as he lived in the Lord.

In sum, Verhey's use of Scripture for ethics cannot be reduced to the shaping of character by community narratives. That is because he wants us to be formed by the message of Scripture as a whole. And the ethical import of Scripture is surely broader than the shaping of character.

Scripture/Hermeneutics

To see this we must consider more fully the issue of biblical hermeneutics. Beyond stating his worries about historical hermeneutics, Verhey says very little about this topic in his introduction. He does, however, recommend recovery of the community of faith and its traditions as the proper context for interpreting Scripture (132). Following his advice, I want to say something about historical Reformed hermeneutics and its relation to ethics. In the process I will join up with other things Verhey says later in his paper about Scripture and its proper interpretation.

Enlightenment hermeneutics not only opened an ugly ditch between the historical text and its spiritual meaning; it also eliminated the belief that in Scripture we have a direct address from God. At best special revelation became a category of general revelation. At worst the Scriptures became a contradictory hodge-podge of human reflections on purported religious experiences—totally human, historical, and fallible.

The Reformed tradition has upheld the view that the "God-breathed" character of Scripture (2 Tim. 3:16) must be recognized while at the same time acknowledging its human diversity and historicity. As Coles' friend says, the Bible is not just human words; it is also the Word of God (138). The notion of "organic inspiration" is one way the Reformed tradition has understood the Bible's divine and human origin. Although the Scriptures were written in a variety of ways in a variety of times and places, their writing was divinely superintended so that through them God himself was speaking and still does speak.

This understanding of inspiration allowed Reformed scholars to maintain a high view of the authority and trustworthiness of Scripture while at the same time benefitting from the insights of modern scholarship concerning the structure, formation, and historical circumstances of the biblical books. Traditional grammatical-historical method was enhanced and improved.

Organic inspiration also allowed the unity of Scripture to be maintained. Because the Spirit of God is the primary author of Scripture, there is a single, comprehensive, coherent message in the canon. As Verhey points out, "In reading Scripture discernment is the ability to recognize the plot of the story, to see the wholeness of Scripture, and to order the interpretation of any part toward that whole" (142). The individual books may come in different genres, written by different people of different cultures in different languages at different times for different purposes. But they all contribute strands and patterns to the marvellous tapestry of the whole. They in turn must be interpreted within the framework of the whole.

Verhey is right. The message of the whole is, I think, a narrative, a single grand story. It is the history of God's earthly kingdom. It is the story of how God came in Jesus Christ to redeem and sanctify his whole creation, but especially his people, from the consequences of the fall and bring them again into his kingdom. This is the grand narrative within which we find the location and meaning of our own lives as the people of God. In the end it interprets us, not we it.

Verhey is also right that Scripture as a whole should shape our ethical lives. Let me suggest a good Reformed account of how this goes. In the biblical narrative we begin with God creating humans with a nature: they are earthly images of God, male and female, called to love God above all and one another as themselves. They are to fill the earth and to have dominion over it as God's earthly stewards. God's will for their lives is that they do and be what he created them to do and be. Doing what they are purposed for is good for them and for the rest of creation and for God's honor. This correlation of created nature, purpose, and goodness is at the heart of the Reformed understanding of natural law or the creation order.

God's revealed law, focused in the ten commandments, restates the basic contours of what God willed for us in creation: love. It is not an arbitrary test of obedience or a mere prohibiter of certain behaviors. In the history of redemption various Old Testament applications of God's abiding will are superseded, but his basic intentions are not. Christ keeps the law for us and fulfils all righteousness so that it no longer condemns, but the law itself is not rescinded. It is now a guide for Christian living. Various New Testament writers emphasize that love for the Lord is expressed by keeping his commandments. Someday the law will be written on our hearts.

But Scripture also promotes the formation of virtuous character and proper dispositions. This is no way conflicts with creation order or divine commands. For virtuous character and holy dispositions are God's intention for our nature from the beginning. They are necessary for fully imaging God and for human flourishing, especially since the fall. Like proper actions, they are therefore commanded by God. The virtues are again possible for us in Jesus Christ and actualized by the power of the Holy Spirit.

On this retelling of the story, there is no conflict between creation order, divine commands, and the virtues as norms for human ethical life. In fact they are complementary parts of the biblical whole. This is the point I wanted to make with respect to Verhey's illustration of how Scripture shapes medical ethics. All these norms have roles in the grand biblical narrative.

Of course the gaps remain. Scripture is sometimes silent and strange and diverse. Here Reformed hermeneutics has approached the biblical story as a whole and has attempted to sort out which biblical norms change and which remain constant through history and across cultures. Scripture speaks more directly and frequently on some issues than on others. Sometimes the distinction between what is a constant and what a variant, between what is an abiding principle and what is merely its application, is straightforward. Sometimes it is difficult and takes centuries to perceive. And so we must take Verhey's advice and read Scripture together with reverence and mutual love in order to discern God's will. We must neither legalistically oversimplify what is complex nor rationalize away what is quite plain. Scripture is an infallible rule. But we must read it aright.

Thus shaped by Scripture, we have clear if not always specific guidance in making the straightforward as well as the difficult ethical decisions we face in post-modern society. Then too we will know what it means to show compassion. For as Verhey suggested, true compassion "fits" with a full account of God's will for our lives.

In Defence of Hermeneutics
and Compassion

A Response to Allen Verhey

Sylvia C. Keesmaat

Our old hermeneutical gods have failed us, suggests Allen Verhey, and the reason they have done so is because "the university [has] displaced the community of faith as the context of interpretation" and "unqualified reason has displaced tradition as the test of interpretation" (132). By and large, this analysis is correct. Modern biblical scholars—or perhaps I should say postmodern biblical scholars—have been coming to the realization for a number of years now that our old hermeneutical assumptions and methods—the historical-critical method, redaction-criticism, form-criticism, literary-criticism—these methods are proving inadequate. In short, biblical interpretation is in crisis. This crisis is intimately connected to the current crisis in Western society as a whole.

As Verhey has carefully pointed out, biblical scholarship has been shaped by post-enlightenment western rationalism and intellectualism. I would add that this shaping has taken place not only in the academy, but also in the believing community (and the two are not as distinct as is commonly made out). As we look to the society around us and see how the modern worldview has resulted in death, and in cultural and global collapse, it is not surprising to be told that the same modern worldview has resulted in emptiness in a field such as biblical studies. It is no wonder that our methods of scholarship, rooted as they are in a scientific tradition which assumes one can objectively discern truth, have failed to bear living fruit.

So in the face of this crisis, how do we view the hermeneutical enterprise as such? Well, in addition to acknowledging that hermeneutics in the past has been less than adequate (as does Verhey), we urgently need to find a life-giving response; we need to articulate a hermeneutic which meets not only the crisis in biblical studies but which also speaks to the crisis of the postmodern world.[1] And indeed, in spite of Verhey's suspicions regarding the present state of hermeneutics, such a response is already being attempted in the world of biblical scholarship, not only in the work of those focusing on narrative, tradition, and community (to which Verhey refers), but also in the work of feminist biblical scholars (e.g. Trible, Schüssler Fiorenza), in the work of liberation biblical scholars (e.g. Croatto), in the work of those who engage in what, for lack of a better word, is termed a sociological approach to the text (e.g. Gottwald, Brueggemann),[2] not to mention the various studies which defy easy labelling but which are published in series such as *Overtures to Biblical Theology*.[3] In addition, recent interpretive studies have outlined hermeneutical responses which endorse specific hermeneutical agenda or advise a particular ethos for interpretation which directly engages our postmodern crisis situation.[4] In short, those involved in biblical studies today are looking for a new hermeneutical context in which to do their scholarship.

In keeping with that search, the organizers of this conference have suggested "an ethos of compassion" as a possible context for our hermeneutical enterprise. I turn now to an evaluation of that suggestion.

Allen Verhey presents us with misgivings about compassion, misgivings which are shared, incidentally, by Oliver O'Donovan in his book *Begotten Or Made?*[5] Both argue that compassion on its own is not enough, that compassion as a feeling is an inadequate basis for action, and hence dismiss it. As Verhey puts it, compassion is insufficient because when it "is exercised in the context of a medicine which is regarded as a marketplace commodity, as value-free skills with which to do the bidding of the one who pays, and when medicine is charged with the awesome task of eliminating suffering and our vulnerability to it" then the result is death (133). What this description makes evident, however, is not that compassion is inappropriate, as Verhey asserts, but that the current cultural definition of compassion is indeed deathly. A scientific value-free context has determined the fruits of modern compassion. With Hauerwas we could say that this *is* a killing compassion. But after death comes resurrection. I want to suggest that compassion needs to be shaped by a different community, a community which is itself shaped by something other than the modern worldview. We need to articulate a vision of compassion which is shaped by the biblical story, by the biblical examples of a compassionate God and a compassionate Christ. What would such a biblical picture be?

It is not too difficult to discover that at the heart of the biblical story we find a God who is compassionate (let me say here that I am not talking about the biblical *idea* of compassion or a biblical *motif* of compassion; I'm talking about the biblical *God*). The confessional statement about God which occurs most often in the Old Testament is this one, quoted here from Exodus 34:6,7: "The Lord, the Lord, a God *compassionate* and gracious, slow to anger and abounding in steadfast love and faithfulness, keeping steadfast love for thousands, forgiving iniquity and transgression and sin, but who by no means will clear the guilty."[6] And the compassion and graciousness of this God is appealed to as a basis for deliverance throughout the Psalms,[7] is the basis for God's remembrance of God's people,[8] is the basis for God's forgiveness,[9] and, perhaps most striking, compassion will be central to the restoration and reconciliation of God with the people of God.[10]

It is no surprise, therefore, to discover that compassion is frequently described as the motivation for Jesus' actions. Jesus had compassion on the crowds, we read in a number of places, and began to heal them, or he had compassion and began to teach them. He had compassion on them because they had gone without food for three days—so he fed them.[11] In two parables which have become definitive in Christian reflection and liturgy, compassion is central. First, in the parable of the Good Samaritan we read that the Samaritan, when he saw the wounded traveller, "had *compassion* and went to him and bound up his wounds ... and brought him to an inn and cared for him" (Luke 10:33-34). Jesus ends this parable with a few simple words: "Go and do you likewise." Similarly in the story of the prodigal son, while the son was still far off the father had *compassion* and ran and embraced him and kissed him (Luke 15:20). In this last parable Jesus makes clear that compassion is at the heart of God's forgiving and loving action towards God's people; in the former parable he makes clear that compassion should be at the heart of the Christian's actions towards others. In the story in which these two parables are grounded, the gospel story of Jesus' death and life again, we see that the motivating compassion not only results in healing and feeding and teaching others, but in a passion which is truly com-passion because it should be *our* passion. That compassion ends in the forgiveness and death which lead to life.

In light of this very quick biblical overview, it is more than evident that to be compassionate is to be God-like, to bear the image of God as revealed in Jesus the Christ.[12] In God and Jesus the very compassion we are to practice is defined as a compassion not which feels sorry and acts unthinkingly (which O'Donovan and Verhey critique) but which is a suffering with, a suffering for,[13] which results in faithfulness, forgiveness, reconciliation, healing, new life.

In light of this we see that Verhey's own conclusions are better than the misgivings he has about compassion—for his picture of a wounded healer who suffers with the one she heals has many similarities with the picture of compassion we have outlined above (see Verhey 146-47).

An ethos of compassion, then, seems to provide a solid, biblically based ethos in light of which we may undertake our hermeneutical enterprise. But before I go on to outline how an ethos of compassion speaks to biblical hermeneutics, and especially to the problems which Verhey raises in his paper regarding the diversity, strangeness and abuse of Scripture, I would like to point out that while compassion is *essential*, it is true that it isn't *enough*. An ethos of compassion which is biblically shaped needs to be directed by something, needs to be striving for and constrained by a good creation. To put it in terms of this conference, an ethos of compassion needs the integrity of creation.

Let me give meaning to the terms "integrity of creation" and "ethos of compassion" in relation to biblical hermeneutics by addressing three of the four problems which Verhey describes as inhibiting our use of Scripture—they are the diversity of Scripture, the strangeness of Scripture, and the abuse of scripture.[14]

First, the diversity of Scripture. How does the integrity of creation affect the fact that the book which is our Scripture speaks to us in many voices, in diverse ways and through various speakers? The integrity of creation should result in an acknowledgement of the integrity of the biblical text. In this context that means that we should acknowledge the importance of the various biblical voices; we should realize that these voices need each other. We should realize that the story of Abraham and Sarah's cruel treatment of Hagar is not complete without the story of the enterprising Moabite Ruth and the tender care Boaz shows towards her.[15] We should realize that knowing God as father is incomplete without knowing God as a mother who cannot help but nourish her children, as the one who groans with the pain of her creation and people.[16] We should realize that the descriptions of Israel's cultic life are incomplete without the prophetic call for mercy rather than sacrifice.[17]

An acknowledgement of the integrity of this diversity which is itself rooted in an ethos of *compassion* should shape our attitude towards such diversity, should make us struggle with it, should give us the freedom to suffer the ambiguity and the tensions which are central to the text. In short, the integrity of creation and an ethos of compassion should give us the grace to acknowledge that although we may not like the "other" emphases, we need not only to acknowledge them but also to struggle with them not only in our mind but in our heart and soul.

Scripture, however, isn't only diverse. It is also "strange." It is a two-thousand year old document from a near eastern culture. It doesn't seem to be on our wavelength in places. This means, of course, that in addition to recognizing the integrity of the text, we also need to respect the integrity of our own cultural situation; we need consciously to read this text in terms of our own cultural needs and times. We bridge the chasm of strangeness by consciously creating a dialogue within our communities between the text and our own cultural needs. Such a dialogue is unlikely to occur without conflict and struggle.[18] Perhaps this means in a twentieth century postmodern culture that we look around at the incredible destruction and suffering that we have created and we read this text in terms of that situation. When we read the text in that context, we realize that (in Gilkey's terms) we are no longer reading the text in order to defend ourselves against secular challenges emanating from this culture, but in order to provide succor to a culture in travail.[19]

When we engage in such a dialogue within the context of an ethos of compassion, we should be able to acknowledge and correct sympathetically, rather than merely ignore or judge, the various cultural limitations which have shaped this text and which shape us. But more than that, an ethos of compassion should ensure that the dialogue we engage in between text and culture is not merely an intellectual exercise but rather a dialogue in which we suffer through and struggle with the tensions between the text and our culture, one where we profoundly identify with the malaise of our culture. In that profound identification we may perhaps finally be vulnerable enough to hear the biblical word of hope.

The last problem associated with the use of Scripture in Verhey's case study is that of the abuse of Scripture. Abuse is a violent act of control, often born out of insecurity. In the context of postmodernity, where little seems secure, abuse, including abuse of Scripture, is rampant. We ourselves are likely to come to this text with our own "latent value-conflicts and power-complexes" (to use the phrase of Matthew Lamb).[20] No matter how much we respect the strangeness and the diversity of this text, it is still possible that we may interpret the text in an abusive way. A hermeneutic which acknowledges the integrity of creation and an ethos of compassion speaks to this problem also, I believe.

First of all, the integrity of creation implies that we acknowledge that this text, in all its strangeness and diversity, has a message to communicate,[21] and hence has a specific function. The message of the Bible seeks to evoke a new social possibility, to change hearts and lives, to create a community of reconciliation and compassion.[22] A hermeneutic which does not enable this new social possibility is a hermeneutic which does not respect the function of the text and is likely to be abusive.

But acknowledging the function of the text is not all that is necessary to protect the integrity of the text from abuse. We also need to acknowledge the integrity of the text in its written form. It is here that methods such as historical-criticism, form-criticism, and rhetorical-criticism, alongside narrative and literary analyses of the text, provide a valuable service. An interpretation which results in a new social possibility may in itself be an abuse of the text if it does not respect the actual argument of the text, the context of the passage, the flow of the narrative or song with which we are dealing. The integrity of both the text's form and function provide a safeguard against abuse.

Moreover, biblical interpretation which occurs within an ethos of compassion acknowledges that a text which is diverse and strange has many possible interpretations. The violent control of the text which insists on only one right interpretation is countered within a compassionate ethos which is already struggling with the diversity of the text and its appropriation in our culture. An ethos of compassion provides a context where the integrity of the text has a certain sensitive flexibility. This is a flexibility which is limited by the text itself and its call to shape a community modelled on the crucified messiah.[23]

The hermeneutic I have just outlined acknowledges the integrity of the text and the challenges it provides, as well as the integrity of our situation and the problems it raises, and tries compassionately to suffer through the tension created by the two. Such a hermeneutic, I would argue, is appropriate for a people who image a God who is in relationship with God's people and world. In that relationship, on the cross and in the Spirit, God is torn by these very same tensions.

Notes

1. Cf. Werner G. Jeanrond, *Theological Hermeneutics: Development and Significance* (London: MacMillan, 1992), 172.

2. Phyllis Trible, *God and the Rhetoric of Sexuality* (Philadelphia: Fortress, 1978); Trible, *Texts of Terror: Literary-Feminist Readings of Biblical Narratives* (Philadelphia: Fortress, 1984); Elisabeth Schüssler Fiorenza, *In Memory of Her: A Feminist Theological Construction of Christian Origins* (New York: Crossroad, 1984); J. Severino Croatto, *Exodus: A Hermeneutics of Freedom* (Maryknoll, NY: Orbis, 1981); Norman K. Gottwald, *The Tribes of Yahweh* (Maryknoll, NY: Orbis, 1979); Gottwald, "Social Matrix and Canonical Shape," *Theology Today* 42 (1985): 307-21; Walter Brueggemann, *Hope within History* (Atlanta: John Knox Press, 1987); Bruggemann, *The Prophetic Imagination* (Philadelphia: Fortress Press, 1986); Brueggemann, *Israel's Praise: Doxology against Idolatry and Ideology* (Philadelphia: Fortress Press, 1988); Brueggemann, *Interpretation and Obedience: From Faithful Reading to Faithful Living* (Minneapolis: Fortress, 1991). On narrative, tradition and community see also Richard B. Hays, *Echoes of Scripture in the Letters of Paul* (New Haven & London: Yale University Press, 1989); N. Thomas Wright, *The New Testament and the People of God* (Minneapolis: Fortress, 1992); Marcus Borg, *Jesus: A New Vision* (San Francisco: Harper and Row, 1987); James A. Sanders, *From Sacred Story to Sacred Text* (Philadelphia: Fortress 1987).

3. Published by Fortress Press. A few representative works are the two by Trible in note 2 above; Fretheim in note 6 below; Walter Brueggemann, *The Land* (1977); Dale Patrick, *The Rendering of God in the Old Testament* (1981); Beverly Roberts Gaventa, *From Darkness to Light* (1986); Charles B. Cousar, *A Theology of the Cross: The Death of Jesus in the Pauline Letters (1990).*

4. E.g., J. W. Rogerson, " 'What Does it Mean to be Human?' The Central Question of Old Testament Theology?" in *The Bible in Three Dimensions*, David J. A. Clines, Stephen E. Fowl, and Stanley E. Porter, eds. (Sheffield: JSOT Press, 1991), 285-98; Gerald West, "Reading 'The Text' and Reading 'Behind the Text': The Cain and Abel Story in the Context of Liberation" in *The Bible in Three Dimensions,* 299-318; J. B. Metz, "Theology in the New Paradigm: Political Theology" in *Paradigm Change in Theology,* Hans Kung and David Tracy, eds., Margaret Kohl, trans. (Edinburgh: T&T Clark, 1989) 355-66; David Tracy, "Some Concluding Reflections on the Conference: Unity Amidst Diversity and Conflict?" in *Paradigm Change in Theology,* esp. 463; Jeanrond, 162-80; Walter Brueggemann, *Interpretation and Obedience: From Faithful Reading to Faithful Living* (Minneapolis: Fortress, 1991) esp. chs. 1, 5, 6; Breuggemann, *Texts Under Negotiation: The Bible and Postmodern Imagination* (Minneapolis: Fortress Press, 1993); Chris Rowland, "Open Thy Mouth For the Dumb," An Inaugural Address delivered at Oxford University, 11 May 1992 (Oxford University Press, forthcoming); Elisabeth Schüssler Fiorenza, "The Ethics of Biblical Interpretation: Decentering Biblical Scholarship" (1987 SBL Presidential Address) *JBL* 107/1 (1988): 3-17. Although the Reformed tradition has acknowledged the need for the application of the Bible to our present time (see 'Report on Hermeneutics and Ethics' published by the Reformed Ecumenical Council [Grand Rapids, 1990], 2), the accepted ethos in this tradition is one which emphasizes "doctrine and characteristic lifestyle" (10).

5. Oxford: Clarendon Press, 1984, 10f.

6. See also Neh. 9:17,32; Ps. 86:15; 103:8; 111:4; 112:4; Joel 2:13; Jonah 4:2. Also Terence E. Fretheim, _The Suffering of God: An Old Testament Perspective_ (Philadelphia: Fortress, 1984), 25f; R. Denton, "The Literary Affinities of Exodus 34:6f," _Vetus Testamentum_ 13 (1963): 34-51. Also on the compassion of God see Trible, _God and the Rhetoric of Sexuality_, 38-59.

7. E.g., Psalm 40:11; 51:1; 69:16; 77:9; 79:8; 102:13; also Isa. 63:15-16.

8. E.g., Deut. 4:31; 2 Kings 13:23.

9. E.g., Psalm 78:38; 1 Kings 8:50; Micah 7:19; Hosea 2:21,23; Isa. 49:13; and most of the biblical references in n. 6 above.

10. Hos. 2:19; Zech. 1:16; cf. Zech. 12:10.

11. Healing: Matt. 14:14; 20:34; cf. Mark 1:41; Luke 7:13. Teaching: Mark 6:34. Feeding: Matt. 15:32/Mark 8:2.

12. See also Rom. 12:1; 2 Cor. 1:3; Phil. 1:8; 2:1; Col. 3:18; 1 John 3:17.

13. On the suffering of God with and for the people of God see Fretheim, _The Suffering of God_.

14. For the purposes of this response, I have considered the fourth problem which Verhey raises—the silence of Scripture—to be a sub-set of the strangeness of Scripture. It hence will not receive separate treatment.

15. On these passages see Trible, _God and the Rhetoric of Sexuality,_ ch. 6.

16. See e.g., Hosea 11:3-4; Deut. 32:10-12, 18; Isa. 42:14-17; Rom. 8:22-26. On female biblical imagery for God see Trible, _God and the Rhetoric of Sexuality_, especially chs. 2 and 3.

17. See e.g., Amos 5:21-24; Micah 6:6-8; Isaiah 1:12-23; 5:1-7; 58:1-14.

18. See Paul Ricoeur, "Response to Josef Blank" in _Paradigm Change in Theology_, 285. On the dialogue between the biblical text and our modern situation see: Croatto, 3; David Tracy, "Hermeneutical Reflections in the New Paradigm" in _Paradigm Change in Theology_, 39f; Jeanrond, 1; James H. Olthuis, _A Hermeneutics of Ultimacy: Promise or Peril?_ (Lanham, MD: University Press of America/Toronto: Institute for Christian Studies, 1987), 35f; Anthony Thiselton, "On Models and Methods: A Conversation with Robert Morgan" in _The Bible in Three Dimensions_, 348; Frank Kermode, "Secrets and Narrative Sequence" in _On Narrative_, W. J. T. Mitchell, ed. (Chicago and London: University of Chicago Press, 1981), 82; Walter Wink, _The Bible in Human Transformation: Toward a New Paradigm for Biblical Study_ (Philadelphia: Fortress Press, 1973), 43f; H. Baarlink et al., "Report on Hermeneutics and Ethics" (Grand Rapids: Reformed Ecumenical Council, 1990), 2, 18-20. See also J. A. Draper, " 'For the Kingdom is inside of you and it is outside of you,' Contextual Exegesis in South Africa" in _Text and Interpretation: New Approaches to the Criticism of the New Testament_, P. J. Hartin and J. H. Petzer, eds. (Leiden: E. J. Brill, 1991), 243: "It is only when we read the Bible in our own specific context that the many meanings it could have are narrowed down into a specific meaning." I have decided to risk talking about "meaning" in spite of the current trend to dismiss "meaning" in favour of "different interpretive interests." See most recently Stephen Fowl, "The Ethics of Interpretation or What's Left Over After the Elimination of Meaning" in *The Bible in Three Dimensions*, 379-98.

19. Langdon Gilkey, "The Paradigm Shift in Theology" in *Paradigm Change in Theology*, 379. Schüssler Fiorenza in "Ethics of Biblical Interpretation," 14f, advocates the necessity of a double ethics in reading: an *ethics of historical reading* (i.e., what sort of readings do justice to the text in its historical contexts) and *an ethics of accountability* (which stands responsible for the ethical consequences of the biblical text and its meanings); italics in the original.

20. Matthew L. Lamb, "The Dialectics of Theory and Praxis within Paradigm Analysis" in *Paradigm Change in Theology*, 79. James Olthuis refers to the "emotional anxieties and hidden desires" which shape our reading of the text in Olthuis, 37.

21. Francis Young, *The Art of Performance: Towards a Theology of Holy Scripture* (London: Darton, Longman and Todd, 1990), 19. See also Olthuis, 37f.

22. See further on this Walter Brueggemann, "Imagination as a Mode of Fidelity" in *Understanding the Word: Essays in Honour of B. W. Anderson,* James T. Butler, Edgar W. Conrad, and Ben Ollenberger, eds. (JSOT Supp 37; Sheffield: JSOT Press, 1985), 30; Wink, 61, 73; Hays, 154-92.

23. See Hays 154-92.

When Is "Against Nature"
Against Nature?

Calvin B. DeWitt

Introduction

In this time of increased environmental awareness, and growing understanding of the workings of the earth at all levels, from the energy transfer functions of the biosphere to wetlands to individual species, there is increased interest in working in accord with nature rather than against it. This interest is being heightened greatly by our growing knowledge of major environmental degradations of the biosphere and the widening recognition of their human causes. We human beings are informed by scientists, and even by the earth itself, that our activities may be tearing at the fabric of the very biosphere that is our planetary home. We have become interested in working with nature rather than against it.

And so a number of questions are becoming relevant to us. How do we know when what we are doing is working "with nature?" And when is what we are doing working "against nature?" Or, as stated in the title of this paper, "When is 'against nature' against nature?" But our response to this question is one that, while perhaps compatible with that of the secular world, must be fully informed by Christian biblical teaching, rooted in acknowledgement of God as creator.

God as Creator and Creation's Testimony

In the Reformed and Christian tradition, and in keeping with the Scriptures, we profess that God is the creator of all things, and that God is a just and right God whose creation itself thus has integrity and rightness, so much so that God can repeatedly declare creation to be "good" and "very good."[1] Beyond God's declaration of creation's goodness, we in this tradition also profess that the creation itself gives such testimony that all human beings are left without excuse but to know God's divinity and everlasting power;[2] that creation itself proclaims God's glory in a powerful and pervasive speech, that while not human speech, yet goes out through all the the earth.[3] Creation's testimony not only proclaims God's divinity, everlasting power, and glory, but also declares God's everlasting care and provision for God's creatures as the creator waters the earth and provides creatures their food and habitat.[4] God not only creates all things, God also has compassion for the creatures.

God's Sovereign Goodness and Compassion

But this is not to say that God's goodness and creation's goodness is "goodiness" or that God's compassion is weak and servile, that God's compassion is subservient or obeisant. As creator and sustainer of all things God is sovereign. Thus God is compassionate as God wills, giving food to the creatures thereby giving them life, withholding their food with resultant death.[5] God's compassion is sovereign compassion.[6]

God's Justice and Wrath

God's sovereign compassion does not stand by itself, for God is more than compassionate. Blatant and flaunting human disregard of the creator's justice in society and creation—of the works of the Lord and what his hands have done[7]—may bring not God's compassion, but God's wrath. As creator and sustainer of all things God is sovereign; and God's wrath also is sovereign. Violation of God's justice may bring the antithesis of compassion, it may bring God's sovereign wrath and anger.[8] And since God is God of creation, the expression of this anger can range from a direct blow to an individual violator to the enlistment of creatures and creation to bring impact upon a whole society.[9] God's sovereign compassion is balanced by God's sovereign wrath. While sympathetically conscious of the discomfort of the creatures and having a loving desire to alleviate it,[10] God also is jealous and protective of the integrity of creation and of God's sovereign justice.[11]

God's Good Pleasure

Thus our compassionate God does not only administer compassion; God also administers justice. But beyond God's compassion and justice is God's pleasure and glory. Thus in God's good creation great storms are generated that, coming in from the sea, tear apart the forests, shake the mountains, and frighten the forest creatures—expressing God's sovereign power so magnificently that the heavenly beings respond with "Glory!"[12] As the song conveys, "And for thy pleasure they were created. Thou art worthy, O Lord!" The Lord is enthroned as sovereign forever, giving strength to God's people and blessing them with peace.

God's compassion, justice, and pleasure: these are expressed in God's work in the world—in the world that God loves. These are important aspects of the context in which we consider all that God has made, God's and creation's goodness, and the integrity of creation. These also are important aspects of the context in which we consider all that human beings have done, both for and against nature.

Reformulation of the Question

And this brings us to our question, "When is 'against nature' against nature?" First, we cannot be satisfied with this formulation of the question, even though we understand why it may be formulated this way by many. Professing that God is the creator of all things, we acknowledge as creation all God has made. And thus, we might reformulate our question as "When is 'against nature' against God's creation?" Or, professing that God is just and right, through whom creation thus has integrity and rightness, we can ask "When are our actions and inactions in creation contrary to the integrity of creation?" Going beyond this, we might reformulate our question as "When are our actions in the world in contradiction to the will of the creator and sustainer of all things?" In so doing, of course, we broaden the scope of the question from "nature" to "creation," thereby assuring inclusion of all creatures and their interrelationships—including human creatures—and we elevate the question from the level of "creation" to the level of "creator."

Discernment between the Integrity and Degradation of Creation

"When are our actions and inactions in creation contrary to the integrity of creation?" or "When is 'against nature' against nature?" Implicit in both these formulations is that human beings are capable of acting contrary to nature and creation. This we find confirmed in history[13] and by present-day observations. Also implicit in these questions is the assumption that "nature is right," or "creation is right." Again, from a Christian and Reformed perspective, we can say that nature and creation are right insofar as they reflect the rightness and goodness of their compassionate and just creator. But not everything we see reflects such rightness and goodness. Human beings have decided to go their own way, transforming a good creation to meet selfish ends.[14] And so, what we see around us is both creation in its integrity and creation degraded by people in pursuit of selfish ends. And this points up the important problem of discernment between what constitutes integrity and what constitutes degradation; it raises the problem of what comprises the benchmark of creation-with-integrity (of nature undegraded) from which we can measure creation's degradation—the "nature" against which we can judge if a given human action is "against nature."

Integrity of Creation

Creation's Teaching of its Own Integrity

Even though we often behave as though our understanding of nature and creation comes from textbooks, the ultimate source of the understanding of nature and creation, as given in our secular textbooks, is nature and creation. This of course follows from what is done in scientific research. It is through such research that nature and creation are observed, are given tentative explanations, are used as the observational base against we test these explanations and, insofar as they are not contradicted by our observations, nor by accumulated scientific knowledge, are ultimately described in our textbooks and papers. Nature and creation in this sense are our teachers, with textbooks and professors as translating intermediaries. Knowledge thus derived from nature and creation is critical to understanding how the world works. And understanding how the world works is foundational to answering our question, "When is 'against nature' against nature?"

The Bible's Teaching of Creation's Integrity

In the Christian and Reformed perspective, both the creation and the Scriptures are foundational for understanding how the world works, what constitutes the integrity of creation, what is "in accord with nature and creation." The scriptural and creedal formulation of these things, however, is elevated above nature and creation to the level of the creator[15] of all things, whose justice, compassion, and glory provide the context for the goodness and integrity of creation and the context for living in obedience and gratitude to God. Thus from this perspective, to "live in accord with nature" is to walk rightly in God's creation, to do the will of the one through whom all things are created and sustained. For us in this tradition to determine what is "against nature" is to determine what is "against God's will"— against the will of creation's creator and sustainer.

But the Scriptures teach us more. They teach us that God loves the world, despises human-wrought injustice and degradation in creation, desires restoration and renewal, and sacrificially and compassionately gives of self to restore and reconcile all things.[16] The one through whom and for whom the world was made,[17] responding to degradation of creation by human creatures, is given by God as redeemer and reconciler—given to make all things right again. And thus, what is "against nature" not only is what is "against God's will" as creator and sustainer, it also is what is "against God's will" as reconciler—"reconciler of all things to himself."

When, then, is "against nature" against nature? In the view of the Bible, it is when it is against God's will as creator, sustainer and reconciler. When is "in accord with nature" in accord with nature? A Mennonite carpenter pastor friend of mine puts it this way, "We should so behave on earth that heaven will not be a shock to us!"

Specific Challenges to Creation's Integrity

But this only partially gets us to where we want to be. We have made some broad strokes in dealing with the question, "When is 'against nature' against nature?" But we still are some distance from being able to answer this question with regard to the issues that confront us today, such as: Is tropospheric ozone depletion against nature—against God's will for creation? Soil erosion and desertification? Destruction of tropical rain forests? Species extinction? Groundwater pollution? Global toxification? Human and cultural degradation?

Responding to Creation's Degradation

Secular Response to Creation's Degradation

The secular world of informed and disciplined natural science has an answer to these questions (sometimes to the surprise of Christians). More specifically, environmental scientists who make it their business to study biospheric and planetary processes and who investigate environmental degradations not only have answers, but answers with which they are largely in agreement. Contrary to what might be conveyed in the media and "gray literature," the content of the primary scientific literature shows a remarkable consensus on the nature and scope of environmental degradation.[18] But beyond mere answers, these scientists are calling for cessation and reversal of these degradations. They are by their statements and actions declaring such degradations not merely to be scientifically interesting, but to be wrong—to be (in the jargon of this paper) "against nature." Curiously, not only are environmental scientists telling us that our world is in critical shape but also that people are chiefly to blame for it.[19] And it is in response to this determination that *The Joint Appeal by Religion and Science for the Environment* proclaims,

> We humans are endowed with self-awareness, intelligence and compassion. At our best, we cherish and seek to protect all life and the treasures of the natural world. But we are now tampering with the climate. We are thinning the ozone layer and creating holes in it. We are poisoning the air, the land and the water. We are destroying the forests, grasslands and other ecosystems. We are causing the extinction of species at a pace not seen since the end of the age of the dinosaurs. As a result, many scientific projections suggest a legacy for our children and grandchildren of compromised immune systems, increased infectious disease and cancer rates, destroyed plants and consequent disruption of the food chain, agriculture damaged from drought and ultraviolet light, accelerated destruction of forests and species, and vastly increased numbers of environmental refugees. Many perils may be still undiscovered. The burdens, as usual, will fall most cruelly upon the shoulders of the poorest among us, especially upon children. But no one will be unaffected. At the same time, the human community grows by a quarter of a million people every day, mostly in the poorest nations and communities. That this crisis was brought about in part through inadvertence does not excuse us. Many nations are responsible. The magnitude of this crisis means that it cannot be resolved unless many nations work together. We must now join forces to that end.[20]

How is it that, without reference to the Scriptures or some other moral code, such a statement can be made with full concurrence of scientists, including those who are agnostic or atheistic? It comes from an understanding of the world itself, and more particularly an understanding of its integrity. The integrity of creation is everywhere apparent, perhaps more so to natural scientists than to many others, since it is because of this repeatedly demonstrated integrity that science is made possible. Everything is found to be consistent with everything else, so much so that Einstein, in objecting to some new theory that was inconsistent with creation's integrity, is able to say, "Raffiniert ist der Herrgott aber boschaft ist Er nicht,"[21] thereby affirming creation's lofty integrity.

Biblical Response to Creation's Degradation

The Bible also has an answer to the problems of environmental degradation. While this is surprising to some, it should not be, given the fact that many human cultures based upon the Bible have stood the test of time and thus have likely been appropriately informed on how to live rightly on the earth. The root cause of the problems we are facing are not new; people, we learn from the Scriptures, long ago decided to go their own way, to cut out on their own, to their own and creation's ultimate detriment. And the Bible calls them back to live lives of integrity, obedience, and compassion—it urges their return to ecological soundness and integrity.

Of the many teachings of the Scriptures, some stand out for their ecological and environmental importance. To pursue these biblical teachings is to contribute towards doing God's will in creation, for the integrity of creation. To do otherwise is to be "against nature." In my listing of these below, the beginning italicized statement of each principle is given in a form that may be evaluated and adopted by all people irrespective of their religious or irreligious tradition.[22] This is followed by direct references to the Scriptures.

1. **Reflection**—*As we are kept through the provisions of land, air, energy flows, and water, so must we keep the earth. People and others do not merely occupy an ecosystem, but are integral parts who contribute to and benefit from its nurture. People must mirror this nurture in their care for creation.*

This Reflection Principle (or Keeping Principle) is a long-standing one. In the Torah, the Aaronic blessing, "The Lord bless you and keep you ..." (Numbers 6:24-26) uses the same word for "keep" (*shamar*) as is used in God's stated purpose for human beings: to keep and take care of (*shamar*) the Garden (Genesis 2:15). Re-enforcing this is use of the Hebrew word *abad* in Genesis 2:15 (to serve, e.g., to till), translated as "to work" in the New International Version. In the Geneva Bible (1560) Genesis 2:15 is given, "Then the Lord God toke the man, and put him into the garden of Eden, that he might dresse it and kepe it."[23] The "dominion passage" (Genesis 1:26-28) can be seen as supporting this principle, by observing that dominion ceases if that which is ruled is destroyed; furthermore this passage describes people as imaging God who is the one who "makes springs pour water into the ravines.... They give water to all the beasts of the field.... The birds of the air nest by the waters; they sing among its branches.... The earth is satisfied by the fruit of his work" (Psalm 104:10-13). Thus, we can conclude, the earth should also be satisfied by the fruit of human work. The concept of dominion as service (*abad* in Genesis 2:15) is reinforced in the Christian tradition (Philippians 2:5-8).

2. **Leadership**—*We must follow those who work to prevent and reverse the work of creation's destroyers, who work to preserve and restore creation's integrity. People relate differently to creation: some vandalize it by intent or degrade it by making and*

accumulating things—careless of destroying the homes and breaking the lineages of biotic species; a few people are benign; and some preserve, restore, and nurture ecosystems of which they are part. It is the last of these types that promote ecosystem and species continuity; it is these we should emulate.

The Leadership Principle in the Christian tradition can be stated as "We must be disciples of the Last Adam, not of the First Adam." This comes from the teaching that people are part of a lineage that has fallen short of the glory of God (Romans 3:23). "But," affirms this Scripture, "Christ has indeed been raised from the dead.... As in Adam all die, so in Christ all will be made alive" (1 Corinthians 15:20-22). The importance of this comes clear in that it is through him that all things are reconciled (Colossians 1:19-20). As disciples of the one, "by whom all things were made, and through whom all things hold together," (John 1:3; Colossians 1:16-17) people participate in undoing the work of the first Adam, bringing restoration and reconciliation to *all things*, doing the tasks the First Adam failed to accomplish (cf. John 1 and Colossians 1; 1 Corinthians 15 and Romans 5; Isaiah 43:18-21, Isaiah 65 and Colossians 1:19-20, 5:17-21).

3. **Fruitfulness**—*We may enjoy the fruits of creation but not degrade or destroy its self-reproducing or self-sustaining fruitfulness. While acceptable to gain sustenance from the creation's fruits, it is wrong to destroy its ability to be fruitful—to destroy its ability to reproduce plants and animals after their kinds and its restorative and self-sustaining capacity. Over-exploitation or disregard for the household of life is wrong; so is human fruitfulness pursued at the expense of other creatures.*

The Fruitfulness Principle clearly distinguishes between fruit and fruitfulness. The book of Genesis relates how the abundant gifts and fruitfulness of God's creation did not satisfy; in their pressing creation, the fruitfulness of creation may be degraded or destroyed. Ezekiel warns, "Is it not enough for you to feed on the good pasture? Must you also trample the rest of your pasture with your feet? Is it not enough for you to drink clear water? Must you also muddy the rest with your feet?" (Ezekiel 34:18; see also Deuteronomy 20:19 and 22:6-7). As people are expected to be fruitful, so is the rest of creation: "Let the water teem with living creatures, and let birds fly above the earth and across the expanse of the sky.... Be fruitful and increase in number and fill the water in the seas, and let the birds increase on the earth" (Gen. 1:20-21). With these words, the creator lavishes blessing upon the creatures, calling forth their fruitfulness, providing blessed impetus to their biological and ecological development, and divinely empowering them to bring fulfilling completeness to the earth. And thus Isaiah warns: "Woe to you who add house to house and join field to field till no space is left and you live alone in the land" (Isaiah 5:8). Expansion of human developments may not be at the expense of fruitfulness of the rest of creation. Moreover, people are expected to prevent extinction of the creatures, both economic and uneconomic, even at tremendous cost, as in the case of Noah (Genesis 6:9-9:17).

4. **Restoration**—*We must not press creation relentlessly, but allow for its self-sustaining, self-controlling, and developmental functions to operate fully. Providing rest for ourselves and other creatures permits continuation of ecosystem homeostasy—its self-sustaining means to achieve its development and maintain integrity. Providing rest liberates the restorative and regenerative provisions of creation to make all things new.*

The Restoration Principle for those traditions that respect the Torah (Judaism, Islam, and Christianity) can be stated: "We must not press creation relentlessly, but must provide for its Sabbath rests." The Torah teaches that, as human beings and animals are to be given their sabbaths, so also must the land be given its sabbath rests (Exodus 23:10-12). People, land, and creatures must not be relentlessly pressured. "If you follow my decrees ... I will send you rain in its season, and the ground will yield its crops and the trees of the field their fruit" (Leviticus 26:3). Otherwise, the land will be laid waste, only then to "have the rest it did not have during the sabbaths you lived in it" (Leviticus 26:34-35)!

The Report of the Pre-Assembly Consultation on Subtheme I, "Giver of Life—Sustain Your Creation!" held at Kuala Lumpur, Malaysia,[24] makes an important contribution to this principle:

> At Kuala Lumpur, we discovered that our theological work gives rise to a new vision— yet one with ancient roots imbedded in the biblical tradition—concerning the pathways to a hopeful and sustainable future for the world.... Out of the rich variety of biblical material, beginning with Genesis and ending with Revelation, that could guide our vision we would like to draw special attention to the concept of *Shabbat* (the Sabbath), Sabbatical and Jubilee Year.... On *Shabbat*, all divisions, separations and hierarchies among human beings are relinquished and an integral community of resting, adoring, and worshipping is established which also comprises non-human life.... *Shabbat* reminds us that time, the realm of being, is not just a commodity, but has a quality of holiness, which resists our impulse to control, command, and oppress. In Genesis 2, God's creation does not culminate in the creation of human beings but in the rest of *Shabbat* and in contemplation and appreciation of all. This close unity of social and ecological reconciliation, restoration, and renewal becomes even more clear in the concepts of Sabbatical and Jubilee Year. In the seventh year, even the earth can rest, poor and wild beasts can eat from it, whereas slaves are freed. In the 50th year, however, this vision of an overall eco-social restoration is extended to the land: a redistribution of land property and an overall liberation is meant to re-create a just and equitable society (Exodus 23; Leviticus 25). Thus, the biblical concept of *Shabbat* joins social justice to environmental stewardship, and law to mercy, to create a model of harmony for all spheres of life.

5. **Precedence**—*We must seek first the wholeness and integrity of creation, not self-interest. Whatever is gained for self should come as a result of caring for and keeping*

the creation—of diligent working to preserve and restore creation's integrity. Pursuit of material things as first priority will impoverish creation, reducing creation's wealth, making us poorer. Seeking creation's integrity first brings sustainable wealth.

The Precedence Principle (or Priority Principle) is expressed in the Christian tradition in its most widely-used prayer: "This, then, is how you should pray: 'Our Father in heaven, hallowed be your name, your kingdom come, your will be done on earth....' " (Matthew 6:9-10). The Scriptures show how tempting it is to follow the example of those who accumulate great gain to creation's detriment. But they also assure people: "Trust in the Lord and do good; dwell in the land and enjoy safe pasture.... Those who hope in the Lord will inherit the land" (Psalm 37; Matthew 5:5). Obtaining food, water and clothing—fulfillment of human needs—is a *consequence*, not of seeking these things directly, but of seeking God's kingdom (Matthew 6:33).

6. **Contentment**—*We must seek to maximize contentment, not material gains, and be able to discern the difference. It is not right to have so little food and clothing that we are in jeopardy; thus we should work for these basic needs, moving us toward contentment. But as we move along the spectrum from nothing to more and more, we must not pass the point of contentment or we will degrade human beings, others, and all creation. All we have is procured from creation; seeking more than what provides contentment degrades creation; an important measure of true wealth is the richness of creation itself.*

The Contentment Principle is supported by the prayer "Turn my heart to your statutes and not toward selfish gain" (Psalm 119:36) and by description of what constitutes true human gain: "... godliness with contentment" (1 Timothy 6:6-21; also see Hebrews 13:5). This is set against the biblical observation that the fruitfulness, grace, and gifts of creation did not satisfy (Genesis 3-11), resulting in disobedience to the law, doing creation "one better," making things "bigger than life."

The Report of the Pre-Assembly Consultation on Subtheme I, "Giver of Life—Sustain Your Creation!"[25] puts it this way:

> This includes a new vision of community and sharing. Stories like those of the *manna* in the desert (Exodus 16) tell us that the bread distributed for need and not by greed is the only bread that can sustain life. We sincerely believe that the food we eat while our neighbor is hungry, and the wealth we consume at the expense of others, separate us from the realm of life and have self-destroying effects. Our vision is that those with enough material goods start to look for fulfillment in spiritual life, and that those having economic and political power make decisions based on the needs of all of creation, leading to a fuller life for all.

7. **Action**—*We must not fail to act on what we know is right. There must be integrity—wholeness and oneness—between our knowledge and our actions. Knowledge of the right does no good unless put into practice. Knowledge of ecosystem science, conservation, and stewardship is meaningless if it is merely accumulated and not acted out. The test of human quality is not in our knowing; it is on what we do with what we know. It is the degree to which we use knowledge for perpetuation and restoration of creation's integrity.*

The Action Principle is supported by scriptural teaching that knowing God's requirements for stewardship is not enough; hearing, discussing, singing, and contemplating the Scriptures is insufficient. They must be practiced, or they do absolutely no good. The hard saying of Scripture is this: We hear from our neighbors, "Come and hear the message that has come from the Lord." And they come, "but they do not put them into practice. With their mouths they express devotion, but their hearts are greedy for unjust gain. Indeed, to them you are nothing more than one who sings love songs with a beautiful voice and plays an instrument well, for they hear your words but do not put them into practice" (Ezekiel 33:30-32; see also Luke 6:46-49).

Summarizing Statements

These teachings are reflected in the summarizing statement of Aldo Leopold's secular classic, "A Land Ethic,"[26] and also in a statement from a meeting of scientists, theologians and fourth-world people at Kuala Lumpur, as follows:[27]

When is a thing right?

A thing is right when it tends to preserve the integrity, stability, and beauty of the biotic community. It is wrong when it tends otherwise.

What is just, what is right, is that which maintains the integrity of the ecosystem—that which maintains the social, biological and physical components and their inter-relationships. Development that degrades any of these components or their inter-relationships, fosters injustice. Thus, injustice done by people to people degrades the ecosystem; injustice done by people to plants or animals also degrades the ecosystem. In any such degradation the whole, and eventually every part, suffers.

When is "against nature" against nature?

When it erodes the integrity, stability, and beauty of the biotic community. (Leopold)

When it fails to maintain the integrity of the ecosystem—fails to maintain the social, biological and physical components and their inter-relationships. Development that degrades any of these components or their inter-relationships, fosters injustice and is "against nature." Injustice done by people to people degrades the ecosystem; injustice done by people to plants or animals also degrades the ecosystem. In any such degradation the whole, and eventually every part, suffers, and thus is "against nature." (Kuala Lumpur)

When Is "Against Nature" Against Nature: Some Practical Illustrations

Forsaking Innocence

When we choose to leave the Garden we commit ourselves to having to know the world. In the early chapters of Genesis human beings are described in their innocence, innocently eating the good fruit, innocently relating to each other and to their Maker, innocently serving and keeping the Garden. Such innocence does not require knowledge of floods, landslides, volcanoes, and geological faults; such innocence does not require knowledge of pests, disease, hunger, and poverty; such innocence does not require knowledge of pollution, toxification and extinction.

The Need to Know How the World Works

Need for Knowledge of Good and Evil

But the choice to go one's own way, "to do creation one better," "to make things bigger than life," brings with it the need for new knowledge—the knowledge of good and evil. Failure to achieve this knowledge in a world of lost innocence and of banishment from the protective and nurturing Garden portends dis-ease, degradation, and disaster—for ourselves and for the systems we affect. Once in harmony with nature's Garden there was no need to know what was "against nature." Once having disharmoniously left the Garden for the world of floods, pests, and pollution, there was need for immensely greater knowledge—of resuscitation, eradication, purification; of creeping slopes, condoms, and toxification.

We human beings have chosen, and continue to choose not to be innocent, and like it or not, we now must learn to know both good and evil.

If we do not gain such knowledge, we find ourselves spreading our residences and businesses across the flood plains of rivers whose very character and position guarantees flooding; cultivating the land and monoculturing our crops in such a manner that we convert otherwise harmonious creatures into pests; and concentrating our wastes in such quantities and locations that assure pollution and fouling of our own habitats.

If we do not gain such knowledge, we find ourselves building on slopes whose soil properties guarantee that our houses will slip downslope during the first large rains (San Francisco); destroying our immune systems, and thus also our bodies' ability to fight off disease; and eroding our physiological and psychological abilities to control our own behavior.

If we do not gain such knowledge, we find ourselves going against nature.

Symptoms and Stratified Symptomatic Relief

But our going against nature in such situations may go even further. We human beings can mislead ourselves and each other by confusing—through selfish intent, ignorance, or denial—highly visible symptoms with the underlying disease. One of the examples close to us all is that of human pain. While we might see pain as a curse to be removed, the case of leprosy shows pain to be a blessing. In leprosy the sensation of pain is destroyed, and responses such as pulling one's hand away from a hot stove or sharp object do not occur, with oftentimes tragically damaging results.[28] Pain is an important component in eliciting a corrective response to what might be degrading and destructive. Debilitation of the ability of pain sensors to signal danger, and inappropriate application of pain killers may be life destroying. Yet, in some cases of "physiological pain" and in many instances of "ecological pain" our response is to destroy the symptoms rather than addressing their underlying causes. In the latter instance, not only are symptoms often eliminated, but the symptoms of additional problems that are generated by treating only the symptoms themselves are given only symptomatic relief, producing—layer upon layer—what can be called "stratified symptomatic relief."

Thus, **pest generation** induced by continual monocropping may lead to increased pesticide use, reduced predator populations, still greater pest populations, extirpation of earthworms and other soil organisms, increased fertilizer applications, increased runoff of biocides and fertilizers to streams, stream eutrophication, groundwater contamination, increased miscarriage rates, and replacement of rural wells with rural water pipeline distribution networks supplied by central water purification plants.

Or, **flooding of homes built on river floodplains** may lead to the building of levees and dikes, making settlement in the floodplain more secure, bringing more development and greater paving of the watershed surface with rooftops, parking lots and roadways, increased deforestation and wetland destruction, still greater flooding downstream, repetition of this sequence downstream, and increased flooding due to similar actions upstream, raising the levees and dikes and further increasing flooding.

Or, **converting our lawns into monocultures** through the use of herbicides and fertilizers, increased leaching of applied chemicals to the groundwater and increased runoff of applied chemicals, achieving greater growth of the grass, extirpating earthworms and other soil organisms that normally consume and recycle grass clippings, creation of "thatch" and the need to collect grass clippings, removal of thatch by machine and grass clippings by bag to the regional landfill, corresponding removal of nutrients gained from fertilizers to the regional landfill, complication of yard management, hiring of all or some of the lawn management to an outside firm, reinforcement of this chain of events by the firm and others who may benefit by the greater throughput and higher complexity of management.

When we limit our responses to environmental degradation by merely treating its symptoms we show a lack of understanding of how the world works.

The Need to Know What is Right

When we choose to leave the Garden we also commit ourselves to having to know what is right. It certainly is true that we can learn much of what is right in creation from creation itself. But much of this is painful and difficult learning. Some of it is learning that comes from retributive justice by the earth itself—retributive justice that is summarized nicely in Leviticus 26: "If you follow my decrees and are careful to obey all my commands, I will send you rain in its season, and the ground will yield its crops and the trees of the field their fruit (vs. 3). But if you will not listen to me and carry out all these commands, and if you reject my decrees and abhor my laws and fail to carry out all my commands and so violate my covenant,... (vs. 14) your land will be laid waste, and your cities will lie in ruins (vs. 33b). Then the land will enjoy its sabbath years all the time that it lies desolate and you are in the country of your enemies; then the land will rest and enjoy its sabbaths (vs. 34). All the time that it lies desolate, the land will have the rest it did not have during the sabbaths you lived on it (vs. 35).

In the assessment of these two questions—How does the world work? and What is right?—Herman Daly observes that it is insufficient to know only the answer to one of these questions.[29] If one knows how the world works but does not know or care about what is right, one's knowledge likely will be used to exploit creation to the exploiter's benefit and at creation's detriment. On the other hand, if one knows what is right but does not know or care about how the world works, one might do such a thing as eliminate the dead wood and dead leaves in a forest, and while rooting out "death" destroy the forest's life.

The Need to Put What We Know Into Practice

But knowledge of the answers to these two questions does absolutely no good unless such knowledge is put into practice. Thus, a third critical question is "Then what must we do?" This is the teaching of the Scriptures that I have summarized as the Action Principle.

Degradations of Creation as Impoverishment

It is crucial to recognize environmental degradations for what they are: the impoverishment of creation—of land, nature, and people. People and other creatures, unable to obtain the means to maintain life and habitat, are compelled to live at the margins of land and life. This impoverishment is exacerbated by degradation of ability of creation—its ecosystems and its people—to sustain and restore itself. It reduces creation as provider. Degradation may even extend to impoverishment of the human spirit, to diminution of human dignity, respect, and integrity. This has been poignantly expressed by Russian physicist Irena Erevlua in reference to the explosion of the Chernobyl power station: "Planet Earth is very small. It is important to protect it from Chernobyl. Chernobyl produces daily destruction; it is eroding our souls. It is most terrible for our culture."[30] Such impoverishment can and should engender compassion.

Reflecting and Keeping the Integrity of Creation

Three Basic Questions

What then can we conclude about our basic question, "When is 'against nature' against nature?" and its antithesis "When is 'in accord with nature' in accord with nature?" It would appear to be this:

How Does the World Work?

First, our question cannot be legitimately answered unless we know how the world works. Thus we need to be firmly rooted in a clear understanding of the natural sciences that is comprehensive enough to deal with the issues at hand. This means that the natural sciences, and in particular, the environmental and ecological sciences are of critical importance as subject matter in education and in the conduct of our work in the world.

What is Right?

Second, our question cannot be legitimately answered unless we know what is right. While we can learn some of this answer from creation's retribution, this can be an extremely painful approach, and beyond its painfulness is the very real possibility of irretrievable loss—such as in species extinctions—and the loading of immense problems onto the third and fourth generations that follow us. Thus our knowledge of what is right must be informed by Scripture. For a start in determining the right course we can heed what in this paper are called the biblical principles of Reflection, Leadership, Fruitfulness, Restoration, Contentment, and Action.

Living in Accord with Nature

In our application of our knowledge of creation and knowledge of what is right, we find ourselves attempting to live in accord with the way the world works. And this is why our basic question, "When is 'against nature' against nature?" is a relevant one. In the Christian and Reformed tradition being "against nature" means being "against God's will" as creator, sustainer, and reconciler. What is "accord with nature" is that which maintains the integrity, biodiversity, and beauty of creation's ecosystems—that which maintains the social, biological and physical components of creation together with their interrelationships. Does this put us into bondage? No. Living in accord with creation does not put us and other systems into bondage, but provides true freedom (the freedom of the children of God). It opens to us creation's dynamic interactive systems in which dynamic design and choice guarantee variety and diversity of form and action.

Then What Must We Do?

Then What Must We Do?
What then does living in accord with creation mean? What should our response be? It would seem to include the following:

Describing the World

What then must we do? We must describe to the world our abusive behavior toward creation and its degrading consequences—our going against nature, our striving against God's intended integrity of creation. (David Ehrenfeld observes that the prophet today is the one who honestly describes *the present.*)

Loving the World

Our response should be to love the world as God does. Our compassionate love for the world should go so far as to be sacrificial, even if it results in re-shaping the vocations of our daughters and sons. (So great a love for the world is this that God gave his only Son, who in compliance with his Father's loving will, suffers even unto death—death upon a cross—through which this Lamb of God takes away the sins of the world and reconciles *all* things.)[31]

Imaging God

Our response should reflect God's compassion, justice, and pleasure as these are expressed in God's work in the world—in the world that God loves. These are important aspects of the context in which we consider all that God has made, God's and creation's goodness, and the integrity of creation and the context of creation's degradation—in which we determine whether "against nature" is against nature.

Following the Last Adam

Thus our response should include our being disciples, not of the First Adam, but of the Last Adam, Jesus Christ, "in whom all will be made alive" (1 Corinthians 15:20-22), "by whom all things were made, through whom all things hold together," (John 1:3; Colossians 1:16-17) and by whom all things are reconciled (Colossians 1:19-20). Imaging God we reflect God's compassionate love for the world, keeping the earth, mirroring God's nurture of creation, its land, air, energy flows, water, creatures and their integral interrelationships. Our response is an imaging of the One who "makes springs pour water into the ravines [that] give water to all the beasts of the field.... The birds of the air nest by the waters; they sing among its branches ... the earth is satisfied by the fruit of his work" (Psalm 104:10-13). We should respond so that the earth is satisfied by the fruit of our work, in service modeled after the Last Adam who takes the form of an obedient servant (Philippians 2:5-8).

Administering Compassion

Our response should be so to administer compassion that it goes beyond the symptoms to address the disease, such that the salve giving symptomatic relief quickly becomes unnecessary. And we should so administer compassion that it takes into account the temporal and spatial context. Rather than being merely a matter of reacting to the particular, in the here-and-now, recognition must be given to the possibility that "narrow compassion" may be discordant with the health and survival of the larger system, and thus might in the longer run or larger arena even counter particular interest. Our compassion should be so administered that it does not become the antithesis of compassion.

Being Children of God

Our response should be so to behave on the earth that the creation, rather than cringing at our coming, says "Aha! Here they come, the children of God, for whom we have been looking with eager expectation."[32]

Restoring Creation's Witness

We must unveil and restore creation's evangelical witness to God's eternal power and divinity where this has been obscured by environmental degradation and alienation from creation.

Reflecting the Kingdom

We must make our lives living reflections of our Lord's prayer, "Thy kingdom come, thy will be done, on earth...." And, in gratitude to God—as disciples of the Last Adam, Jesus Christ—we must work to set things right in creation, so behaving on earth that heaven will not be a shock to us.[33]

Creating Creation Awareness Centers

As living testimonies of gratitude, our churches can proclaim his holy and divine Word and, as "Creation Awareness Centers," open human eyes to the universe as "that most elegant book in which all creatures, great and small, make us ponder and see clearly the invisible things of God, even his eternal power and divinity." Thus, while taking enormous comfort in the fact that we, and our world, belong to God, we are not and cannot be indifferent onlookers in this time of degradation of creation, impoverishment of creation's ability to bring God praise, and alienation of human beings from creation's testimony.

Responding in Gratitude

Our response should be motivated out of our gratitude for God's love for the world, for his sustaining care for the world, and his reconciliation of the world that brings us to join with all creation to serve and praise him. By so doing we profess that God's sustaining love for the world, and his reconciliation of the world, has also enveloped us, setting us free from the bondage of sin and misery—bringing a freedom that opens our lives and churches to be living testimonies of gratitude to God, honoring him as creator and imaging his goodness, his sustaining care for all creation, and his reconciliation of all things.[34] As living testimonies of gratitude, we become disciples of the Last Adam whom we follow and with whom we work to undo the works of the first Adam, doing what the first Adam was supposed to do[35]—God be praised![36]

Environment, Development, and the Integrity of Creation

Enterprise and Development

Enterprise in our times not only must sustain creation's integrity, it must win back what was lost, *restore* integrity where degraded, allow creation to re-claim its self-control and re-establish creation as teacher. This is to avoid the overwhelming alternative to assume the impossible task of earth management and education—of which we are incapable. The prevalence of impoverishment (embedded in the very fabric of much present-day "development" and "progress") means that any enterprise now envisioned must be redemptive. It must undo impoverishment produced and allowed by current enterprise, relieve the biosphere of the relentlessness of exploitation, and allow intrinsic recovery systems to operate. It must be sustained, and be sustainable. It must humbly give back to creation the opportunity and rest necessary to restore, employ, and sustain its intrinsic ability to heal. Redemptive enterprise must in some sense do as a doctor does for a great teacher brought down in battle: establish and maintain the conditions for self-healing so that the patient can be restored to life as a supportive benefactor of life and community.

Enterprise thus must achieve a full reversal of impoverishment. It must give people significant control over life and environment. It must respect and save the means for sustainable households, including for example, transfer of oral tradition, and maintaining and re-establishing seeds and roots of locally-adapted stocks. It must protect and provide inheritors with the means to continue as long-standing transmitters of knowledge on sustainable living within particular habitats and ecosystems. It must restore dignity and respect to people sustaining themselves within long-standing cultures; it must protect their lands and habitats for their use and our education.

At the time of this writing, June 3, 1992, leaders of 160 nations have just begun meeting for the The Earth Summit (the United Nations Conference on Environment and Development). The major item of discussion and debate is "sustainable development." Given this important event and its potentially enormous consequences, how do we address our question, "When is 'development' against nature?" Given our analysis, we can say: When the Precedence Principle is violated; when wholeness and integrity of creation is not sought first, but something else is.

While it is often true that structures within which we currently operate leave us with no recourse but to degrade creation—be they church, government, business, or university—it also is true that we find insufficient time and give insufficient effort to reform or replace these structures. Somehow the integrity of creation—in its human and creaturely fullness—has not been, and is not, our goal. Application of the Precedence Principle would find enterprise—economic, governmental, juridical, charitable, ecclesiastical, educational—putting pursuit of wholeness and integrity of creation first. Its success would be measured by the degree to which it met *this* goal. Such enterprise would be real, earnest, and life would be its goal.[37]

How would what we have said be translated into action at the The Earth Summit? The following resolution is an example.[38]

A RESOLUTION ON DEVELOPMENT AS ENTERPRISE IN SERVICE TO THE INTEGRITY OF CREATION

(1) That development be defined as enterprise; (2) that consistent with its status as enterprise, it be given a definitive and unclouded goal; (3) that this goal be integrity of creation in all the richness and fullness of its meaning, including (a) the mutual integrity of people, human society and the biosphere and (b) justice and peace throughout creation; (4) that consistent with its status as enterprise, it have a bold and comprehensive strategy to meet this goal, including (a) the halting of creation's degradation in its many aspects, (b) restoring creation's integrity where degraded, (c) the qualitative development of this integrity in societies that have reached material maturity, (d) both qualitative and quantitative development of this integrity in societies that have not yet reached material maturity, and (e) encouraging and enabling each person to engage in the care and keeping of some part of creation; (5) that it provide for discernment between growth and development, between price and value, between job and vocation, and between activities that lead to creation's integrity and those that do not; (6) that means be instated for using the results of these discernment provisions to implement actions that continually direct and re-direct enterprise toward its goal of creation's integrity; (7) that education in (a) the integrity of creation, (b) knowledge and naming of both its local ecosystem components and its global biospheric components, (c) knowledge of their degradation, and (d) knowledge of stewardship as the means of creation's care and keeping, be enabled on a direct experiential level through the full use of the talents of all peoples and professions; (8) that each human community be encouraged and supported to guide and direct activity toward enabling creation as teacher of integrity, sustainability, and community; (9) that all institutions—economic, governmental, juridical, charitable, ecclesiastical, educational, and others—be enabled and encouraged to develop the means for making the goal of creation's integrity their highest priority; and (10) that the United Nations, with the expectation of full support and cooperation of all governments and institutions, declare integrity of creation as its highest priority and make provision and opportunity for each of its member nations to do the same.

Conclusion

When is "in accord with creation" in accord with creation? When it joyfully respects, honors, and obeys the creator, when it administers compassionate love to all creation, restoring and preserving its God-given integrity.

Notes

1. Cf. Genesis 1-2.
2. Rom. 1:20.
3. Psalm 19:1.
4. Acts 14:17; Psalm 104:10-18, 27-30.
5. Psalm 104:28-30.
6. Cf. Psalm 107, 116, 117, and 136, esp. Psalm 116:5.
7. Cf. Psalm 28:5.
8. Cf. Jer. 8:4-22.
9. Cf. Jer. 8:13, 14, and 17.
10. Webster's Seventh New Collegiate Dictionary (Springfield, Mass.: G.& C. Merriam Co., 1963) defines compassion as "Sympathetic consciousness of others' discomfort together with a desire to alleviate it."
11. Cf. Rev. 11:18, "The time has come ... for destroying those who destroy the earth."
12. Psalm 29.
13. See for example Genesis 1-11.
14. Cf. Genesis 1-11 where there are repeated examples of people deciding to act contrary to God's will from the eating of the forbidden fruit through the building of a tower.
15. The Belgic Confession, Article 2, describes the means by which God is made known unto us: "We know him by two means: First, by the creation, preservation, and government of the universe; which is before our eyes as a most elegant book, wherein all creatures, great and small, are as so many characters leading us to *see clearly the invisible things of God,* even *his everlasting power and divinity,* as the apostle Paul says (Rom. 1:20). All which things are sufficient to convince men and leave them without excuse. Second, he makes himself more clearly and fully known to us by his holy and divine Word, that is to say, as far as is necessary for us to know in this life, to His glory and our salvation." "Doctrinal Standards of the Christian Reformed Church," in *Psalter Hymnal* (Grand Rapids, MI: Christian Reformed Church Publishing House, 1959), 3.
16. Cf. John 3:16-17; Col. 1:15-20.
17. John 1:1-5; Col. 1:15-17.
18. Note for the non-technical reader: The primary scientific literature is distinguished from what is commonly called the "gray literature." The primary scientific literature is technical scientific writing that is subjected to review by three or more anonymous professional referees in the appropriate field of study, and subject to the discipline, standards, and control of professional scientists and professional scientific societies that are recognized for integrity within their scientific area. The gray literature includes publications in proceedings of professional meetings, contributions of chapters to books, technical reports of agencies and offices, and articles written for the purpose of popularizing scientific findings. Publications in the gray

literature may or may not be subject to review, but generally are not recognized by scientists as rigorously evaluated and authoritative.

19. This is the observation of Douglas John Hall in his book *Imaging God: Dominion as Stewardship* (Grand Rapids: Eerdmans, 1985).

20. Declaration of the "Mission to Washington" of the Joint Appeal by Religion and Science for the Environment, Washington, D.C., May 12, 1992, signed by 115 leaders in religion and science, including scientists Dr. James Hansen (Goddard Institute for Space Studies), Dr. Henry Kendall (Stratton Professor of Physics, Massachusetts Institute of Technology), Dr. Richard B. Norgaard (Professor of Energy and Resources, University of California at Berkeley), Dr. H. Ronald Pulliam (Director of the Institute of Ecology, University of Georgia and President, Ecological Society of America), Dr. F. Sherwood Rowland (Donald Bren Professor of Chemistry, University of California at Irvine and President, American Association for the Advancement of Science), Dr. William Schlesinger (Department of Botany, Duke University), Dr. Stephen H. Schneider (Head of the Interdisciplinary Climate Systems Section, National Center for Atmospheric Research), Dr. Stephen E. Schwartz (Senior Physical Chemist, Brookhaven National Laboratory), and Dr. Edward O. Wilson (Baird Professor of Science, Harvard University). Joint Appeal by Religion and Science for the Environment, 1047 Amsterdam Ave, New York, NY, 10025.

21. "Subtle is the Lord, but malicious is he not." Meaning that while creation is not quick to give up its secrets and while consistencies may not be immediately or clearly evident, everything that is found is in accord with everything else; the Lord has not put inconsistent things into creation—God is not malicious. On the contrary, the God the creator is just and true in everything and every way throughout the whole of creation. See Abraham Pais, *"Subtle is the Lord...."* in *The Science and Life of Albert Einstein* (Oxford: Oxford University Press, 1982), 113-14.

22. These principles were presented earlier in "Ethics, Ecosystems, and Enterprise: Discovering the Meaning of Development and Food Security" in *Growing Our Future: Food Security the Environment*, Katie Smith and Tetsunao Yamamori, eds. (West Hartford, CT: Kumarian Press), 6-26. Here material originally presented in footnotes is moved to the body of the text and edited to fit the purposes of this paper.

23. *The Geneva Bible. A Facsimile of the 1560 Edition* (Madison: University of Wisconsin Press, 1969).

24. Held in Kuala Lumpur (Petaling Jaya), Malaysia, May 12-20; report available from Subunit on Church and Society, World Council of Churches, Geneva, Switzerland, 1990.

25. Ibid.

26. In: Aldo Leopold, *A Sand County Almanac* (New York: Oxford University Press, 1949).

27. From the Report of the Pre-Assembly Consultation on Subtheme I, "Giver of Life—Sustain Your Creation!" held in Kuala Lumpur, Malaysia, May 12-20 (Geneva, Switzerland: World Council of Churches, 1990).

28. This example was first brought to my attention by Dr. Paul Brand, former chief of the Leprosarium at Carville, Louisiana.

29. Herman Daly, unpublished manuscript.

30. Ibid.

31. Abraham Kuyper puts it this way: "God loves *the world*. Of course not in its sinful strivings and unholy motions. As such is enemy of God whoever is called a friend of the world. But God loves the world for the sake of its origin; because God has thought it out; because God has created it; because God has *maintained* it and *maintains* it to this day. Not we have made the world, and thus in our sin we have not maltreated an art product of our own. No, that world was the contrivance, the work and the creation *of the Lord our God*. It was and is his world, which belonged to him, which He had created for his glory, and for which we with that world were by him appointed. Not to us did it belong, but to Him. It was his. And *His* divine world we have spoiled and corrupted.

"And herein roots the love of God, that he will repair and renew this world, his own creation, his own work of wisdom, his own work of art, which we have upset and broken, and polish it again to new lustre. And it *shall* come to this. God's plan does not miscarry, and with divine certainty he carries out the counsel of his thoughts. Once that world in a new earth and a new heaven shall stand before God in full glory. But the children of men meanwhile can fall out of that world. If they will not cease to corrupt His world, God can declare them unworthy of having any longer part in that world, and as once he banished them *from Paradise,* so at the last judgement he will banish them from this earth, and cast them out into the outermost darkness, where there shall be weeping and gnashing of teeth. And therefore whoever would be saved with that world, as God loves it, let him accept the Son, whom God has given to that world, in order to save the world." From "God So Loved the World!" Chapter 7 as translated from the Dutch in 1928 by John Hendrik de Vries in *Keep Thy Solemn Feasts: Meditations by Abraham Kuyper* (Grand Rapids, MI: Eerdmans, 1903), 70-71.

32. Cf. Romans 8:18-21.

33. These three tasks can be fruitfully compared with those of prophet, priest, and king. Some of this material is taken from the conclusion of the paper I published called, "Creation's Care and Keeping: A Reformed Perspective," *Theological Forum* (Reformed Ecumenical Council) 19, no.4, 1991: 1-7.

34. Our gratitude to God means that we will not fail to act on what we know is right. Knowing God's requirements for stewardship must be practiced, or they do absolutely no good. Hearing, discussing, singing, and contemplating God's message is not enough. The hard saying of Scripture is this: We hear from our neighbors, "Come and hear the message that has come from the Lord." And they come, "but they do not put them into practice. With their mouths they express devotion, but their hearts are greedy for unjust gain. Indeed, to them you are nothing more than one who sings love songs with a beautiful voice and plays an instrument well, for they hear your words but do not put them into practice" (Ezek. 33:30-32; see also Eph. 5:8-10 and Luke 6:46-49).

35. For a full discussion of Jesus Christ as second Adam, see the chapter by Ronald Manahan in *Environment and Christian*.

36. Cf. Matt. 5:16 and Heidelberg Catechism, Lord's Day 32, Question 86.

37. It may not be clear to some that integrity of creation is a worthy goal, due to confusion of our ideas and models with reality. It is common in recent times to view nature as something to be transformed to match our own model or idea—something we have to a large extent been able to do. But we are making two very significant discoveries: (1) that it is beyond our capability to do so in many areas—for example, comprehensive management of global circulations and world weather patterns; and (2) that, more importantly, it is beyond desirability—many things in this world are better left to its own management systems so people are free to do other things. Thus increasingly we transform our ideas in accord with the principles upon which ecosystems are based and upon related ethical principles.

38. From the original manuscript for "Ethics, Ecosystems, and Enterprise: Discovering the Meaning of Development and Food Security," in *Growing Our Future: Food Security the Environment*, Katie Smith and Tetsunao Yamamori, eds. (West Hartford, CT: Kumarian Press, 1992), 6-26. (The original U.N. draft resolution that was developed in this paper, and which is presented here, has been edited and moved to the final section of this book.)

When Is Sex Against Nature?

James Olthuis

Our discussion about the integrity of creation order and the ethos of compassion would be incomplete without our talking about sexuality. But it's not an easy topic. Talking about our sexuality and its mysteries tends to be precarious and makes us vulnerable at the best of times. When such discussion involves basic differences of outlook and conviction it is even more difficult. The difficulty is magnified for Christians if there is difference in what is considered to be a position faithful to Scripture. All of these factors are present in discussions about homosexuality.

Indeed the volatility of the subject in today's Christian community often makes an edifying discussion seem impossible. Yet silence is really not an option for the Christian community. There is too much suffering and hurt that needs attending. Increasingly, we have in our midst gay and lesbian brothers and sisters in Christ who, tired of waiting and begging for recognition and acceptance, say they often feel like lepers in the church, stereotyped, misunderstood, abused and rejected. At the same time, there is the deep pain of confusion and betrayal which many Christians feel when some voices in the Christian community argue for more open acceptance of homosexuality. On the one hand, many homosexuals and gay-positives are deeply hurt by what they perceive as dogmatic or misinformed, or even pharisaic judgments and attitudes. On the other hand, many are pained and astonished at what they perceive to be the minimizing or even tailoring of the Bible to be more accommodating to homosexuality.

There is also another group which may even suffer the most in the controversy. I mean those who agonize about their sexual identities, not knowing if they must change to live in Christ, or whether to live in Christ means to accept who they are and then live responsibly.

In this context, as we seek the truth in love, the first and last word I need to inscribe—and we all need to embody—is "compassion." And the middle words—also for communal embodiment—are "empathy" and "forgiveness." We have to listen with empathy to all those who fear that the church is in danger of losing its moral soul. And we need to ask forgiveness of those homosexuals who have been persecuted and ostracized. I write this as a discussion piece, setting forth my own struggle with this difficult matter, hoping to keep open the lines of communication even with those who may strongly disagree.[1]

Anyone who begins to explore the topic of homosexuality in the Christian church is faced almost immediately with the fact that those who are opposed to any form of lesbian or gay relationships in the Christian church seem to focus largely on the exegesis of seven or so Scriptural passages. At the same time many of those open to certain forms of homosexual relations, convinced that the particular passages do not speak about committed gay relations, seem to engage in a wider ranging hermeneutic exercise to determine how the more general biblical exhortations to respect, love, and honor our neighbors are to be embodied in our contemporary situation.

In this context my focus will be to explore whether, when looked at exegetically, hermeneutically, and ethically there may be a welcoming, congenial space in a biblically-informed ethic for committed same-sex relations. The guide for my discussion will be an important article by well-known New Testament scholar Richard B. Hays on Romans 1, which in exemplary fashion combines and emphasizes both exegetical and hermeneutic concerns.[2] Working through Hays's discussion seems especially apropos, for even though he makes clear that the Scriptural references to homosexual practice are uniformly negative, he emphasizes that this does not yet decide the wider hermeneutic concerns for obedient life today. In so doing, Hays opens up, I suggest, a much-needed space where the various parties may meet in the middle without accusation and acrimony.

As we begin, it is worth quoting Hays at some length.

> Because there remain open questions about precisely *how* the Bible functions as an authority for normative ethical judgments, we cannot relieve ourselves of the responsibility for moral decision by appealing to the plain sense of a single prooftext; nor, on the other hand, should we feel constrained to force Paul, through exegetical contortions, to say what we think he ought to have said. We must let the text have its say, whether for us or against us: then we must decide what obedience to God requires (205).

As I read Hays, he is saying that whereas in many or most cases in Scripture there is little doubt about the meaning of a text, there may be more doubt as to what that text means in its larger canonic context, and even more doubt, sometimes tremendous disagreement, as to the normative force such a text should have in shaping our vision of the obedient life. For example, women are not allowed to teach and should remain silent (1 Tim. 2:11-12), women are to wear veils on their heads (1 Cor. 11:2-16), members of the body of Christ are to wash one another's feet (John 13:14-15) and are not physically to resist evil (Matt. 5:38-41), etc., etc.

In each case, Christians have been and continue to be divided in various degrees as to how these commands are to be received today. Are they to be taken as binding norms, or are they time-conditioned expressions of abiding norms which require changing expression in changing times? Fundamentally the debate about normativity turns, not so much on what this or that text says, but on the "appropriation of the biblical teachings in later historical settings"(205).[3]

It is around the matter of appropriation that the discussion becomes difficult and complex.[4] For, although I agree that Paul's portrayal of homosexual relations is indisputably negative, I am not sure this is to be taken as a universal condemnation of all kinds of same-sex relations. And if his negative judgments do not have that universal scope, it may be biblically responsible to come to a positive rather than a negative moral judgment about certain kinds of homosexual relations (i.e., committed ones of mutuality and equality). To get this issue before us as clearly as possible, I propose to consider Romans 1, the text generally considered to be the most general judgment on homosexual relations.[5] After briefly highlighting some of the most trenchant exegetical features of Romans 1, I want to place the text historically in the context in which Paul wrote. Finally, with a view to determining what directions are open for us as we give shape to our vision of the obedient life for today, I hope to engage in a hermeneutic discussion of what we have found in the light of the overall redemptive thrust of Scripture.

Romans 1:26-27

The main reason, it seems, why many Christians feel called to resist the morality of loving same-sex relations is the judgments on homosexual practice contained in Scripture coupled with the absence of any affirmation of such practice. Moreover, it is the talk of homosexual practice as being "against nature" in Romans 1 that is often taken as the blanket, or global judgment on homosexuality:

> Because of this [idolatry] God gave them over to shameful lusts. Even their women exchanged natural use for use against nature. In the same way men, too, abandoned the natural use of women and were inflamed with lust for one another. Men committed shamelessness with other men, and received in themselves the due penalty of their error.

Since my interest here is not primarily exegetical, I will limit myself to considering features of this text which have particular relevance for the broader hermeneutical discussion.

1. First of all, as Robin Scroggs affirms and Richard Hays confirms, in the larger structure of Paul's argument homosexual behavior serves "a secondary and illustrative" role. Homosexual practice is portrayed as a symptom or *result* of, and not the reason for, idolatry. It is because of idolatry that people are given over to the unnatural. As Hays puts it, homosexual practice is seen to be one of the "*manifestations* (not provocations) of the wrath of God.... Paul is not warning his readers that they will incur the wrath of God if they do the things that he lists here; rather, speaking in Israel's prophetic tradition, he is presenting an empirical survey of

rampant human lawlessness as *evidence* that God's wrath and judgment are already at work in the world" (190-91).[6]

Already at this point an important hermeneutic question suggests itself in our contemporary situation: do all kinds of homosexual practice, i.e., practice in committed relations of mutuality and equality, serve as evidence of human lawlessness and idolatry? Certainly, indiscriminate or unequal or coerced homosexual practice gives evidence of such idolatry, as do "wickedness, evil, greed and depravity, ... envy, murder, strife, deceit, malice" and so forth (vs. 29-30). But does same-sex relating within the bounds of loving commitment by confessors of Christ who elsewhere in their lives exhibit the fruits of the Spirit fall automatically into the same category?

2. Since the brunt of exegetical attention has been focused on Paul's usage of the terms "natural" and "contrary to nature" in verses 26 and 27, I need to attend to these terms. The flurry of exegetical activity is engendered by the fact that their meaning is not simple in Paul's writings, nor in the New Testament as a whole. The term "nature" does not occur in the Gospels. In the Epistles of Peter and Jude unrighteous men are said to be like "natural brute beasts" in their destructiveness. In Paul's writings there are a number of occurrences (Rom. 1:26, 27; 2:14, 27; 11:21, 24; Gal. 2:15; 4:8; 1 Cor. 11:14; Eph. 2:3). Paul talks of those who are "by nature" without law (Rom. 2:14), uncircumcised (2:27), or Jewish (Gal. 2:15). Most of these writings receive consistent interpretation, when nature is taken, as Countryman recently claimed, to indicate "the continuity of an organism with its past."[7]

However, 1 Corinthians 11:14 is somewhat of an exception. Here "nature" clearly has a normative character: "Does not nature teach you that if a man wears his hair long it is a disgrace?" But since most Christians today do not consider it immoral if women have short hair and men long hair, "nature" in this instance is not to be read as creational order, but as custom, tradition, or convention.

It is in Romans 1 and 11 that Paul uses the phrases *para physin* (against nature) and *kata physin* (according to nature). In Romans 11:21, 24 he distinguishes branches attached to an original tree (according to nature) and those grafted in by God (contrary to nature). Since here it is God, not a human, who is acting "against nature," it is clear that the "phrase does not by itself mean 'immoral.' "[8]

This leaves the meaning of "against nature" in Romans 1 to be largely determined by contextual considerations. Thus, William Countryman reads verses 26 and 27 as Paul repeating in other words what he had previously said: Through the punishment of God for their idolatry, Gentiles have changed their " 'nature,' that is, lost a certain continuity with their remotest past," and exchanged their natural practice of heterosexual desire for homosexual practice.[9] Richard Hays argues that it is the "standard Hellenistic Jewish polemic against Gentiles" (194) from which the "thought-patterns of Romans 1:18-32 emerge"(196).[10]

It is clear that the opposition between what is "natural" and "unnatural" did play a role in many Greco-Roman texts of the time. As Boswell argued and Hays concluded, " 'natural law' was not in Paul's time a fully developed topic within Christian theology" (196). Hays, therefore, surmises that in Stoic thought nature may mean "something like the orderly structure of ideal reality, and other times it appears to mean ... 'convention as understood by me' "(196). Moreover, even if Paul's use of natural has Stoic connotations, Countryman reminds us this does not necessarily mean a direct reference to the creation order because "*para physin* in Hellenistic Jewish writers refers not to a theology of creation but to the issue of whether sexual acts are procreative."[11] Scroggs concludes that since Paul is dependent on Greek rather than Jewish sources, his contra-nature judgment does not ultimately rest "... on some doctrine of creation ... but on what seemingly is thought to count as common-sense observation."[12]

More recently Pim Pronk has argued that since Paul does not use the term "nature" earlier in Romans 1 when talking about knowledge of God from the works of the creator, it is not obvious that his use of "nature" in verse 26 is a clear reference to Genesis 1.[13] In contrast, although Hays acknowledges that Paul "offers no explicit reflection on the concept of 'nature,' " he does think it "clear that in this passage Paul identifies 'nature' with the created order" (194).

Looking at the extensive debate as to the meaning of "against nature" in Romans 1 that we have briefly canvassed, I am struck by the fact that whether one agrees with Hays's strong connection with creation order or takes Countryman's argument that nature in Paul's usage generally has the meaning of continuity with "remotest past," all agree that Paul at a minimum is saying that homosexual practice is against the accepted, ordinary, and traditional way. No matter what the details, the judgment against homosexual behavior is unequivocal and weighty.

Indeed, from this viewpoint, the gap between considering Paul's "against nature" reference as referring to the remotest past or to the creation order may even appear rather small. However, as we look more closely, the full significance of the different interpretations emerges. Those who (for example, Scroggs[14] and Pronk[15]) interpret the reference as accepted practice see Paul making an empirical observation of what is actually happening, while the others (for example, Hays) see Paul as appealing to an "intuitive conception of what ought to be, of the world as designed by God" (194).

Although hermeneutically the precise nature of the connection between Romans 1 and Genesis 1 and 2 remains an issue for discussion, it does seem important, on the one hand, that those who prefer the weaker connection would have to give full value to the fact that Paul as a Jewish thinker could not make an empirical observation outside of his understanding of creation as foundationally given in Genesis. By the same token, on the other hand, those insisting on the strong connection need to keep in mind that most everyone interprets Paul's "by nature" argument in 1 Corinthians 11 as meaning "convention." Moreover, all of this means that our discussion will be incomplete without paying some attention to Genesis 1 and 2.

3. Concerning the expressions "shameful lusts" and "inflamed with lust," Hays points out that "the usual supposition of writers during the Hellenistic period was that homosexual behavior was the result of insatiable lust seeking novel and more

challenging forms of self-gratification" (200). In line with this, Paul's talk of "shameful lusts" and being "inflamed with lust" seems to put the emphasis on wanton desire and could easily be an implicit reference to the legendary sexual orgies of first century Rome.[16]

4. Concerning the expression, "the due penalty of their error," Countryman points out that the usual interpretation that the "error" is homosexuality, and the penalty as some evil that punishes it, is extremely unlikely. In every other case when Paul uses the term *plane,* translated "error," it has to do with "wrong belief rather than desire or action."[17] A consistent reading takes "idolatry" as the error, and impurity of Gentile culture as the penalty.

5. Concerning the expression, "women exchanged natural use," a striking feature of this passage which has not received sufficient attention is that the only purported reference to lesbianism in Scripture may, in fact, not be such a reference. The fact that Paul does not say "women with women" (as he says "men with men"), coupled with the fact that there are only a few examples of lesbianism mentioned in the extant literature,[18] raises some doubt. More doubt is raised because, says Eva Cantarella, professor in the Institute of Roman Law at the University of Milan, Roman males believed that "pleasure could only be dispensed by men"[19] and were consequently possessed of an "absolute inability to imagine that there could be women who preferred being loved by other women."[20] Likewise, since for the Greek male sexuality required a phallus, sex without a male organ seemed unimaginable and even impossible.

Although the church fathers—along with society in general—were largely silent about lesbianism, Augustine did warn nuns against it.[21] Noteworthy, however, is the opinion attributed to Anastasius in which the reference to women in Romans 1 is said to mean women offering themselves anally to men, most likely to avoid conception. This would support the idea that Paul's concern in this passage for both men and women is indiscriminate sexual behavior. In fact, Augustine too seems to have interpreted the Romans reference to women in this way.[22] And if that is indeed what Paul meant, we are left with the fact that there is no negative mention of lesbianism in the Bible.

Homosexual Practice in the Ancient World

The fact that there is only one mention of lesbianism in Scripture (and even that one questionable) becomes more understandable in terms of ancient Greek and Roman culture. "The pagan world considered sexual relations between men as an integral part of sexuality."[23] Ancient Romans and Greeks seemed simply to assume that people could be attracted to both sexes. They even debated the merits of the different kinds of love. The idea of a homosexual person as a person dominantly or exclusively oriented to members of the same sex does not seem to have been known. This of course does not mean that there was no same-sex loving until the late nineteenth century. What it does mean is that such behavior until then was understood in a different context.

Before the late eighteenth century, although there were same-sex acts, there were no homosexual persons as identified by either society or themselves.[24] "To be 'homosexual' (in the modern sense of the term, which rules out relations with women) cannot have been easy in Greece."[25] The term homosexual, a neologism combining a Greek prefix with a Latin root, was as far as we know coined in 1870 by Carl Westphal, a German physician, and introduced into English in 1891. Michel Foucault argued that a "homosexual" person, as distinct from same-sex behavior engaged in by people of varying identities, personally and socially, is largely a twentieth-century development.[26] All of this cautions us against naively expecting that what an ancient text such as Romans means is the same as what we mean by homosexuality today.

Before the late eighteenth century sexual behaviors were not perceived on the basis of whether one was homosexual or heterosexual, but along different lines of demarcation. In the medieval world, the major fault line was between procreative and nonprocreative sex. Thus, even in marriage, oral or anal sex is prohibited. Procreation as the demarcation line likewise explains why rape and incest are considered less sinful than oral or anal sex. For the Greeks the important dichotomy was between being active and passive. A free adult male could have sexual relations with both male and female provided that he was the dominant partner. It is this desire to play the active role which was considered "natural." The problem for the Greeks was not same-sex relations as such, but it was fear of effeminacy (read: passivity or submission) in males. The active role had to be that of the older partner, the younger had to be passive. The rigid distinction between the older man who takes the active role and the youth who accepts the passive role points to the use of sexual roles in the maintenance of social structure. "In Greece the sexual relationship was assumed to be a power relationship where one participant is dominant and the other inferior. On one side stands the free adult male; on the other, women, slaves and boys."[27] In other words, it is role, not gender, that is the most salient consideration.

Among the Romans it was not that heterosexual intercourse was permitted and homosexual sex prohibited. An adult male citizen could have sex with male or female, but it was only acceptable to be the giver, not the receiver of seed.[28] "Roman homosexuality, then, was purely and simply, not to say brutally, a matter of bullying and violence, a manifestation of the social and sexual power of the stronger over the weaker, the master over the slave, the victor over the vanquished."[29]

In any case, the love of an older man for a youth, paiderastia, became a rather vital institution in Greek society because male children grew up in mother-dominated environments with absent fathers. By relating to a young man instead of a woman, the Greek male could "still play a phallic male role but avoid the dangerous female,"[30] and the Greek son could gain a surrogate father. Eva Keuls concludes that in male-male relations "a mutual sexual relationship between two men of approximately the same age and social standing" was frowned upon, not because it was unnatural, or even that it breaks the link between sex and procreation, but because, in negating the use of sex as shoring up the power structures, it would be a "rebellion against the social order."[31] Sex as a major instrument of political domination/submission thus helps explain why equal relations of mutuality and reciprocal desire between same-sex partners of the same age seems almost unknown in those times.[32]

Romans 1 and Christian Ethics

Against this background of degradation and moral perversity, it is not difficult to understand Paul's very clear indictment of homosexual practice: "[I]n Romans 1 Paul portrays homosexual activity as a vivid and shameful sign of humanity's confusion and rebellion against God" (Hays, 211). However, the important hermeneutic question is the scope of that condemnation. If the negative passages (including Romans 1) focus on known practices such as cultic prostitution, or other exploitative situations such as male prostitution, orgies, sex with inferiors (i.e., slaves), and pederasty, and if in the culture there were no model of reciprocal sexuality between equals, is it hermeneutically legitimate to read the biblical witness as a universal condemnation of any and every form of homosexuality? Richard Hays again says it well: "This is precisely the point at which genuinely fruitful reflection must begin; ... we still have to decide how to construe the authority of his [Paul's] opinion in the present time" (205).

Robin Scroggs puts the problem this way: "That Paul uses here the argument from nature might mean, of course, that he would have made the same judgment about *any* form of homosexuality. No one can legitimately conclude, however, that he would have done so."[33] Scroggs goes on: "If he [Paul] opposed something specific, then his statements cannot be generalized beyond the limitations of his intentionality without violating the integrity of Scripture (134)."[34] Scroggs's conclusion follows: "*Biblical judgments against homosexuality are not relevant to today's debate ... not because the Bible is not authoritative*, but simply because it does not address the issues involved."[35]

Taking issue with Scrogg's view, James B. DeYoung argues that, since "[t]hroughout Scripture the condemnation is universal and absolute,"[36] committed same-sex relations of mutuality and equality also fall within the ban. DeYoung asks: "If the model of homosexuality makes a difference regarding acceptability or culpability, why is Scripture silent on the matter?"[37] One possible, viable answer would be, as Scroggs suggests, that the model of adult mutuality in commitment was unknown in ancient times. DeYoung responds: "Yet if it exists now, it certainly existed then. Man's nature has not changed, nor has the power of the gospel. Scroggs has no evidence that mutuality is more common today than it was then."[38]

DeYoung's rejoinder is inadequate, both conceptually and historically. Certainly God's call for us to be image-bearers of God, agents of love, has remained constant from the beginning. Nevertheless, historically, ever since the Fall, structures of domination and power-over, not mutuality and power-with, have been the characteristic feature of human culture and history. For that reason the absence of models of mutuality (apart from friendship) in ancient patriarchal cultures is not surprising.[39] Indeed, amazing as it may now seem, both in the world and in the church, it is only in the late twentieth century that patriarchal hegemony is being challenged and mutuality—even in heterosexual marriage—is becoming recognized and acclaimed as a normative model.[40]

In his hermeneutical discussions in moving from the text to today's situation, Hays, too, cautions that "no direct appeal to Romans 1 as source for laws about sexual conduct is possible." He even insists that "in view of the wider framework of Paul's discussion of the normative role of law in the Christian life, any such appeal would be intensely problematic" (206). He does claim from Romans 1 that we "can properly infer the principle that human actions ought to acknowledge and honor God as creator." But that, he adds, is "too general to provide concrete ethical norms"(206).

Nevertheless, in the end, Hays interprets Paul's reference to nature as clear enough biblical testimony which leads him to reject the moral legitimacy today of any form of homosexual relationship. (At the same time, in an article in *Sojourners*, Hays makes clear that he will have nothing to do with discrimination against homosexuals.[41]) He summarizes: "Arguments in favor of acceptance of homosexual relations find their strongest warrants in empirical investigations and in contemporary experience. Those who defend ... [them] may do so only by conferring upon these warrants an authority greater than the direct authority of Scripture and tradition, at least with respect to this question" (211).

As I have indicated throughout, I consider Hays's article to be a model of argumentation and investigation. At the same time, I question his conclusion that anyone who takes a gay-positive position is conferring greater authority upon contemporary experience than upon Scripture and tradition. This would only be the case, I suggest, if it is clear that what Scripture means by homosexual experience corresponds with what we mean. And that, as we have seen, is by no means clear. It appears that in the Hellenistic culture of Paul's day pederasty, male prostitution and owner/slave relationships were widely promoted and flourished. If that is correct, and the weight of the evidence points in that direction, does it not seem somewhat problematic to carry over directly the negative judgment on promiscuous non-equal homosexual experience to those homosexual relations qualitatively different, i.e., non-exploitative, equal, and non-promiscuous? How can we be so sure that his judgment would also apply to gay Christians in trothful relations who claim to experience the grace and not the wrath of God?

In the end, Hays's negative view rests on his judgment that "it is clear that in this passage [Romans 1] Paul identifies 'nature' with the created order" and that this is not "an empirical observation of what actually exists; instead, it appeals to an intuitive conception of what ought to be, of the world as designed by God" (194). In other words, the real telling point for Hays is his view of the creation described in Genesis 1 and 2.

In a similar vein, it is significant to note that the influential evangelical scholar John Stott has recently written that "the reason for opposing homosexual partner-ships is not the six or so negative prohibitions that may be found in Scripture, because they are capable, or some of them at least, of being argued as special cases. The ground is rather the plain, positive, witness of Scripture that the one flesh union of sexual intercourse belongs to heterosexual marriage alone."[42] Thus, hermeneutic considerations lead us to a consideration of Genesis 1 and 2.

A Creational Order of Compassion

In Genesis 1 and 2 we find that God's word for creation is simultaneously a gift and a call. As a gift, the word orders creation, issuing parameters and marking out paths of response and service. But this ordering is at the same time a dynamic calling which invites human participation and partnership with God, not only in keeping but also in dressing the garden of creation. Receiving the order as gift of God, at the same time we receive the order as a call to work with and to work out. That is, we are called to order life as commissioned image-agents of God. Correlative to order as gift and call, imaging God is both a gift and a call.

As the fall recorded in Genesis 3 and the rest of Scripture makes clear, this creational ministry in the renewing Spirit of God becomes a redemptive partnership of love and healing. The order of love becomes in redemption an order of compas-sion.

Compassion, we need to note, is not just a feeling moved by someone or something, as it is often understood. Compassion is to suffer-with. And the root of this compassion is found in God. Indeed, it is striking that the word for compassion in the New Testament, *splanchnizomai*, "... is used only of Jesus or by Jesus to refer to figures in parables who represent God or himself."[43] In identity with this Christ, who alone is the compassionate one, we are called to be compassionate. "Our passion is a participation in Jesus' compassion."[44]

To have compassion means, literally in the Greek, to turn over one's bowels. Such compassion is not letting anything go, or being "soft on sin," or whatever. Compassion is not pity, feeling sorry for. It is more than empathy. To practice compassion is to grow up in Christ, it is to be involved voluntarily and intentionally in a process of struggle, pain, confrontation. Compassion is a thirst for justice, not just for us, but for all of God's creatures. It is a call to non-violence and service, a call to ministry, to love God and neighbor as ourselves. Compassion calls for sacrifice and mercy, a call to go the second and third mile.

Compassion or love is not, however, as John emphasizes, a new commandment, but an old commandment which you have had from the beginning, yet it is new (1 John 2:7, 8). The paradox is crucial. God's good order for life remains in place. Yet because of the disorder and pain caused by the fall into sin, God comes in Jesus Christ to transform us, re-order us, and suffer with us in the pain. This surprise of grace renews the old order, God takes the pain of the world, embraces it. God's love becomes a suffering love, and the order of love becomes, in a new and deeper way, an order of compassion. Agents of love are now agents of suffering love. We are to be compassionate as our Father in heaven is compassionate. We are to be "wounded healers" who share the woundedness of the whole body of Christ. Creational normativity continues to hold but, as I suggest, it undergoes what I will call redemptive re-routing in and through Christ, now as agent of re-creation as well as of creation.

Genesis 2 presents male/female partnership—mutual empowerment, community, and enjoyment—as a gift of God to/for humankind. Verse 24 provides one paradigm example of such partnership: a man leaves his father and mother and cleaves to his wife and they become one flesh. This passage does not talk of marriage as an institution for begetting children, nor is the one flesh simply reference to sexual intercourse. The fundamental focus of the verse is the complete personal community of pledged troth between husband and wife.[45]

Generally speaking, this passage has been read to mean that such intimate sexual conduct is *only* ethically permissible between a male and a female, and never between betrothed same-sex partners, although that is, in actuality, never said in so many words. As George Edwards concludes: "In sum, the creation stories do not provide explicit moral or theological evidence on homosexual practice. Homophobic interpretations of subsequent passages, such as Genesis 19, read back into Genesis 1-3 sexual ideas extraneous to those chapters."[46] In similar vein, Reformed Old Testament scholar Marten Woudstra also felt that Genesis 1 and 2 could not be read as an outright condemnation of any and every form of homosexual relationship.[47]

The question then arises whether the focus on conjugal troth declared in Genesis is only and exclusively and forever tied to a heterosexual orientation. But not everyone has such a heterosexual orientation—for whatever reasons, perhaps in some way a result of the general fall of humanity. However, even if we take heterosexual marriage as God's good creational intention, we need to recognize that God's mission of redemption in a fallen world involves what I will call redemptive re-routings. The Scriptural account reveals Yahweh as the faithful, longsuffering, merciful one who, ever mindful of human limitations and brokenness, opens up alternate routes to obedience and blessing. Indeed, in the same Bible which portrays the very institution of marriage as intended by God for life between one man and one women, divorce is allowed in certain situations (Deut. 24:1-4, 22:13-29; Matt. 19:9), polygamy is tolerated (but not harems Gen. 29, Deut.17:17), and some may be eunuchs for the Gospel (Matt. 19:12). After the fall, the state is given the power of the sword (Rom. 13) and warfare is allowed (with exemptions for many, Deut. 20). Slavery is allowed for a limited time (Deut. 15:12-18). More generally—and I submit, of utmost significance—is not redemptive re-routing in fact the way God worked for the redemption of humankind in the coming of Jesus Christ in the flesh, as the second Adam?

It is this Scriptural narrative of God's redemptive dealings with humankind that leads me to wonder if committed same-sex pairings may not also be a redemptive re-routing, a re-routing making possible mutuality, troth, and sexual intimacies for all of God's children, not only heterosexuals. This in no way would affect or undermine the normativity of the marriage covenant for heterosexuals. What it would do is provide a normative route for sexual intimacy as well for those who find themselves to be homosexual and not gifted with celibacy.[48] For homosexuals are included among the earth-creatures of which Genesis 2:18 says that it is not good that they are alone. Moreover, when we read Genesis 2 as necessarily precluding same-sex covenants, are we not in danger of prematurely foreclosing on the possibilities of the eschatological drama of redemption? We may even be guilty of placing too much emphasis on the complementarity of bio-physical build and fit when compared with the quality of the ethical intimacy. In such cases the humanity, morality, and religious validation of human sexual intercourse seems to be, when all is said and done, too dependent on a certain fit of sexual organs and on procreation.

It is also in the grand sweep of redemptive re-routing that Richard Longenecker calls Galatians 3:28 [There is no longer Jew or Greek, there is no longer slave or free, there is no longer male and female, for you are all one in Christ Jesus.] "the most forthright statement on social ethics in all the New Testament."[49] Galatians 3 presents an eschatological unity of male and female, slave and free, Jew and Greek. This does not mean that the differences are obliterated, that the matter of gender is of no account; it does mean that "the eschatological reality ... must shape the social reality of the church in the present."[50] Allen Verhey notes that this "new perspective called for freedom and love, a harmonious pluralism within the church marked by respect and love for those who were and remained different."[51] The language Paul uses in Galatians 3:28 ("no male and female") is a direct and clear reference to the creation story in which God created humanity male and female. [The "and" instead of "nor" picks up the "and" of male and female of Gen. 1.[52]] Thus, if we keep in mind that partnership and mutuality were God's will for human relations in Genesis 1 and that the fall brought disorder, domination and subordination, it is questionable if Paul tries to balance, as Longenecker in more Lutheran fashion claims, the "redemptive category of new life in Christ wherein freedom, mutuality, and equality are prominent" with the "creation, wherein order, submission and subordination are features."[53]

In more Calvinistic fashion, I suggest that Paul is more likely reminding his readers that in Christ we are the already-not-yet equal partners God intended from the beginning, even as Paul struggles to work out what this means in concrete situations. Here the order of creation as gift and call is redemptively reaffirmed in the cross and resurrection of Christ and eschatologically rearticulated in the Gospel of grace, mercy and justice. In that perspective Paul, for example, sees celibacy as a sign of the new age and regards marriage no longer as a duty, but a gift. And insisting on mutuality in marital relations he not only says, for example, the husband has "power over" his wife's body, but in a move towards mutuality shocking his first century readers, he asserts that a wife also has "power over" her husband's body (1

Cor. 7:4). Paul in Galatians 3 is reaffirming and reframing the creation order in eschatological perspective so that we in hope and with the promise of the Gospel may be inspired to put aside and replace the old fallen structures of hierarchy and domination with new and reformed structures more expressive of the love and mercy of Christ.

Interpreting Genesis in the eschatological sweep of Galatians as well as interpreting Galatians as a redemptive republication of Genesis seems natural, especially for Calvinists, because we have always strongly affirmed that in and by Christ all things were created and that everything holds together in him. Indeed, through Christ God was pleased to reconcile all things (Col. 1:15-20). As Ridderbos explains, a "mystical" explanation of "in Christ" is on the "wrong track." Rather "in Christ" speaks of "an abiding reality determinative for the whole of the Christian life, to which appeal can be made at all times, in all sorts of connections, and with respect to the whole church without distinction."[54]

In this context, I am suggesting that perhaps Galatians 3:28 sets an eschatological horizon in which we can raise the issue of same-sex relations in the body of Christ. If we are all one in Christ, no longer Jew or Greek, no longer slave or free, no longer male and female, may then the freedom to which Christ in Galatians calls us not include a call to a love in which there is no longer straight or gay? Today, in continuity with the direction set by Paul, we are called to apply the central, creational mandates of the Gospel to the circumstances of our day as he did in his day. *"If, "* declares Richard Hays in his brilliant recent treatment of Pauline hermeneutics, *"we learned from Paul how to read Scripture, we would read as participants in the eschatological drama of redemption."*[55] By discerning the way in biblical history the Spirit led people in their time and age, we can have a sense of the way God asks us to go in our day. This means, to be sure, that we may be led to go beyond the letter of certain biblical injunctions to obey their spirit, working out our salvation with fear and trembling. "Above all, Paul provides us with a model of hermeneutical freedom.... Indeed, Paul's own example would lead us to expect that the community, under the guidance of the Spirit, will remain open to fresh readings of the same text, through which God will continue to speak."[56,57] Thus, N. Thomas Wright works with a five-act model of biblical authority (four acts are written, with the New Testament as the first scene of the fifth act which gives hints about the end) in which the church is called, under the authority of the first four acts and guided by the Spirit, to work out the remainder of the fifth act for herself "by speaking and acting with both *innovation* and *consistency*."[58] In this spirit—in the Spirit—the church has done this with the question of slavery, usury, divorce and remarriage, and the place of women.[59] And now we face the question of same-sex relations.

Reminding us that "[w]e are children of the Word, not prisoners," Hays argues that such fresh readings do not need to "overthrow the canon," as many fear, but in reality they may "uphold the canon." At the same time he recognizes that "such reading is dangerous." But, he explains, we have no other choice. In fact, with strong echoes of Gadamer, he asserts that such a view which recognizes the reality of "our own hermeneutical agency" is safer than one which "denies the necessary contribution of the reader and the reader's community in the act of interpretation."[60] Moreover, Hays declares, ironically those who attempt to curtail our hermeneutic freedom are "unfaithful, in the most fundamental way, to the teaching of the apostle who insisted that 'the word is near you, in your mouth, and in your heart.' " Taking "the risks of interpretive freedom," he avers, is to be faithful to Paul's word and example.[61]

"It is for freedom," exclaims Paul, "that Christ has set us free" (Gal. 5:1). Hermeneutically, comments Hays, "[e]ntering into 'knowledge of the glory of God in the face of Jesus Christ' (2 Cor. 4:6) liberates believers from bondage to a circumscribed reading of the old covenant and empowers them to read it with freedom—more precisely, to live it with freedom—as a witness to the righteousness of God in Jesus Christ."[62] Thus in his time Paul, standing in that freedom, judges that in "Christ Jesus neither does circumcision avail anything, nor uncircumcision: but faith, working through love" (Gal. 5:6). Living in the Spirit is what matters: "But the fruit of the Spirit is love, joy, peace, patience, kindness, goodness, faithfulness, gentleness and self-control. Against such things there is no law" (Gal. 5:22).

In line with the freedom to which we are called, I want to suggest that Paul's emphasis on the fruits of the Spirit may open room for us to consider that the ethical quality of a same-sex relationship, rather than the gender of its participants, be the morally decisive factor.[63] I see that as a real option. That would mean, from a moral viewpoint, that the gender of the lovers in a committed relationship is less germane than we may think. Is that going too far? I think not, because we still have a very clear answer to our main concern. Sex is against nature when it is against love and the God of love. The moral norms—troth, justice, integrity, mutuality, choice, non-coercive consent, etc.—remain clear and undiluted. Violence of any kind in sexual relations is condemned; rape, incest, abuse of children, battering of women or children stand judged. The relevance of this call to normativity in our contemporary world plagued with violence and antinormative behavior needs no argument. We have clear normative guidelines for everyone regardless of sexual orientation.

In the hermeneutic process, it is well for all of us—whether we favor or oppose committed same-sex relations—to remember the very real dangers of self-deception and radical discontinuity. Thus Hays, in attempting to formulate the constraints which must guide all who recognize the authority of Scripture, lists three. (1) "No reading of Scripture can be legitimate if it denies the faithfulness of Israel's God to his covenant promises." (2) "No reading of Scripture can be legitimate if it fails to acknowledge the death and resurrection of Jesus as the climactic manifestations of God's righteousness." (3) "No reading of Scripture can be legitimate, then, if it fails to shape the readers into a community that embodies the love of God as shown forth in Christ."[64]

In the light of these excellent criteria I believe that we in the body of Christ need to assess where we are in relation to the homosexuals in our midst. Indeed, what if the traditional reading of Scripture in regard to committed homosexual relations "fails to shape the readers into a community that embodies love as shown forth in Christ"? What if in a growing number of situations our readings of Scripture, instead of serving and enhancing communities of faith, damage and undermine them? What then? Do we not need to take another look, carefully, prayerfully, thoughtfully, communally, compassionately—trusting in the "power of the Spirit to disclose truth and give life?"[65]

Is it just possible that same-sex commitment and mutuality can be a sign of God's abundant grace, a token of God's future in a fallen world? I believe it is. In large measure this is only to say more clearly and more publicly what many of us are already saying privately and pastorally: trothful sex is always to be preferred to promiscuous sex.[66] At the same time, the small difference is important. To affirm straightforwardly that committed same-sex relations may be conduits of blessing would serve to reassure gay men and women that the body of Christ, rather than merely tolerating them, welcomes, embraces, and values them and their gifts.

This is perhaps the place to invite Hays at least to reconsider his own negative judgment on committed same-sex relations. In terms of his own convictions that Paul's "interpretive methods are paradigmatic for Christian hermeneutics,"[67] and in terms of his criteria, it would seem to me that Hays would need to leave the discussion more open than he appears to. His cryptic insertion that Paul's judgment on homosexual relations, "[o]bviously ... leaves open many questions about how best to deal with the problem pastorally" (207) suggests perhaps that Hays may see committed same-sex relations as a pastoral alternative. But if Scripture is clearly against such an approach, how can a pastoral approach—and certainly "pastoral" ought to be "normative," but normative in a developmental pastoral way—move in that direction? Indeed, Hays' third criterion of social embodiment for legitimate readings of Scripture is pastoral through and through.

No doubt many will believe that I am on the wrong track. I invite discussion and correction. But, as of now, I submit that the question is not as closed as many people continue to assume. The ministry of suffering love incarnated by Christ and expected of his followers asks us not to put any burdens on people that are extraneous to the Gospel. Even if their experience is strange to us, do we not need to take seriously the confession of gays and lesbians that they have received the Spirit in faith, and not declare this to be impossible if they do not "change"? May not gays and lesbians belong to the "strangers" that we are to embrace in the compassion and suffering love of Christ?[68] In the end, the depth and measure of our compassion is determined by the degree the center of the body can find place for those on the margins, without marginalizing and repressing them. For we are, as Paul says, the body of Christ, and individually members of it. If one member suffers, all suffer together, if one member is honored, all rejoice together (1 Cor. 12:27, 26). According to a ninth century Latin hymn based on 1 John 4:16, [*Ubi caritas et amor, ubi caritas, Deus ibi est*] where charity and love are found, there is God.

Notes

1. Since interpretation never happens in a vacuum, and since our issues concern people rather than abstractions, I want to affirm the importance of face-to-face experience with gay and lesbian Christians in considering this issue.

2. Richard B. Hays, "Relations Natural and Unnatural: A Response to John Boswell's Exegesis of Romans 1," in *The Journal of Religious Ethics* XIV, 1986: 184-215. References to this article will be included in the text without further identification.

3. In 1992 The Reformed Ecumenical Council adopted a "Report on Hermeneutics and Ethics" which declared in its summarizing statements that "[i]n applying Scriptural ethical directives to concrete life situations, it is necessary to take into account contextual factors in the believer's situation, such as prevailing customs, institutions, and traditions." In doing so "it is necessary to maintain the priority of Scripture, the legitimacy of contextual factors, and the need for spiritual discernment."

4. How the church has dealt with the problem of usury over the centuries is particularly illustrative. Usury was almost unanimously condemned by ancient philosophers as being contrary to "nature." All the scriptural evidence is negative, the church fathers banned it, as did Thomas Aquinas and many church councils, beginning with Nicea. Calvin believed a professional usurer ought not to be allowed in church (see Ronald Wallace, *Calvin's Doctrine of the Christian Life* (London: Oliver & Boyd, 1959), 156. Nevertheless, gradually after the fourteenth century in which Christians became increasingly involved with banking, the ancient prohibitions were read to apply only to the demanding of *excessive* interest. See the discussion of John Boswell in his *Christianity, Social Tolerance, and Homosexuality* (Chicago: University of Chicago Press, 1980), 330-32.

5. For this reason in this paper I will deal directly only with Romans 1:26-27. The other classic passages are Gen. 19, Judges 19, Lev. 18:22 and 20:13, 1 Cor. 6:9-10, 1 Tim. 1:9-10.

6. See Robin Scroggs, *The New Testament and Homosexuality* (Philadelphia: Fortress, 1983), 113-14.

7. L. William Countryman, *Dirt, Greed and Sex* (Philadelphia: Fortress, 1988), 114.

8. Hays, 199. For that very reason, Boswell in his *Christianity, Social Tolerance, and Homosexuality* argues that this speaks for interpreting "against nature" in Romans 1 as the "unexpected, unusual or different." That means, according to Hays, that the phrase itself "contrary to nature" probably did not carry for Paul and his readers the vehement connotation of " 'monstrous abomination' which it subsequently acquired in Western thought about homosexuality" (199) and "... certainly should not be adduced as if it were a warrant for the frantic homophobia which sometimes prevails in modern society" (199).

9. Countryman, 114.

10. Ibid., 113.

11. Ibid., 115.

12. Scroggs, 117.

13. Pim Pronk, *Against Nature?* (Grand Rapids: Eerdmans, 1993), 277.

14. Scroggs, 117.

15. Pronk, 277.

16. See Catherine Kroeger, "The Apostle Paul and the Greco-Roman Cults of Women," in *Journal of the Evangelical Theological Society* 30 (1987): 25-39.

17. Countryman, 115.

18. See Christine Downing, *Myths and Mysteries of Same-Sex Love* (New York: Continuum, 1991), 143.

19. Eva Cantarella, *Bisexuality in the Ancient World* (New Haven: Yale University Press, 1993), 171.

20. Ibid., 217.

21. Boswell, 158.

22. Boswell, 158. Also Peter Coleman, *Gay Christians: A Moral Dilemma* (London: SCM Press, 1989), 77.

23. Cantarella, 211.

24. Downing, 4-5.

25. Cantarella, 216.

26. Michel Foucault, *The History of Sexuality*, vol. 1 (New York: Random House, 1978), 43.

27. Downing, 135.

28. Ibid., 5.

29. Cantarella, 218.

30. Philip Slater, *The Glory of Hera* (Boston: Beacon Press, 1968), 61.

31. Eva C. Keuls, *The Reign of the Phallus* (New York: Harper & Row, 1985), 276.

32. Downing, 144.

33. Scroggs, 122.

34. Ibid., 125.

35. Ibid., 127 (his italics).

36. James B. De Young, "The Meaning of 'Nature" in Romans 1 and its Implications for Biblical Proscriptions of Homosexual Behavior," *Journal of the Evangelical Theological Society* 31/4 (1988): 437.

37. Ibid., 440.

38. Ibid.

39. This does not exclude the fact that individual couples may have enjoyed mutual relations. In a recent book, *Same-Sex Unions in Pre-Modern Europe* (New York: Villard Books, 1994), John Boswell argues that even though many same-sex unions in the Greco-Roman world were of the exploitative older/younger, victor/vanquished kind, there were also bondings of brotherly equals. The significance of his claims (were many of these "friends" actually "lovers," as Boswell suggests?) for our discussion awaits critical reviews of these claims by experts in the field. For a different interpretation of equality in Athens, see Evelyn Fox Keller, *Reflections on Gender and Science* (New Haven: Yale University Press, 1985), 23-30.

40. For a brilliant analysis of how domination (as distinct from mutuality) has been rooted in the human psyche, see Jessica Benjamin's *The Bonds of Love* (New York: Pantheon Books, 1988).

41. Richard B. Hays, "Speaking the Truth in Love," *Sojourners* (July 1991): 17-21.

42. John W. Stott and John S. Spong, "A Dialogue on Christian Sexual Ethics," *Crux,* vol. XXIX (no. 3, September 1993): 20.

43. Andrew Purves, *The Search for Compassion* (Louisville: Westminster/John Knox Press, 1989), 16.

44. Ibid.

45. Claus Westermann, *Gen. 1-11: A Commentary* (Minneapolis: Augsburg Press, 1984), 234.

46. George Edwards, "A Critique of Creationist Homophobia," in Homosexuality and Religion, ed. Richard Hasbany (New York: Harrington Park Press, 1989), 114.

47. From materials appended to personal correspondence with Ralph Blair, Nov. 11 1986.

48. Since the gift of celibacy is rare among heterosexuals, it seems reasonable to expect that the same would hold true among homosexuals. Lewis Smedes believes that "If celibacy is not possible, it is better for homosexual people to live together in committed monogamous relationships of love than not. Homosexual partnerships that are committed offer the best moral option available," *Sex For Christians* (Grand Rapids: Eerdmans, 1994), 243.

49. Richard Longenecker, *New Testament Social Ethics for Today* (Grand Rapids: Eerdmans, 1984), 30.

50. Allen Verhey, *The Great Reversal: Ethics and the New Testament* (Grand Rapids: Eerdmans, 1984), 113.

51. Ibid., 114.

52. Longenecker, 75.

53. Ibid., 85.

54. Herman Ridderbos, *Paul* (Grand Rapids: Eerdmans, 1975), 59.

55. Richard Hays, *Echoes of Scripture in the Letters of Paul* (New Haven: Yale University Press, 1989), 185 (his italics).

56. Hays, *Echoes*, 186-87.

57. Along similar lines, in her inaugural lecture, *Fruit in the Wilderness: The Changing Landscape of Biblical Studies* (Toronto: Institute for Christian Studies, 1995), Sylvia C. Keesmaat suggests that Paul, in not merely repeating stories from the past, but evoking them as he retells them, offers "... a paradigm for our telling of the story anew in our cultural situation" (19).

58. N. T. Wright, "How Can the Bible Be Authoritative?" *Vox Evangelica* 21 (1991): 19.

59. For a good treatment of the hermeneutical struggles within the church in terms of four issues, see Willard M. Swartley, *Slavery, Sabbath, War and Women* (Waterloo, Ont.: Herald Press, 1983).

60. Hays, *Echoes*, 189.

61. Ibid.

62. Ibid., 154.

63. Just as, for example, the majority of the Christian Church—with the official Roman Catholic Church as the big exception—has come to accept that conjugal sexuality receives its validation, not from propagation, but vice versa: propagation receives its moral validation in terms of commitment, choice, consent, and mutuality. Likewise, the reality of what is now being referred to as "marital rape" is making clear that the morality of sexuality, even in marriage, is not decided by marital status alone, but by non-coercive consent and choice.

64. Hayes, *Echoes*, 191. In my *Hermeneutics of Ultimacy* (Lanham: University Press of America, 1987), 84, I put it this way: since "Scripture is a pastoral book, concerned to feed and shepherd the souls of the faithful ... any interpretation of Scripture which does not build the faith is misleading and inadequate."

65. Hays, *Echoes*, 192.

66. As Smedes puts it in *Sex for Christians*: "I still believe that God prefers homosexual people to live in committed and faithful monogamous relationships with each other when they cannot change and do not have the gift of celibacy," 239.

67. Hayes, *Echoes*, 183.

68. For a recent argument for such inclusion, see Jeffrey S. Siker's "How to Decide? Homosexual Christians, the Bible, and Gentile Inclusion," *Theology Today* 51/2, (July 1994): 219-34.

Is Male Dominance Against Nature?

Elaine Storkey

Autobiographical Note

Twenty-six years ago I sat in Paul Schrotenboer's home in Hamilton, Ontario, and was excited by the vision for a Christian Institute in Canada. Shortly after my return to England, that vision became a reality.

My encounter with reformational philosophy while in Canada prompted me to visit the Free University for three weeks once I was back in Europe. I visited to ask some questions of Dooyeweerd and Vollenhoven and to seek out the wisdom of John van der Hoeven among others. During that brief visit I became aware of two things. First, that I was English, and second that the worldview, vision and direction articulated by the Philosophy of the Law-Idea had profoundly changed my life.

Encouraged by these godly people, I decided to pass on what I had already assimilated in Canada to any in England who would be interested in working with me through some of the literature and ideas. We formed a small group of like-minded people, and two years after that I married one of them.

Twelve years later, committed as ever to the Reformation vision and now with three sons, Alan and I came to Calvin College to join the sociology faculty for a year. Since then, not only have others from England come over to the Institute and learned more than I ever did, but there has been a steady flow of two way traffic. Meanwhile, in England the reformational worldview has been disseminated and forms a significant part of our own developing Christian culture.

I'm acutely aware of the tensions raised by the subject of male dominance and all of the questions surrounding it and, as someone who is at heart a reconciler and peacemaker, I'm wary of the possibility that I may actually fuel dispute. Certainly, we encounter strong disagreement in England on this matter, albeit on slightly different questions. Currently, much heart-searching is going on over the issue of the ordination of women within the Church of England. Those most vehemently opposed cite sexuality and nature in their defence. For them, men are by their very nature more fitted for the sacramental service of the church. Indeed, Anglo-

Catholic men often take the view that they are closer to God than women are, even if this is just in an advisory capacity.

However, many of these gender problems are rooted in our tendency to erect stereotypes and in our failure to listen. For me, this is admirably illustrated by the story of an English archdeacon, well-known for his opposition to the ordination of women, who was attending an Anglican conference in Canada. The centre where the conference was to be held was high up in the mountains in Alberta, and so the archdeacon was required to negotiate sharp hairpin bends in a rented car. For quite a few miles the sight of the great drop beneath him every time the front of his Buick edged over the bend made the archdeacon feel sick. He was just starting to relax when a Ford convertible came down the other side of the road at a crazy speed. Horrified, the Archdeacon watched the car wavering across the road, only to realise that the driver was a woman wearing a clerical collar. The archdeacon, furious at the woman's driving, was unable to move further over, and so she had to brake rapidly in order to avoid a collision. He watched numbly as the woman swerved and screeched past his car. As she did so, she yelled "Pig." Disregarding his status as an English archdeacon, he bellowed back "Cow!" It was with great anger and a rising temperature that he set off to take the next corner too fast and proceeded to hit a pig! Of course, the moral of this story is that we need to judge less and listen more, for when we do so perhaps we will hear something which is advantageous to us.

A Question of Definition

As I seek to discuss whether male dominance is against nature, I find myself encountering a second difficulty: I do not know what "nature" is. It was from you that I learned, more than twenty-five years ago, that nature is indeed a complicated concept. For example, do I understand it to be some sort of irreducible essence which is central to our ontological personhood? Or is it that which was seized upon by the Enlightenment in its emphasis on natural rights, natural religion, the state of nature and the natural light of reason? Perhaps it is the "autonomous nature" which is set over and against the "freedom of the human personality"? I have no linguistic access to an unambiguous "nature" which is not already located within an unfolding worldview and undergirded with philosophical assumptions.

Even with this mapping out of territory, the task is not a great deal clearer, for the term "male dominance" brings its own problems. It carries unfortunate overtones and receives a bad press. In England at least, those who argue in favour of male dominance as opposed to priority, responsibility over creation or headship over women find that they have few followers. Asking people to vote for dominance is comparable to staging a U.S. election campaign under the slogan "Clinton for Despot." Of course, the end result might be the same whatever words we select. This is the point made by those who attack the Christian church. They say that we may call it what we like, but the underlying concept remains one of dominance and oppression.

Male dominance is generally referred to as "patriarchy." Those who use it most argue that the term is imprecise and global because of the global nature of the system itself. Patriarchy is denoted by the concentration of power, control, privileges, decision-making and even the means of decision-making in male hands. Of course, this is not in individual male hands, for it is the corporate structure of patriarchy which gives it its power and vehemence. Wherever there are structures of authority, whether in business, commerce, the state, then university, the home, the trade union or the church, they are all invested in the male. Consequently, even in advanced western societies women in the workforce can earn considerably less than men, are less likely to be promoted and have to struggle for recognition in the professions. Besides this, women experience a far greater degree of poverty than men and are the ones who usually suffer the ill consequences of divorce. (In the U.S.A. fewer than a fifth of divorced men continue to pay maintenance for their children after one year.) Women are also more likely to experience physical or sexual violence. The pattern is the same in the world's poorer countries. Women suffer disproportionate poverty and are most heavily exploited as cheap labour in the production of luxury goods to be sold to rich countries. When they have nothing left to sell but their bodies, they are forced into prostitution. On a recent trip to Brazil, it struck me that nearly all of the street children were boys. When I asked where the girls were, suggesting that their parents protected them at home, my naivete was met with incredulity.

The point I am attempting to establish is that patriarchy has multifarious faces. Of course, some are kind. Benign husbands and fathers would never dream of abusing their wives or daughters, but perpetuate the status quo by remaining silent in the face of what they know to be injustice. Others are greedy. They push the pornographic industry to its very limits, demonstrating indifference towards the dehumanisation of the women portrayed in magazines and video nasties and the enslavement and destruction of men who become addicted to anonymous, fantasy sex as a cheap but pathetic substitute for the intimacy of troth and commitment.

Male dominance then is about more than who preaches the sermon in church or gives thanks for the food at the table. It is a ubiquitous system which decrees that male is normal; that men have the right to control and define; that women are given their meaning, definition and identity through men. Many women who have grown up even within Christian circles will testify to having seen themselves through male eyes and evaluations. When they wrestle to free themselves, they are able to see themselves in the light of the face of the incarnate God, Jesus Christ, and suddenly glimpse a new womanhood and a new humanity. All too often the church has colluded with those outside it in defining women as sexual, erotic and instinctual, while viewing men as more rational and normal and therefore more capable of justifying the ways of God to man.

It is precisely this powerful ability to define the meaning of women which places the church in the firing line of many feminist writers. Mary Daly is a post-Christian feminist whose writings have encouraged many women to leave the church. She is merciless in her attack, arguing that the system of male dominion undergirds all religious systems, just as it undergirds all political and economic systems. For her, the notion of male dominance holds sway not only in Marxism, Hinduism, Judaism and Islam, but in Catholicism and Reformed Protestantism. Her allegation is indicting: "Patriarchy is the prevailing relation of the entire planet."

Male Dominance Is Against Nature

For many of those who assume a feminist stance, male dominance is indeed against nature. Among this group are Susan Griffin, Mary Daly, Carol Christ and even the Canadian novelist Margaret Atwood. Images and metaphors of nature are employed in their identification of women. They appear to accept the dichotomy between the sexual and the rational, spurning male rationality because it is represents exploitation—exploitation not just of women, but extending through the whole of life. In that the planet is particularly adversely affected, male dominance is, for those occupying this school of thought, profoundly in conflict with nature. And so, for these women a new religious language develops. Mary Daly speaks for many others in saying:

> This is a period of extreme danger for women and for our sister earth and her other creatures, all of whom are targeted by the maniacal fathers, sons, and holy ghosts for extraction by nuclear holocaust, or failing that, by chemical contamination.... Yet at this time, somehow living/longing through, above, before and beyond it, thousands of women struggle to remember ourselves and our history to sustain and intensify a biophilic consciousness. Having once known the intense joy of woman—identified bonding and creation, we refuse to turn back.

The sense of a bond between woman and the basic life of earth is a theme constantly revisited. On the Greek island of Lesbos, under the radioactive cloud caused by Chernobyl, Carol Christ writes:

> I know this earth is my sister more deeply than I feel and know anything. My spirituality stems from a sense of connectedness to this earth.

This theme is taken up by indigenous women in North and South America. They blame the patriarchal and capitalistic West for robbing them of their land rights and violating their mother, the earth, and so depriving them of a close relationship with the sweet, fresh winds and the clean, pure air.

For these writers and for many others—including to an increasing extent those within the church—the culprit can now be named. Male dominance in all its colonising and aggressive forms is profoundly anti-nature, for it is against body and against the motherhood of humanity. Therefore, a true woman-spirituality must go back to the earth and embrace. According to one Canadian speaker at a conference of Christian women which I attended, this is the source from which the Holy Spirit emanates—woman-spirit, giver of light and life to all who love her.

The vociferous attack on the supposedly male God of Christianity was launched in the 1970s by Mary Daly's book *Beyond God the Father*. It has deepened into a permanent sense of alienation, whereby Christianity is seen as aggressively and irredeemably sexist and responsible for unleashing untold harm on the entire planet. For these women, the traditional God upheld by such a religion will no longer do.

Male Dominance in Obedience to Nature

The route taken by these feminists—choosing to identify women with nature—is a costly one. They may be rejecting the male implications drawn from it, but at the same time they are reinforcing the male/female division which has penetrated various branches of the church for very many years. Thomas Aquinas articulated this split:

> Woman is defective and misbegotten, for the active force in the male seed tends to the production of a perfect likeness in the masculine sex, while the production of woman comes from defect force or some maternal indisposition, or even from some external influence—such as that of the south wind, which is moist.

Aquinas's view was, of course, something which he had inherited from Greek dualism. Aristotle asserted that the male semen gave Form to the Matter provided by woman, so effectively giving her a rational soul. Aquinas modifies this, stating that God gives the soul to the fetus, while the male simply prepares the matter in so far as it is ready to accept the soul. In either case, the active principle is the prerogative of the man, for the woman offers matter and in that sense the body is defective.

By no means was Aquinas a solo voice. Attitudes which deemed women to be bodily and sexual proliferated in the early church. Clement of Alexandria believed not just that women's bodies were passive, but that they were potentially contaminating: "Woman is a temple built over a sewer." Jerome expressed concern that women's rouge might "inflame lustful passion." There are many more quotations identifying women as sexual, passive and possessing the capacity to defile while pinpointing rational, active and prior qualities as idiosyncratic to men. Perhaps the ultimate is a remark made by Odo of Cluny in the twelfth century: "To embrace a woman is to embrace a sack of manure."

Similar notions can be located in certain social/psychological and biological theories, according to which male dominance is rooted in biology, anatomy, physiology and hormones. A single example from the sociobiological school of thought (one which has been gaining more adherents in recent years) will suffice to make the point.

Sociobiology

Sociobiology places the identity of our human personhood in our biology and, while acknowledging the need for social adaptation, particularly in our genes. We are driven by our evolutionary need to ensure our genetic survival and require optimum conditions to make certain that our own genetic material is passed on rather than that of others. For sociobiologists, it is here that the explanation for male-female dissonance lies.

Stress is placed upon the fact that, presupposing sufficient sexual energy and a plentiful stream of human partners, the human male can produce two hundred offspring. Women, on the other hand, can produce no more than twenty or so children at best, and most settle for two or three. This discrepancy forms the basis of the sociobiologist's assertion that men and women have incompatible genetic needs. Men, they state, need more women with whom to copulate, while women need a safe environment in which to raise their limited number of children. From this, the conclusion is drawn that the fundamental power in society is patriarchal not matriarchal. Women have claimed victory via social taboos, religion and the development of the appeasement tactic for domestication of the male. The latter means that the natural sexual aggression required by the male in order to compete for sexual partners has been channelled into sport, national wars, business, politics and the church. There is, however, a price to be paid for this victory: because aggression and promiscuity are deeply engrained in the genetic makeup of the male, they will periodically surface. Such surfacing will produce rape, assault and various forms of sexual attack. No level of sophistication within our societies will enable us to eradicate these, simply because male dominance is in keeping with nature.

I do not intend to produce a critique of this position. A great deal of evidence countermanding such a view could easily be cited, besides which its reductionism will be evident to all. I merely wish to draw attention to fact that, despite considerable research in the fields of both psychology and sociology about the development of identity and the formation of structural power, biologistic explanations for social phenomena continue to find a hearing.

Rather than becoming caught up in adjudicating between various responses to the question of whether or not male dominance is against nature, I'd like to step back and examine a bigger issue which lies beneath the entire discussion. The question I actually want to ask runs, "Is our emphasis on creation order out of step with a commitment to compassion in the area of gender?" Many would say that this is indeed the case, arguing that rigid acceptance of the "order of creation" places women in subordination to men, and by doing so has contributed substantially to the patriarchal oppression of women throughout the ages. Moreover, the argument proceeds, this emphasis alone has enabled a wedge to be placed between men and women and assigned to each different identities and values. As such, it has not only provided and inadequate basis upon which to build relationships, but it has also failed to facilitate the exercise of empathy and compassion. The very Christian basis which might have offered liberation and meaning has been one which has increased the suffering and pain of women.

Yet, I am deeply reluctant to concede that we must jettison a substantial part of our own tradition and framework and make a new departure. I remain unconvinced that a paradigm shift is necessary, but suspect that that same tradition could itself offer a better way forward for fuller understanding of the issues and resolution of the pain. Even the cosmonomic law idea, I believe, could provide greater help and insight if only we would allow adequate breathing space. We need not chase after some rumour of gold in a distant country, but rather we should examine more carefully the metal which we have quarried from our own mine and discarded as dross. To employ a more environmentally acceptable metaphor, we need to listen to our own stories and hear the joys and heartaches of the sisters and brothers of our own family before journeying off to foreign lands in search of new scripts. We possess so much love, so much commitment, so much experience, so much sorrow and so much loss. We need only to find words to articulate them and ears to listen.

Our own tradition offers highly valuable insights which can act as a useful starting point. It offers, for example, deep analysis of the nature of our human personhood, which includes human sexuality. It doesn't root our identity in the earth, in our biology, in form or matter, in our separateness or autonomy. Instead, our identity is rooted in our fundamental experience of ourselves as beings created in God's image and so linked to eternity. We are all creatures, for, along with the earth, the winds, the trees and the animal kingdom, we are in a relationship of dependency with the creator God. Yet, the God upon whom we depend creates us, both male and female, in his own image—an image of unity, reciprocality, mutuality, distinctiveness and respect. We are in every sense persons in relationship—relationship with God, with one another and with the creation itself as it groans and travails.

Our own tradition bears testimony to the diversity both of creation and of our own lives. But by not rooting our identity in that diversity, it enables us to see in perspective those who would.

While as created persons, both male and female, we function in every modal aspect, our tradition does not locate our identity in any of those functions. It tells us that men are not to be placed in the rational/logical and women in the biotic or physical. Such an approach is apostasy, for together we think thoughts, experience emotions and come to know and appreciate our sexuality. We are called in a union of love and obedience to the God who has created us and who, through Jesus Christ, is redeeming us.

Finally, it is crucial that we recognise that the Christian gospel cannot be Good News for both men and women, nor the reformational movement celebrate this same Good News in every area of life simply through the articulation of the Law Word of God in his diverse creation. It is also to be achieved through the worship of Jesus Christ, the word made flesh, the one who is before all things, the one for whom all things were created and the one in whom all things are held together. Through this we recognize that Jesus Christ is the integration point and unity of our lives, our church and the world order; we acknowledge that we are Christ's body, brought into redemption and into reconciliation with God, with each other and with creation itself though the cross. In Jesus there is freedom and recovery of integrity.

When we put aside our words and seek Christ's face in worship we begin to experience something profound about compassion and shalom. As we see Jesus, we are brought into contact with God who does not break the bruised reed or quench the smoking flax, but who believes in the integrity of creation. Those of us who have been oppressed by the egoistic exercise of power can begin to feel the warmth of love which the Saviour offers and which his modern disciples so often distort. The fundamental model of both creation order and compassion is one of creatureliness, servanthood, and humility. It is a model which requires reverence for Christ, submission to and love for one another, expressed in seeking the interests of the other before our own. As such, the model precludes dominance of any kind: "By this shall all people know you are my disciples, if you show love one to another."

Order and the Transcendence of Order

A Meditation on Order, Sin and Grace

Langdon Gilkey

Order is a most important aspect of creation, though it represents by no means all of created reality. Correspondingly, order or law are crucial aspects of God but—thank God—not all there is of God. This dialectic of order or law and what transcends order and law in nature, in human affairs and in God is my central concern in this essay.

I hardly need to remind you that the dialectic of law and gospel, of the *order* of God, transcended but not negated by the justifying *mercy* of God, is the center of what is often called the biblical gospel. It certainly was the center of the Reformation, of its great uncle Augustine, and of its veritable progenitor St. Paul. Order is truly of God; law is God's law, but because of sin, order becomes a principle of divine condemnation and also of human depravity and death (Romans 5:20; 7:7-8, and 7:10). Hence it is God alone who fulfils and justifies God's own law, and God does so precisely by going beyond the law in the atoning work of Christ and in God's justifying and sanctifying grace to us. Order is fulfilled—as it must be fulfilled—not by its denial but by its transcendence and transmutation in mercy and love, and only thus can it remain order, God's order. This is a paradox, but there is not much in sacred theology that is not.

If, on the one hand, order and law are ignored or omitted, then understanding and self-discipline are alike impossible, creation is unravelled, chaos results and there is no mercy anywhere. But, on the other hand—and this for us in the middle classes is far more surprising—if order or the law, or in the Republican reversal, "law and order"—are all there is to nature, to morals, to God's revelation to us and God's message to us, then veritably all is lost in condemnation, in injustice and in sin, whatever the leaders of the neo-Calvinist tradition, or of the Catholic natural law tradition, for that matter, may have said. This is unexpected. Is not order the first necessity for any being, for any science or knowledge, for any social peace or harmony, for "rights" of any sort, and so for equality and freedom? What is wrong with order, or in religious language, why are not God's laws, God's holy ordinances for creation, for society, for the home, for the church—and for salvation itself—enough? Why is not the clear revelation of "God's universal principles of justice and righteousness," of "the immutable laws of the divine maker of all things"—these laws seen in nature, repeated in the Word, and assented to in the heart—sufficient for understanding, for a creative and serene soul, and for true piety?

When we reread Paul, or Paul's descendent Augustine in his great *On the Spirit and the Letter*, we see the answer: the omnipresence of sin in all of us. Sin is estrangement from God and neighbor, a curving in on ourselves in radical self-interest. It results in a consequent pride, obscures and corrupts the law. Sin, so the Bible tells us, is something we all participate in, whether we are aware of it or not. And thus it is sin that transforms God's law into a vehicle at once of our unrighteousness and so of the divine commandment (e.g., Galatians 3:19). Sin therefore makes it necessary for grace to replace law, to transmute it and so in the end to fulfil God's law. Order and law are sacred but not *God*. Hence both can, because of sin, become demonic unless God's grace infuses order with love, law with a higher compassion. Sin renders God's law ambiguous at best, and it turns us not to law but to grace for relief.

Let us be clear, sin is not so much disobedience to recognized law as it is that which distorts and warps recognized law into an instrument of destruction and not of salvation. The world is fallen partly because it disobeys the law of creation, but even more because it corrupts and distorts that law. Surely this is what Paul said in Romans 5-7 and repeated in Galatians 3: law without grace and love—both divine and human—means the death of both body and spirit. This is the rock on which the Reformation churches were established. Were it not for sin, law would have no need for grace, nor the Catholic church for a Reformation! (As an aside, I am bemused that the intervention of sin into God's creation had to be brought first to our evangelical, Reformed conference by a representative—if a poor one—of the Chicago school. Such are the surprises of history!)

This gospel theme, the dialectic of sin, law and grace, is *seen* only in revelation, principally for us in the life and death of Christ. Yet I also believe it is seen in God's covenantal relation to the Hebrews of creative gift, judgment, and promise—though that is another story. I believe that this theme or dialectic is, however, the best pattern or paradigm for all of God's activity in our world. It is best for the mystery of creation and so of nature, for the even deeper mystery of history and so of providence, and for the strangest stories of all, the stories of our lives together in search of ourselves and of each other. If once seen in faith, as we say, this pattern can then be seen everywhere. As Calvin repeatedly said, "Once we have put on the spectacles of Scripture, we can see clearly the presence and work of God in all of creation." My point is that *what* we can see there are no so much God's universal principles or laws—though they are surely there, if clouded or obscured—as this dialectic, initiated by sin, of law, sin and gospel, of created order, disruption and compassion, of order and the transcendence and transmutation of order in love. I shall make my point by beginning with the *sacrality* of order, proceeding to the *ambiguity* of order through sin, and ending with the consequent need for the *transcendence* of order, and illustrating this theme in the two overwhelmingly important social issues of our day.

The Sacrality of Order

Order has always disclosed itself as a sacred aspect of the reality outside and inside us, along (let us note) with power and life. We habitually trace this sense of order—as families are wont to do—back only to our own cultural ancestors, in our case to the earliest Greeks and the Hebrew wisdom literature, these two streams surprisingly uniting later in the divine Logos through whom all things were created. But the sense of sacred order permeating all and giving each entity its value is quite universal in human experience. In the earliest primal religion of which we know, a sacred order binds all entities together, an order understood by the shamans, carefully followed out in religious rites, and renewing life whenever it was obediently repeated. A quite different sacred order rules all change and all life in Sumeria and Egypt (as professor Wolters noted), in ancient India, the Dharma, and then in another form in China as the Tao. I mention this to emphasize how universal is this disclosure of order or law, in each case a law governing not only nature, history and society but giving normative principles and rules to each individual life as well. Of course in each case the understanding and expression of this sacred order varies with its culture, but the perception of reality as order is universal.

For all of these cultures life is to be renewed and fulfilled only if the sacred law is obeyed, and correspondingly life disintegrates into suffering and ultimately into non-being when this order is flouted. The Greeks and the Hebrews certainly believed this, but they were not the only ones. Nor is all this only metaphysics, though metaphysics quickly expressed it. Basically it was a *religious* intuition or manifestation. It has been interesting to me to see how vigorously and enthusiastically the neo-Calvinists apparently returned to this long tradition: creation embodies the divine law originally thought by God, a law that governs, or should govern, all of life, namely science, technology, aesthetics, morals and religion. Hence true piety is to study, recognize, acknowledge and embody this divine law in all aspects of life: in the body politic, the home, the university and the religious community.

Let us note that modern culture, in moving away from this *religious* and *normative* interpretation of law, has by no means denied the rule of law. In fact modern science and its sibling, modern scientific technology, as professor De Witt said, are established on the firm belief in a universal order pervading all of space and time, an order making the existence of our universe and its life possible, an order discoverable by human inquiry and expressible in human mathematics, an order which, when carefully obeyed by those who uncover and know it, will—as Francis Bacon prophesied—grant nearly infinite power to the knower. For us moderns the shaman, the Bramanic priest, the Confucian scholar, the Rabbi, and the neo-Calvinist have been transmuted into the priest in the white coat, the scientists, the "expert" through whose knowledge comes power. Through that power will come in turn infinite well-being. Few myths about order and its benefits have been more persuasive than this one, and yet more naive! Other echoes of the older tradition that united order and value remain with us: the eternal laws of the free market, as known by the scientific students of these laws, the economists, will, if obeyed, bring universal prosperity; and in yet another, the Catholic, tradition, God's natural law is our only guide in family and sexual matters.

On the whole, however, modern scientific, academic and professional culture represents, so it seems to me, not so much a "natural law" tradition as a confused dualism, a kind of poor man's Cartesianism. For most of the academy reality is defined and only defined by science. On the one hand, therefore, whatever is real is what can be discovered by science, a system determined by necessitating, purposeless and valueless law; hence reality in itself, "what is the case," is valueless. On the other hand, the objective science that knows that the impersonal system of law is itself conducted by a knowing, intellectual *subject*, and that subject follows, or "uses," a quite different set of laws (the rules of logic or of thinking) and acts according to an entirely different set of principles, namely (hopefully) the humanistic values of the democratic tradition. The objective mind that *does* science, and the moral idealism that *directs* the use of science exist, therefore, in a different "world" than does the determined reality that science studies and uses. Object is thus here sundered from subject, nature from the science that studies and manipulates nature. That second world of the subject is ruled by the intellectual laws of objective logic and the moral laws of democratic idealism—at least so it is claimed. This latter realm is not at all deterministic but in fact is radically Platonic and Pelagian, so long, that is, as one dons the white coat that is necessary for entrance into that realm of rationality and freedom. Frankly, I'm not sure which social world seems to me to be worse: a theocratic society ruled by ulemas (or their Christian equivalents) schooled in ancient and barely relevant religious laws, or a technical society ruled by experts in *our* secret laws, the so-called laws of nature, the laws of society, and the laws of the psyche! Modernity and its laws provide no answer to the modern search for order and for a humane order. So let us return to our theme: the sacrality and the ambiguity of order.

The Ambiguity of Order

Order is sacred, of God, and yet deeply ambiguous. For the law without grace "brings about wrath" (Romans 4:15), *kills*, says Paul (Romans 7:10-11), becomes a cause of death, that is, it reveals and encourages sin, and so it is a law that condemns us all. What do these familiar but bizarre biblical thoughts *mean*: for they *are* bizarre (foolishness) to all the cultures we have rehearsed, not least to modern scientific and technological culture. How are we really to understand them, as well as repeat them dutifully? That is, what do they *mean* in our actual experience? For I believe that these thoughts about the ambiguity of law—or the dialectic of law, sin and grace which they presuppose—provide the only real clue, the only true paradigm, that can illuminate the mystery of our common experience.

We can sense this deep ambiguity of order—even the demonic possibilities of order—in our most common political apprehensions and intuitions. We speak of "world order," an "old" world order and a "new" world order. The old one was ambiguous enough: the former colonial order—what we who had empires called "peace"—which stifled, exploited and oppressed most of the peoples of the world. Then there was briefly the "new" order of Asia promised by the resurgent Japanese and in Europe promised by the Third Reich. Or possibly we mean the communist order dominant for seven decades throughout the Soviet Union and for four decades in Eastern Europe, an order so oppressive and stagnant that even the anarchy that may follow it seems a relief. "Our order," be it that of the British colonial past or of the recent American century, appears to us as justice as well as peace; to those whom it ruled it has appeared once, and it still does, as oppressive and exploitative. The same is true of the order, an order of creation it was called, that established the priority and supremacy of men, in society and home alike. In most male eyes this was a divine and creative ordinance, but hardly so for women, once a higher law can reveal the *sin* of this law!

The prime example of the ambiguity of order is from our most recent history, namely, the "law and order" manifested to all the world—except to the propertied classes and their government in America—an oppressive and destructive system, an order established on and representative of rank racial and economic injustice, and hence inevitably one that bred violence if not revolution. Unless that order is transformed into one moving toward justice, it will, we may be sure, disintegrate into permanent disorder. So it has in fact been throughout our century: an established order is always and also an *ambiguous* order, in fact a "fallen" order, an order tainted and warped by sin. It thus breeds protest, violence and ultimately revolution; hence, if it will not transform itself, it breeds its own ultimate demise. The righteousness and justice of God are not absent from history. Nor do they reside only in the holy law. More often—according to the biblical word—the divine judgments are illustrated in the condemnation visited on those who represent and enforce the law, on all unjust rulers when, like the tallest trees, they are cut down and burned.

Sin Corrupts Order

How is this possible? How can order, which brings unity and peace, and hence is the only condition for security, creativity and fulfilment, for family dependence and individual independence alike, how can order become so destructive, so much the instrument of suffering; how can order or law *kill*? The answer in both testaments is, of course *sin*. On the one hand, sin breeds disobedience and disorder and so sin *requires* order if there is to be peace. Were it not for sin there would be no need even for law—a theological point well recognized and respected in Los Angeles and in Washington. On the other hand, and on a more fundamental level, sin *corrupts* order—a point quite unknown among the ruling classes, though one, may I hazard, familiar to the French and the native Canadians in Canada. Sin transmutes order into injustice and oppression. Let us see what this means: how *does* sin corrupt order?

Each community, said Augustine, strives for unity, harmony and peace—it yearns in all it does for the order and love of the Kingdom. But the order it establishes over another community favors itself. Or if we speak of a domestic order, the order it establishes over itself favors its own ruling class, as the order men establish in the home sustains and encourages a male dominance. Order represents the interests of those who rule, and it overlooks, if it does not entirely negate, the interests of those who are ruled. Hence each actual peace is never real peace but in part an unjust peace; each actual order is not real order but in part an oppressive order. Marx saw this, as had Augustine; Marx did not see, however, that the oppressive ruling class is not just those who have once owned property, but as Karl Popper reminds us, the ruling class is those who rule, whatever their origins. Thus could the communist elite be their ruling class as in another society the ruling class could be, and still is, the bourgeois elite—who still (at least in the United States) think *the* only ruling classes are the European nobility! In all of these cases when we speak of sin we refer to an overweening, an inordinate self-interest, the self making itself, or its community, the center of the world; a grasping after power, wealth and privilege, and a fierce determination to hang on to all of this; and finally identifying its order with God's order, the rule of its law with the rule of God. It is this inordinate self-interest on the part of the powerful that corrupts each historical order. Thus nowhere in actual history do we have the divine law *itself*; in every tradition we have only its strangely warped form—as a feminist critique of even scriptural law will show. In this at least theological "religion" joins hand with historical relativism and so the historical consciousness—once in a while John Dewey and Reinhold Niebuhr shook hands across Broadway!

Religious communities can also sin, as history shows, not only secretly by coveting their private vices, but openly by identifying their own law with God's law. Again, we can all see these religious failings in other religious communities: in the authoritarianism and inquisitorial persecution of the late medieval and counter-reformational Catholic church, in a number of present Islamic communities, and in potentiality even in Israel. We have much more difficulty seeing this in ourselves, or even as a possibility for ourselves. But let me say to this probably politically liberal readership that this is the grave sin tempting your American evangelical second-cousins at the moment: the lure of a theocratic rule by the saints—God's own order; a rule, if not directly, then at least via a captured right-wing Republicanism. To me this is one of the darkest of our many nightmarish scenarios for the future. A religious order, even a "correct" religious order, can and almost certainly will fall into injustice and oppression; the law of God, even in our innocent hands, even in the hands of the saints, can become the instrument of social destruction. This is hard for us to believe—in the New Testament is not this warning addressed only to the Jews?

But you do not need to sin to be religious in this way. I am reminded of the bakery advertisement in New York city that said, "You do not need to be Jewish to eat bagels." Secular communities, too, especially their ruling groups, can identify their own interests with those of history, of justice or of peace, or all three together, as any nationalist fervor, as the fascists and the communists have in our century all shown. Sin is here the interest of a part of the community over against the whole, and the insistence by that part that it represents the whole. Hence it follows that the aggression, the dominance, the privileges of this group are warranted. In society it is the part claiming to be the whole that constitutes social sin, the part that creates, sustains and preserves social injustice, and that finally leads to ultimate disorder and chaos. Interpreted theologically this is the self, the social self, usurping the role of God. To preserve itself over time, order must become *more* than order; order must incorporate *justice* into itself. Thus begins the dialectic with which we started, the dialectic through which order is transmuted into what transcends order, namely into justice and then into law, an order fulfilled only by grace.

The Transcendence of Order

We said we would examine, or illustrate further, this dialectic, this gospel paradigm or order, sin and grace, in terms of two overwhelmingly important social issues of our time, the problem of social justice on the one hand and the crisis of the natural environment on the other. We could well have taken the issue of gender, but I do not know how well I would do that.

In both of these crises (social justice and the environment) the role of order is crucial. But in both of them an untranscended order, making order central, becomes fatal because of the intervention of sin. It is because of sin—radical self-interest— not because of a lack of knowledge or ignorance, that both problems are so intractable. Possibly this closer look at both will help us see precisely what the place of "compassion" may be in the justification, the redemption of order—or in Calvin's terms, what in our day might be the "third function of the law," the function that unites law and grace.

Let us begin with the issue that presently dominates our minds, that of social justice, and—as if it were necessary—let us recall the recent riots in Los Angeles as an example of our theme. The ultimate causes of that event were racism and neglect: racism that consigns our minorities to large-scale poverty, unemployment and hopelessness, and neglect on the part of two administrations who refused, because it would cost a little tax money, and because there were few votes for them there, to do anything for the inner cities. In fact they stopped doing the little that was then being done. Then came the insane verdict that the police who beat up Rodney King were innocent, a clear result of racial prejudice and the blind defense of one's own racial tribe. The resulting violence tore that society apart briefly. For a brief time we in the United States looked into the monstrous face of anarchy, as we have recently seen in Azerbijan, Bosnia and Croatia. Order, as we have said, is an absolute necessity, but an unjust order becomes tyranny and will not survive. Sooner or later it gives way to anarchy, its terrible opposite.

The diagnoses and the prescriptions of the administration in Washington represent classic—and fatuous—reactions of a now worried upper class: outrage at the violence their own neglect and covert racism have caused; blame that "socialist" or "liberal" ideals have twisted the minds and the goals of an otherwise contented underclass; and most common of all in such social upheavals, urgent appeals to those suffering in the inner city to shore up and round off their decaying "spiritual life," their "family values"—as if those values were as easily available to persons facing grinding poverty, joblessness, prostitution, abandoned children and hopelessness as it is to the affluent middle classes. Of course family values and the spiritual life are important. As I am urging here, no social order is possible without the strongest sort of moral character (of justice and even of law) in its people. But it is sheer hypocrisy when that is the only message that comes from affluence to poverty, from the well-fed to the starving, from those "in" the society to those dependent on it but quite outside it. What in effect it says is: though you cannot come into our working midst, you are on your own; we who profit from the social order will not share one dime of its rewards with you who cannot so profit; and we are not in any way responsible for your plight or for its alleviation—the sharpest sort of denial of any sort of real family values.

Let us recall with some repentance that this message of "spiritual values" rather than any sort of difficult and costly social transformation was precisely what most Christians, in fact most "evangelicals," preached from the 1890s through the 1920s to the growing poor in American cities, and also in Europe. It was, let us also recall, only that convert to liberalism, Walter Rauschenbusch, who showed churches the way to a new *communal* understanding of the gospel, a social understanding of the responsibility of the Christian for that Christian's neighbor. Our American evangelicals still repeat the old words, "Give them a spiritual message but not bread"! Reagan, Bush and Quale have said the same thing from a more prominent platform, and will reap the same worldwind for us all!

Order must be qualified by justice, shaped by justice, if it is to represent order, if it is to *be* over time. But in a society which by its very creative dynamic breeds inequality, unfortunately justice requires ever and again some *sharing*, sharing in some way of one's substance with the other who is in need. It never hurts us to share something that is non-essential to our being, like small change, a can of beer, or an extra piece of cake, and thus we consider ourselves generous. It does hurt, however, to share of one's substance, of one's essential property, place and power. Such essential loss in favor of the other makes one more insecure, hence more anxious about the morrow, less able to have all one wants, less able to provide for one's own—all *good* reasons to resist sharing, unfortunately. This sharing requires some genuine measure of sacrifice. It means admitting a new range of responsibilities, a larger circle of "neighbors." Justice, being just, *hurts* those who enjoy privilege. That is why privilege always has to be *pushed* unwillingly into reforms, if not *prodded* there by revolution.

It is far easier for the middle and wealthier classes to disclaim responsibility for anyone else ("all for their own good," of course), continue to accumulate as much of this world's goods as possible, to call righteously on law and order to deal with the results, and to appeal to the ideology of a natural order of the free market which prohibits interference in the economic realm. Thus does every ruling class "justify" its actions in its own interest by such appeals to order, the order that secures and enhances its own well-being.

We can see clearly in this tragedy that order requires justice, but further it is plain that justice requires a measure of love, of *agape*, of concern for the other, whoever or whatever she or he may be, accompanied by a humble and repentant acknowledgement of our own complicity in the suffering and violence. Compassion is not just added to order. Compassion—I prefer repentance and love—must be ingredient in any actual order for order itself to survive. This is the transmutation I spoke of, the weird dialectic of the sacred: order, beset by sin, moving into justice in order to be and remain order, and both—order and justice—necessarily qualified by repentance and grace if they are to remain alive. No wonder—since, as Calvin said, the gospel presents us with a hard and arduous road—social problems are intractable!

I have called all this "sin"; that is our traditional and biblical word, but it is the only one that fits. In our usual, everyday usage sin tends to mean lawlessness and vice, and so is usually applied only to the untutored classes, to a few "unrespectable" people in the middle class, and above all to the kind of rioting and looting that we have here rehearsed. This, however, is *not* its biblical usage, and we should note that. In the Bible sin characterizes us all, good and bad, pious and impious alike. In the New Testament the publican, the woman taken in adultery, the thieves on the crosses are, if not "better," at least they are more acceptable (though they too are sinners) than the Pharisees, the moralistic judges that condemned the woman, and the upholders of the Sacred Law and the Roman Imperial Courts that crucified Jesus. In fact, as Reinhold Niebuhr pointed out, the biblical view has a kind of bias *against* the mighty, the rich, the wise and the good as the prime examples of "sin." Their pride as well as their power are greater, and so the effects of their self-interest on the sufferings of others are more devastating. It is they who make radically unjust the order they helped to create and which they rule, and thus is they who initiated and now perpetuate the conditions that lead to suffering and violence.

So it is with our present case. The immorality in American life is greater at the top than at the bottom, more evident among the respectable and law-abiding than among the poor in the cities. It is the immorality of greed, of wealth—those who will not pay more taxes—in order to alleviate the poverty and despair of our cities. This is also, to be sure, *pride*; they have, they assure us, earned their wealth, and they deserve it all—it is not a gift—and their view of the economic order is *the* correct view. But above all, it is that other major form of sin which is endemic to a consumer society: *concupiscence*, the greed that seeks the whole world for itself, wealth, power pleasure, especially more and more goods: "you can have it all!" Here is the form of sin besetting our present social order rendering that order in the end disorder. What is needed is more self-awareness of our actual situation of judgment and repentance, and a new sense of responsibility for our neighbor even if it hurts, a new willingness to sacrifice. These latter virtues: self-awareness, repentance and responsibility take, as always, faith, courage and compassion. But without them our secular world will come to naught. These moral virtues are possible, fortunately, in "secular" form as humility, responsibility and a moral concern for justice. But as we have tried to show, fundamentally they are the evangelical virtues, the third use of law for our age. With them—note that they *are* "spiritual values"—political and economic programs can be devised that can render our situation more just, our order more secure and creative. Incidentally, there is plenty of evangelical material here to preach, possibly even in Canada!

Order and the Crisis of Nature

Let us now look briefly at another great social issue of our time, the crisis of nature. The problem of social justice is as old as history, as is that of gender. But this one is new and very scary. Clearly we are progressively upsetting the order of nature by our intervention which, we have recently discovered, in fact oppresses and exploits nature, to use metaphors from social injustice. As a result, continued life within nature, and so our own life within nature, is endangered.

Order is thoroughly intertwined with this crisis. It is through our scientific knowledge of the order of nature that we humans have developed in the first place the technological ability to control nature, to extract and use her materials, to create new compounds, to redevelop forests and lands, and so on and on. Knowledge of the order of nature ironically allowed us to "transcend" that order in "creative" work designed to answer, so we thought, "all our needs." As a result this crisis has been created. The biblical admonition that it is the *creative* in human life that can also become the *demonic* is astoundingly validated here. As in so much of history, human creativity unites with the urge for power on the one hand, power over our destiny, and on the other hand with greed, to drive, and to drive endlessly whatever productive machine in our ingenuity we can devise. Our scientific understanding of nature is rational, the instruments we use to deal with nature are rationally designed, the productive process itself is eminently rational. In fact we *define* rationality in precisely these terms of inquiry, tool-making and systematic organization! Yet since the entire mechanism is driven by this infinite urge, this desire to devour and consume endlessly, the net result, as we are now discovering, represents the most radical *irrationality*, the virtual destruction of our own home. The pictures we have all seen from Eastern Europe give us evidence of the actuality of this unbelievable irrationality.

Science is perhaps our most brilliant human achievement. With uncanny accuracy it penetrates into the order of nature and lays that order before us in human symbols, formulae and language. Its remarkable validity is shown continuously by the undeniable fact that it works: bridges hold, planes fly, messages are communicated. But it does objectify whatever it knows. It omits the *subject*, intellectual and moral, and it abstracts away from whatever inwardness, openness, diversity, and depth its object manifests. Its picture of nature represents an abstraction, and what's more, it's a picture of an empty system of objects, a rational maze of hurrying parts. We reduce in order to understand, we kill in order to dissect, as Coleridge disdainfully put it. Hence the scientific understanding of nature's order, as an order of empty objects, leads to and makes possible the technological manipulation of nature. Thus both together, in objectifying nature, they prepare it as a fit object for use. In effect they reduce nature to the role of mere raw material for our productive needs. Science not only gives us the knowledge and the tools to exploit nature, it provides us with the attitudes towards nature that have made that exploitation possible.

Our religious tradition, let us admit, has not done much better on this issue. Emphasizing God's covenant with and love for men and women—the creative center of our cultural inheritance—it has desacralized nature and then proceeded to ignore its values for itself, its value for God, and even its value for us. Let us note again: the most creative aspects of our common cultural inheritance have together helped, along with greed, to bring on this crisis.

Something must be done. Again, however, as with social justice (and gender), the main problem is not devising solutions; there is much that can be done and done immediately. The problem is once more that any resolution *hurts*. Every solution means a sacrifice of some sort: perhaps it will raise production costs, and so jobs will be lost. As Robert Heilbroner gloomily prophesied, no society will voluntarily lower its gross national produce or its standard of living. There are no solutions that are cheap, none that are free. Hence policies that save the trees, clean the air or the water, reduce toxic waste, rescue the ozone layer—whatever—these policies all *cost* something precious, they hurt someone and perhaps they hurt all of us. Good policies require sacrifice. Thus, whether it be a capitalist or a communist society, these policies tend to be ignored, their evidence is disputed, other experts are called in. And so we delay, and in the end we endanger our world, our children's future, our species itself. In both societies, capitalist and communist alike, it has been the rational and responsible managerial class and the governments that represent that class, not the so-called irresponsible poor, that have refused to act, that ever and again balk at these policies.

Once more—note—self-interest, "sin" dominates the upper, respectable levels, not merely the lower: the managers, the investors, the employed workers, the governments that represent then. Above all, and most interesting, this radical self-interest, this "sin," prevents us precisely *from* being rational, even from a simple prudence about our survival. As Augustine said, it blinds us to our own real self-interest. In fact a rational self-interest in ecology itself represents a moral and spiritual achievement of some dimension. It requires—for us to see the problem, to believe the evidence, to embark on a painful cure—it requires a concern for nature, repentance from our past attitudes and assumptions, and above all the willingness to sacrifice some of our precious security and well-being in order that we may survive at all! No wonder that virtue, even prudence is so rare; it most always hurts.

The gospel message that order is of God, and that order brings fulfilment to life, is true. But that message must be seen within the entire gospel context if it is to be properly understood and effectively proclaimed. Order *is* of God: the order of nature, of society and of family and individual life. Our knowledge of and adherence to that order represent great and creative virtues. But order is continually warped by our pride and our greed, and order without justice and love merely breed disorder and destruction, as the biblical theme of judgment reiterates. Only if order is transmuted by justice—justice to the poor and justice to the earth—can order become creative. That transmutation will only come if through common grace we are given repentance, courage and love.

A Summing Up

Jonathan and Adrienne Chaplin

The organizers of this conference have invited us to explore whether the ethos of creation order which has guided this institution since its inception is any longer up to the challenges facing us at the end of the second millennium. The doubt, the discomfort felt, it seems, by many in the reformational Christian tradition regarding this ethos is not that it is in principle intellectually unsatisfying, nor that it is biblically unwarranted, but that it is inattentive to the cries of suffering rising up within our communities and in those outside.

The restlessness and unease with the tradition cannot be dismissed simply as "itching ears," to use the apostle Paul's phrase; it is rather a matter of "aching hearts." As Nicholas Wolterstorff put it, many people have just "had it up to here" with appeals to creation order. Someone close to us, a conservative Reformed person in Dutch reformational circles, once told us that during his youth in the 1940s he and his peers were subjected to such incessant appeals to "covenant" that they "just got sick of it"—that biblical notion has since then lost much of its power to move him.

We have to acknowledge this as something of a tragedy. When people become deaf to the liberating power of any of the words of God, that is tragic. There is in fact a biblical precedent here. Exodus 6:9 records Moses proclaiming the saving promises of God to the enslaved people of Israel. But they could not hear this word of God, the text records, "because of their broken spirit and their cruel bondage." This is the reality we face and we must deal with it redemptively and compassionately, which is how Jesus dealt with the broken spirits of his time.

While recognizing that, perhaps two observations may be worthwhile. First, we need to recognise that different communities suffer different kinds of pain—indeed they generate different kinds of pain. The pain suffered by North American Reformed Christians at the end of the twentieth century, generated by the abuse of the metaphors of order and law, may not be same as that suffered by other Christian communities elsewhere whose controlling metaphors have been different. Indeed, the metaphor of creation order has often proved a dynamic and liberating power to those coming into this tradition from outside, who are often among its most enthusiastic advocates.

Second, turning to communities outside the church, the situation is different again. It could be argued that the main characteristic of a postmodern culture is not, after all, the experience of a crisis following the abandoning of traditional norms. Rather it is the celebration of diversity and fragmentation. Postmodern people are insensitized to much of their pain, swirling as they are in a sea of endlessly changing images which numb them to their own pain and that of others. A gospel message in which compassion is the dominant note may not engage such people. Perhaps what they most need to hear, or rather see, are living examples of the fruit borne by well-ordered lives.

But let us deal with the problems as they have surfaced within this community. Insofar as other communities have been shaped by similar metaphors to ours, our experience may well have much wider significance. Different reasons have been given for the sense of dissatisfaction with the traditional understanding of creation order.

One is that excessive appeal to creation order breeds a joyless sense of duty which quenches the human spirit and breeds a deadening sense of guilt. A second is that appeals to creation order have been utilized to legitimate oppressive hierarchical structures, whether in the family, church or state. Langdon Gilkey forcefully reminded us of this as others have throughout the conference.

A third reason is that to perceive reality primarily as a testimony to a meaningful creation order prevents us from truly acknowledging and entering into the depths of human suffering, which to the victims cannot but seem meaningless.

Linked to this is a fourth misgiving: that conceiving of creation primarily in terms of an order of law, and of God primarily in terms of law-giver, would lead us to explain the brokenness of creation exclusively in terms of human rebellion against that order—surely the book of Job, if not the inexplicable, arbitrary tragedies many of us have experienced, should cause us to question that.

Finally, making creation order the controlling metaphor in biblical hermeneutics is to fail to grasp truly both the narrative character of Scripture and the narrative character of our own lives.

These diverse misgivings may be part of a more fundamental problem endemic in the reformational worldview. We are familiar with reciting the well-known trilogy of biblical motifs: creation, fall and redemption, each integrally linked to the others. But perhaps what our conference has suggested is that we have simply been paying lip-service to this integrality, loudly proclaiming their inner connections but in practice letting creation set the dominant tone. Perhaps we have allowed our celebration of the creation-motive (as Dooyeweerd called it), our amazement at the splendour and majesty of God shown in his created works, to squeeze out a full confrontation with the destructive power of sin, and to muffle the radicality and transforming power of Jesus Christ. We have often accused Barthians and others of Christomonism; but perhaps there has been a creation-monism within ourselves, denied intellectually but at work spiritually; and perhaps it is now bearing its own bitter fruits.

Much of the critical discussion of the reformational tradition in the last few days can perhaps be seen as urging us to practice what we have preached, to recapture—perhaps even to discover for the first time—the full integrality of the biblical narrative of creation, fall and redemption.

Two of the major substantive proposals made in this conference can also perhaps be seen in this light: Hart's proposal to replace an ethos of order with an ethos of compassion, and Allen Verhey's recommendation of a new "narrative" hermeneutic. Hart seeks an ethos that serves redemptive ends, and Verhey wants a hermeneutic that arises out of the story of salvation.

Since Hart's proposal for an ethos of compassion generated much controversy here, we'll organize our thoughts around that. Several central questions emerged from Hart's proposals.

First, why must we choose a single biblical metaphor as a way of capturing the ethos we seek? Hendrik Hart claimed that we must, because we need a spiritual centre, a focus around which our communal practices can cohere. But is this quest for such a single metaphor not misplaced, others asked. Might not an ethos of compassion eventually go dead on us just as an ethos of order seems to have done? Why not simply try to hold all biblical metaphors together simultaneously? Or better, keep them all together in our quiver but then judiciously select the arrow most appropriate to the situation before us at a particular time. This is surely what Paul did and, it seems, so did Jesus. If we are persuaded of the fundamental unity of Scripture, we should be able to convey the whole truth of the gospel through any one of its parts; and we may feel free to do so.

A second question is the relation between compassion and truth. Hart's strictures against legalism and intellectualism were, it seems, well taken, with one exception. Johan van der Hoeven questioned Hart's claim that Dooyeweerd, for example, exemplified the logocentric rationalism which has done so much of the damage here. That issue needs clarifying.

But many raised the question: If compassion transcends order, as Hart suggested, what is left of the content of compassion? Could we even recognize suffering as suffering if there were not order of which it was a violation? Of course there is a radical difference between God's order and our own necessarily fallible human responses to that order. Certainly compassion must transcend fallen human order. But in doing so it must itself be guided by God's order, otherwise it could, at best, fail correctly to identify the needs of the sufferer or, at worst, turn into the murderous compassion that Stanley Hauerwas and Allen Verhey warned of (each in his own distinctive manner).

This leads us into a third question, difficult to express adequately: how specific is God's order? How much detail is there in the normative design of creation? And how wide is the scope of free human response to that order? Another way to put the question is: how much of the order that we need in order to live are we required to construct ourselves? Consider marriage. If the creational norm for marriage is heterosexual monogamy, humans have relatively limited discretion in deciding on the nature of the marital bond. If however the norm for marriage is simply "troth," then both heterosexual and homosexual bonds are permissible. The same kind of question arises when we consider the state, or any other supposed creation structure.

Now it became quite clear that both sides in this debate wish to affirm both given order and subjective human response. But there is a deep disagreement over where the boundary is to be located. This disagreement certainly exists regarding particular questions. The most prominent of these at this conference turned out to be homosexuality, the discussion of which generated considerable unease. But the issue of the environment also throws up the same question, yet did not generate the same unease—it is interesting to ask why, when the implications of the environmental crisis are no less urgent than issues of sexuality—perhaps more so.

But the disagreement is not only over particular aspects of creation order, it is also evidently a general problem. Those who seek to defend the traditional interpretations of where the boundary between divinely given order and free human response lies are accused of a fearful conservatism. By refusing to embrace the freedom God gives us, they necessarily end up clinging to merely human conceptions of order which serve the interest of the powerful. By contrast, those who seek to widen the scope of the human response beyond that which has been regarded as acceptable in the tradition, are accused of hubristic relativism. In insisting that order should serve foreseeable consequences for human well-being—shalom—they end up living, not by faith but by sight. After all, by what criteria do we assess what constitutes shalom? Perhaps this might have been a more profitable starting point for the conference than a putative contrast between order and compassion. It is certainly a fundamental challenge this tradition must face head-on. Particular issues like that of homosexuality will not be adequately addressed until this deeper one is clarified. Or perhaps some would argue that it's the other way round.

Finally, this issue leads us directly back to that of hermeneutics. Most would accept that we can only interpret creation through Scripture; we can only interpret our own creaturely experience in the light of Scripture. But most would also want to say that we cannot interpret Scripture apart from our creaturely experience. The traditional position has been that Scripture must control our interpretation of experience in a way that our experience must not control Scripture. But some are uneasy with this way of stating the issue.

Allen Verhey sounded a new note which those rooted and raised in Reformed hermeneutics have not sounded before. He sang a new song. The question turned out to be whether his song was simply a variation on well-loved Reformed tunes, or whether it's a quite different one, impossible to harmonize with those old favourites.

John Cooper was optimistic about the possibilities of harmonization, though Allen Verhey was a little uneasy about simply joining the existing chorus, adding no more than a little literal embellishment to a rather tired old piece from the *Psalter Hymnal*.

There's no time to deal adequately with this issue here. What is clear, though, from these last few days, is that biblical hermeneutics remains central to the task of creational hermeneutics. Whoever is appointed as Senior Member in biblical studies certainly has his or her work cut out.

Finally, we want to say something about the spirit in which this conference has taken place—its ethos. Some have been hurt by some things said here; many, perhaps, are disappointed about one or other feature of our gathering. Perhaps painful issues have been raised without a way of expressing and dealing communally with that pain. Perhaps other issues ought to have been addressed.

Immersed in the tradition and its limits, however, we may not see how remarkable these few days have been. Nicholas Wolterstofff remarked that he thought that none of his colleagues at Yale Divinity School would ever have had an experience like this, of a believing community wrestling together, and wrestling around Scripture, sometimes with deep divisions, and yet somehow staying together. That makes me proud to belong to this community and to have been part of its story.

DATE DUE